D0241814

The High Middle Ages

The High Middle Ages 1200–1550

Trevor Rowley

AVON COUNTY LIBRARY

Class No. 942.03

AR
11/86 Alloc. GE

AVON COUNTY LIBRARY

x [942 04]
x [942 05]

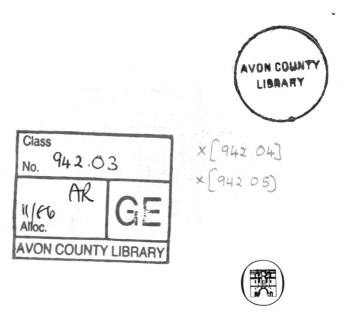

Routledge & Kegan Paul
London and New York

First published in 1986
by Routledge & Kegan Paul plc

11 New Fetter Lane, London EC4P 4EE

Published in the USA by
Routledge & Kegan Paul Inc.
in association with Methuen Inc.
29 West 35th Street, NY 10001

Set in Palatino, 10 on 12 pt
by Input Typesetting Ltd, London
and printed in Great Britain
by The Thetford Press Ltd,
Thetford Norfolk

© Trevor Rowley 1986

No part of this book may be reproduced in any form without permission
from the publisher, except for the quotation of brief passages in
criticism

Library of Congress Cataloging in Publication Data
Rowley, Trevor, 1942–

    The high Middle Ages, 1200–1540.

    (The making of Britain, 1066–1939)
    Bibliography: p.
    Includes index.
    1. Great Britain—History—Medieval period, 1066–1485.
2. Great Britain—History—Tudors, 1485–1603.
3. Anthropo–geography—Great Britain. I. Title.
DA175.R73   1986   941   85–28304

British Library CIP data also available
ISBN 0–7100–9815–4

Contents

Illustrations

Figures

Tables

Acknowledgments

I would like to thank all those who made the writing of this book possible, in particular Anne Marriott who undertook much of the background research. Grateful thanks are also due to Melanie Steiner who prepared many of the plans for publication. I have benefited from discussions with many colleagues over various aspects of medieval life, but most of all my post graduate tutor, W.G. Hoskins, who taught me as he has taught so many others, how to read the landscape. I would also like to thank Jean Cook, Shirley Hermon and Linda Rowley for their considerable help in preparing the finished text.

The author and publishers would like to thank the following for permission to reproduce illustrations: National Monuments Record for plates 6, 8, 12, 21, 62, 70, 72 and 73; Committee for Aerial Photography, University of Cambridge for plates 10, 14, 16, 17, 18, 20, 24, 26, 27, 30, 31, 35, 37, 40, 45, 46, 47, 48, 49, 54, 58, 59a, 60, 67, 68; The National Trust, plate 9; All Souls College, Oxford plates 25a, 25b; Bodleian Library, Oxford plate 61; British Library plate 39; Chelmsford Record Office plate 53. Thanks are also due to Mick Aston for permission to reproduce figures 8, 9, 10, 13, 15, 34, 46, 50 and 51, and James Bond for figures 12, 19 and 26.

General Editor's Preface

To the archaeologist, the notion of material culture, of a society exemplified by its artefacts, is commonplace. To historians it has traditionally had less appeal, although Professor Fernand Braudel's *Civilisation matérielle et capitalisme* marks a foray into unknown terrain. The intention of this series, which follows chronologically from another of more directly archaeological approach,* is to see the history of Britain from the Norman Conquest to the Second World War, partly in human terms – of changing cultural, social, political and economic patterns – but more specifically in terms of what that society produced, and what remains of it today.

Few themes run with consistency through the history of the British Isles, save the land itself. This series seeks to show the way in which man has shaped and occupied the country, and how society has been moulded by the opportunities and constraints imposed by the landscape. The broad theme is of man's interaction with his environment, which is carried through the series.

As editor, I have tried to allow each author to write his approach to the subject without undue interference. Ideally, such a study would have appeared as a large single volume, but we have sought to make the divisions less arbitrary by allowing authors to cover a broad body of material in more than one book. Thus the volumes dealing with the medieval period come from the same hand, as do those spanning the sixteenth to the nineteenth centuries.

One of the most dangerous myths of the medieval age is that of *development*. It was born of the notion of progress, of medieval humanity working its way up from the mire towards civilization, constitutional government, good order and national pride. It was, in essence, a nineteenth-century imposition on the past. But it was supported by a misreading of the material evidence. So much of the High Middle Ages remained – castles and great church

Britain before the Conquest, 5 vols, Routledge & Kegan Paul, 1979–81.

buildings developing and elaborating in style and sophisti-
cation over the centuries – that they seemed to resound
with the truth of the notion of progress.

Re-reading the evidence, as Trevor Rowley has done so
successfully, indicates a different picture. He points to a
society where a whole complex of different changes were
acting upon society, accentuated in varying ways by regional
and local factors. Thus, peasants working on the marginal
lands of the Lincolnshire Wolds simply abandoned their
hard-won but fruitless lands when the Black Death
scoured their population. The experience in a village with
better land, or in the town or city, was quite different.
All experienced the pestilence and suffered from it: the
consequences of the suffering were different. Much of this
new picture emerges from a fuller understanding of the
archaeological and material remains of the period.

Trevor Rowley also revises the notion of 'the middle
ages' which ended with Bosworth Field and the accession
of the Tudors. He now makes the transition a generation
later, with the wholesale closure of the monasteries and
the radical reshaping of English landholding in the 1540s.
This accords both with revisionist views of the developments in the fifteenth century and the notion of a Tudor
revolution in government during the 1530s. The pattern
of change which he shows is much patchier than the old
notion of progress. It is also much more convincing.

Andrew Wheatcroft

Preface

This book is intended as an introduction to the High
Middle Ages, the period between AD 1200 and AD 1500.
Conventionally it has been seen in two quite distinct parts,
the first represented by a period of population expansion,
the creation of new towns and a flourishing agrarian
system based on open field arable. The second part has
been seen in terms of economic recession accompanied
by population decline, and the break-up of many of the
institutions associated with medieval society. This
impression that the fifteenth century, in particular, was a
period of decline has been reinforced by the rather peculiar
nature of the surviving documentation from that century,
which tends to be rather stereotyped and at a local level
fails to provide the detailed information that is available
for the previous two centuries. However, one has only to
look at the extraordinarily fine church architecture of the
late Middle Ages to appreciate that all was not gloom
and despondency. Indeed subtle changes in all aspects of
English society were taking place during the later Middle
Ages and the criteria used to measure the health and
wealth of society in the early Middle Ages are no longer
applicable.

Economically it is true that after the middle years of
the fourteenth century there was a sustained fall in the
population. There were a variety of reasons for this development which appears to have been accompanied in parts
of the countryside by the abandonment of traditional
open-field farming and its replacement by either mixed
farming economies or purely pastoral regimes aimed at
wool production. Many towns also seem to have been
affected by the dwindling population. A number of centres
which earlier had enjoyed or had aspired to urban status
reverted to villages and even large centres such as Oxford
and Northampton went through a period of marked
deterioration. This pattern was not universal, however,
because there were both new villages and new towns
created which were geared to the growing textile industry
and where there was unheard-of prosperity during the
later Middle Ages. This wealth was expressed through the

great wool churches of East Anglia and the Cotswolds and even the West Midlands and parts of northern England.

Prosperity came to parts of England not only from wool production and textile manufacture but also from the diversification of trade and the opening of new markets and new commodities which brought wealth to ports such as Norwich, Bristol and above all London. The new wealth was spent not only on churches, and cathedrals as had been the fashion in the previous centuries, but also in secular benefactions such as the foundation and endowment of colleges, schools, almshouses and guild halls. On the domestic side the later Middle Ages saw a change from castle to countryhouse to house the aristocracy and merchants, and the rise of the so-called yeoman farmers in the countryside produced the first generation of vernacular houses that have survived on any scale until today. These include cruck buildings and several other types of half-timbered houses from various parts of England and Wales.

No new great monasteries were established during the later Middle Ages and some were even closed before the great dissolution of the early sixteenth century. However, for most monastic establishments the work of restoration and rebuilding went on throughout the period and economically many of them became extremely wealthy on the basis of diversified economies including textiles, industrial activities and more efficient pastoral farming. Many of the great monastic granges and storage barns date from this period, representing a period when some monastic fortunes, at least, were ascending.

To the landscape historian the High Middle Ages left a wealth of information. Much of the architecture we know as 'medieval' dates from this period, particularly at a parish church level. As to the earthworks which we call medieval, the majority also date from the later Middle Ages, the most extensive of all being ridge and furrow, which, despite the decline in arable farming, continued in use over perhaps as much as half of England. Almost all the villages which are classified as being deserted medieval settlements come from this period providing us with a series of unique reservoirs of stratified archaeological deposits. The earthworks of fishponds, water mills and windmill sites, precinct boundaries, industrial enterprises, failed towns, deer park boundaries and so on can all be dated for the most part to the High Middle Ages.

Until relatively recently this landscape survived more or less intact in many parts of England and Wales. The last two decades, however, have seen a severe diminution in the amount of surviving physical evidence from the period. Urban and rural building projects, new roads, and mineral extraction have all taken their toll, but the greatest threat has come from the intensification of farming. This has been accompanied by the continuous removal of hedgerows and the spread of arable farming into areas where it has been unknown since the Middle Ages, and indeed to levels even higher than those reached during the thirteenth century in places. It is idle to bemoan the loss of such a relic landscape much of which is seen and enjoyed only by a minority. Nevertheless we should recognise this loss and take steps to ensure that at least a representative sample of such a valuable historical resource does survive for the benefit of future generations.

Trevor Rowley
Wheatley, Oxfordshire

The high Middle Ages

The high Middle Ages was a turbulent period in British history. The three centuries between 1200 and 1500 saw considerable and continual political, social and economic change. Politically the period has conventionally been seen in terms of the development from the warring feudalism of King John through to the embryonic united kingdom of Henry VII. Constitutionally it is seen as the period when parliament developed and gradually took over some aspects of government from the crown. Socially it is seen as the period during which many of the trappings of feudalism were shed – in particular feudal services being commuted to paid renumeration. Economically it is seen as the period when the country changed from basic subsistence arable farming to an exporting economy in which wool and textiles played a major role. Although such generalisations do reveal something of the truth, they are inevitably misleading in so far as there was no regular curve of development in any one direction. Over a span of 300 years there were constant false starts, with successes and failures in all spheres of human activity. Not only is the story of human endeavour never a smooth one, but our view of it is tempered and distorted by the nature, quality and erratic survival rate of the evidence which is available to us to recreate the past.

Nor should we deceive ourselves into believing that there is one single history for this or any period. There are countless histories and countless ways of recalling them depending upon what questions are asked and the view-point taken by the historian. Traditionally the story of the later Middle Ages has been written about in terms of the kaleidoscopic political drama of the period. Not a little under the influence of Shakespeare, we have been brought up to think of medieval history in terms of 'good' or 'bad', 'weak' or 'strong' monarchs. It is questionable, not how far the activities of these rulers and of their barons permeated down the social scale – for the effect of their actions had a deep impact on medieval England – but rather how much their activities were themselves the product of underlying economic, demographic and social forces. Conspicuous

power and wealth were still significant characteristics of
the high Middle Ages, but this power and wealth was
more broadly distributed than during the Norman period.
This book is concerned not so much with the checks and
balances of power, or even with the distribution of wealth,
but with the ways in which power and wealth found their
expression through buildings, topography and the landscape of medieval England and Wales. During the later
Middle Ages monasteries, cathedrals, merchants and
lesser nobility joined the crown and the aristocracy in
fashioning town and countryside and in bequeathing to
us some of our finest architecture and some of the most
enduring elements in the landscape.

Considerable attention has rightly been paid to the
wealth of documentary sources which survive from medieval England, which can, in some instances, provide us
with microscopic details of the political, fiscal and judicial
history of the period. So too the great buildings of the
Middle Ages, the mighty castles, the great cathedrals and
the stubborn monastic hulks tell their own story of medieval craftsmanship, aspiration and vision. The missing
element in the analysis has been the landscape. Until
recently scholars have paid comparatively little attention
to the landscape of medieval England. Over the past few
decades the work of pioneers such as W.G. Hoskins and
M.W. Beresford has brilliantly demonstrated the important
role that landscape analysis should play in medieval
studies. The village or town abandoned before the Great
Rebuilding of the sixteenth and seventeenth centuries, the
medieval port choked by silt, the defended borough which
wilted soon after its strategic role passed away, the market
town 'fossilised' by a diversion of routes – these offer
unrivalled opportunities for understanding aspects of the
Middle Ages which are not available from the written
sources. Throughout this book whenever possible archaeological, landscape and building evidence will be used
alongside the evidence available from the more conventional historical record.

From John to Henry VII

To begin with it is necessary to establish the political
framework for the period in question. The high Middle
Ages saw a procession of monarchs belonging to the house
of Plantagenet, a royal dynasty which was descended from
the counts of Anjou. The first three Plantagenets, Henry
II, Richard I and John, are normally styled Angevins. The
right of succession of the subsequent Plantagenets, Henry

III, Edward I, Edward II, Edward III and Richard II, was undisputed, but in 1399 Henry Bolingbroke claimed the throne as the son of John of Gaunt, Edward III's third son, and achieved it by deposing his cousin Richard II to become Henry IV. During the fifteenth century there were two branches of the Plantagenet dynasty, the Lancastrians (Henry IV, Henry V, and Henry VI) and the Yorkists (Edward IV and Richard III) who battled for the throne. The Plantagenet line of kings came to an end with the defeat of Richard III at Bosworth Field in 1485, when it was forced to yield to the first of the Tudors, Henry VII. The year 1485 is one of the seminal dates in English history as it has been taken as the end of the Middle Ages by generations of historians. In recent years the validity of this date in terms of English political history has been questioned. Looked at from the points of view of the economic, social, architectural and landscape historian it appears to fall conveniently near the end of an awkward century and provides an opportunity to start a new chapter, rather than mark a convincing conclusion to the book of Medieval England.

In the late twelfth century under Richard I, England was ruled by a royal dynasty whose network of family alliances encompassed France, Germany, Spain, Sicily and the Holy Land. At the time of Richard's death in April 1199 different parts of the Angevin empire chose different heirs. The barons of England and Normandy opted for John 'Lackland' (King John) while Anjou, Maine and Touraine preferred Arthur of Brittany: Aquitane was held on John's behalf by his mother Eleanor, who died in 1204. From the start John was faced with problems on several fronts. By 1204 he had lost most of his northern French lands and after the Battle of Bouvines (July 1214), he lost effective control of much of the remainder of France with the exception of Gascony. Apart from his overseas failures John's reign also witnessed conflict with the church at home. After the death of the Archbishop of Canterbury Hubert Walter in 1205, John's own nominee to succeed him was passed over in favour of Stephen Langton, the papal candidate. John refused to allow Langton into England, and after placing the kingdom under interdict, the pope excommunicated John and, in 1209, threatened to depose him and to sanction an imminent French invasion. The dispute was not ended until 1213, when England and Ireland became papal fiefs. John also faced increasing opposition from his barons who regarded his rule, in particular his methods of raising revenue, as despotic, and in 1215 he was forced to sign Magna Carta. John's subsequent failure to honour the terms of the charter provoked the barons to offer the crown to the Capetian Louis, son of Philip II Augustus of France. Following Louis's landing in Kent (May 1216), John, who had campaigned successfully in the Midlands and the north, lost most of southeast England. In October the king died at Newark and with the crowning of his son, Henry III, and the re-issue of Magna Carta, prolonged Civil War was averted and the tide turned for the Plantagenets.

Superficially at least Henry III's long reign (1216–72) can be interpreted as a relatively calm one. Nevertheless in 1224 England lost complete control of its last possessions in France, with the exception of Gascony. In Wales a strong Welsh kingdom under Llewellyn the Great and his grandson, Llewelyn ap Gruffydd, was forged into a single political unit, which was reluctantly acknowledged when the latter was recognised as Prince of Wales by Henry III in the Treaty of Montgomery (1267). Meanwhile, in the north a Scottish attempt to reclaim Northumbria was resisted and a relatively stable foreign situation appears to have prevailed.

Despite the length of his reign Henry has been judged a failure in several spheres; he was only nine years old at his succession to the throne and it was not until 1227 that he declared himself of age. His ineffectual government, financial mismanagement and dependence upon foreign, largely Poitevin, favourites provoked baronial opposition. A rebellion led by Richard Marshal, 3rd Earl of Pembroke and Striguil (1233–34) forced Henry to dismiss his unpopular advisors: Peter de Roche who was Bishop of Winchester, and Peter de Rivaux. The Savoyard relations of his wife Eleanor of Provence, whom he married in 1236, appear to have aroused further anger. When Henry demanded an exorbitant sum partly to fulfil a promise to finance papal wars in Sicily, in return for the Sicilian crown for his son Edmund, the conflict came to a head. The barons issued the 'Provisions of Oxford' (1258) designed to limit the king's power and when they were renounced by Henry the second Barons' War (1264) broke out. In May of that year the baronial leader Simon de Montfort captured the king and his son Edmund at the Battle of Lewes and ruled England until he was defeated at Evesham in 1265. After his restoration during the final years of his reign Henry played little part in government, which was largely in the hands of Edward, his eldest son.

Although Henry III's reign saw significant and costly

military activity, it also witnessed the expenditure of very large sums of money on building. It is not possible to say how much Henry spent, for the documents do not permit exact calculations. It is clear, however, that between 1216 and 1272 not less than £113,000 was spent on royal castles and houses plus up to £50,000 on Westminster Abbey. This represents an annual average of nearly £3,000, or about one-tenth of the normal receipts of Henry's government. Although this was not an unduly large proportion of revenue to devote to building, it represented almost three times as much as John's average expenditure on his castles and houses, and there can be little doubt that it was more than Henry could really afford. It was however, political folly rather than architectural extravagance which led to the political crisis of 1258, and it was Henry's method of government, not his over-enthusiastic patronage of the arts, which was the object of baronial censure. Some historians have regarded him as a dilettante king but this charge underrates the seriousness of his military and political ambitions. However it remains true to say that the only campaign in which Henry knew how to succeed was the one of building, and that in the words of Colvin and Brown, 'Westminster Abbey is the truest memorial to a king who was a better judge of sculpture and painting than he was of politics and men.'

The reign of Edward I (1272–1307), whose formidable military talents had been revealed against the rebellious barons at Evesham, was characterised more by external than internal conflict. In two devastating campaigns in 1277 and 1282–3, Edward I overran Gwynedd and secured the defeat or submission of the native princes of Deheubarth. The third Welsh principality, Powys, was in effect already under English control and subsequently was treated as an English barony. Despite a series of revolts the Edwardian conquest of north and west Wales proved final and was to shape many features of Welsh life until the sixteenth century. In particular the building of a series of mighty castles and fortified towns including Harlech, Caernarvon and Conway insured the permanence of military victory. The newly acquired lands in Wales, the Principalities as they became known, were largely retained in crown hands and were divided into shires on the English model. While native Welsh law was still tolerated in certain spheres, the forms and substance of English common law were introduced by the Statute of Wales (1284).

Edward spent some £80,000 on his eight new Welsh castles between 1277 and 1304, but surprisingly the indi-

1 Four medieval kings
with monasteries they
patronised: Henry II
with Waltham Abbey
in Essex, Richard I
with the church of St
Thomas at Acre in the
Holy Land, John with
Beaulieu Abbey and
Henry III with
Westminster Abbey.
The drawings, which
are arranged in a
conventional style,
are by the St Alban's
chronicler, Mathew
Paris

vidual castle upon which he spent most was the Tower of
London, whose reconstruction between 1275 and 1285 cost
over £20,000. The rebuilding of the castles at Cambridge
and Windsor cost a further £5,000 and at Westminster
Palace the accumulated expenditure of the reign totalled
over £10,000. Edward's other religious foundation – Vale
Royal Abbey – was conceived on the grand scale and,
to begin with, received financial provision commensurate
with the conception. To all this must be added the maintenance of many other royal castles and houses
throughout the kingdom and the cost of the works in
Scotland where there were serious and unresolved trou-
bles. Indeed Edward was on his way to subdue the

rebellion of Robert the Bruce when he died in 1307. There
were also problems in France with attacks upon Gascony
which led to a need to raise taxes, which in turn led to
further baronial unrest.

Nevertheless during Edward's reign there were
important legal and administrative reforms. The Statutes
of Gloucester (1278) and Winchester (1285) and the statutes
quo warranto and *quia emptores* (both 1290) were enacted.
These measures were designed to centralise administration
and establish regulations for the maintenance of the peace.
The constitutional importance of parliament was
increasing.

Edward II's rule (1307–27) was no more peaceable than
that of his father and was characterised by a series of
baronial revolts. Born in Caernarvon and the first English
prince of Wales, Edward married Isabel of France in 1308.
Initially he was a popular king but his extravagance and
poor judgment of character made his reign a troubled one.
In 1308 the barons forced the king to banish his favourite
Piers Gaveston to Ireland, and it was the reaction to Gaveston's return in 1309 which helped provoke the appoint-
ment of the lords ordainers, who forced the king to accept
limitations on royal power outlined in the Ordinances
(1311). Gaveston was again banished, and his return, together with Edward's attempts to evade the Ordinances, led
to civil war (1312). Gaveston was executed and a disastrous
Scottish campaign, notably the defeat at Bannockburn
(1314), so weakened Edward's position that he yielded his
authority to his chief opponent and cousin, Thomas, Earl
of Lancaster. Within two years, however, the king had
regained much of his power and by 1318 had found a new
favourite, Hugh le Despenser. Renewed baronial
complaints led to the banishment of Despenser and his
father. However in 1322 the king recalled them and
successfully renewed the war against the barons,
capturing and beheading Thomas of Lancaster. Edward
then revoked the Ordinances, only to encounter opposition from his wife, who in 1325 went to France where
she formed an alliance with Roger de Mortimer, a bitter
enemy of the Despensers.

Edward's reign was brought to an end by a successful
coup by Queen Isabel and Roger de Mortimer in 1326. In
the following year the deposed Edward died in Berkeley
castle and was succeeded by his son Edward III (1327–77).
To begin with Edward did much to revive the prestige
of the English monarchy following his father's disastrous
reign, by conciliating the barons. He pursued an

enlightened commercial policy, and brought about an important reorganisation of the navy. Nevertheless his reign was dominated by the wars with Scotland and France.

The long reign of Edward III was a period of considerable building activity, both civil and military. At his birthplace, Windsor Castle, Edward III spent well over £50,000, the highest figure for any single building operation in the

2 Aerial view of Windsor castle, Edward III spent over £50,000 here, which was the highest figure for any single building operation in the whole history of king's works during the Middle Ages

whole history of the king's works in the Middle Ages. His new castle and town of Queenborough cost him over £25,000. A whole series of lesser but still considerable works were undertaken at the king's favourite castles and houses. These included Rotherhithe, Gravesend and Henley on the Heath, as well as four new hunting lodges which were built in the New Forest. In the course of his

reign he spent some £29,000 upon the palace of
Westminster. Over and above all this, substantial amounts were spent at Clarendon, Woodstock and Havering; Gloucester, Nottingham and York; upon Berwick and the royal castles in Scotland; and upon the fortifications of Calais, which cost an average of £1,000 a year from 1347 onwards. Like his grandfather Henry III, Edward took a personal interest in his buildings. It seems probable that he was present when work began on his castle at Queenborough just as Henry III had been present at the beginning of his castles in Wales. A writ of June 1358 ordering money to be made available for works at Newcastle-upon-Tyne, 'which lie near to the king's heart', underlines the attachment Edward had for his great building enterprises.

Edward III's reign saw the beginning of the 'Hundred Years War' (1337–1453), which was neither one continuous conflict, nor a single dispute lasting a century. It was part of a disjointed series of wars between England and France which had originated at the time of the Norman Conquest. Edward III's expedition to the Low Countries in 1338 marked a new phase of the struggle, which was to last until the mid-fifteenth century. Family ties, commercial and strategic considerations and even differing attitudes to the papacy helped to extend the Anglo-French conflict to the Iberian Peninsula, the Low Countries, Scotland and Ireland. There was extensive fighting from 1338 to 1347 and again in the late 1350s. The renewal of war in 1369 lead to more modest campaigning, with both kingdoms so exhausted in 1396 that they reached a truce which lasted almost 30 years. During the wars of Edward I and Edward II the English crown had developed a remarkable ability to raise large forces, in the form of mercenary armies. They were better disciplined and more dependable than the loosely organised, traditionally raised French forces. The English men-at-arms and archers had a decisive advantage even against superior numbers, which resulted in great victories in the first decades of the wars, as at Crécy and Poitiers where John II of France was captured.

Despite major economic problems, not least the Black Death of 1348, the English financial commitment to the war was considerable. Expeditionary forces, some of them very large, were raised with impressive regularity and as England's military advantage narrowed after 1369, so the government resorted to newer expedients such as the poll tax, which was levied on everyone over 14 years of age and was widely evaded. At the same time England was defending her Scottish border, maintaining the peace in

Ireland and preventing an uprising in Wales. The achievement appears to have owed much to the inspiration of the king and his elder son the Black Prince. Time was not on England's side, however, for after 1369 there were few English victories and at home opinion grew critical of the war and of its conduct. During the latter years of his reign Edward III grew increasingly senile and government was largely in the hands of his fourth son, the Duke of Lan-

3 Fourteenth-century manuscript showing boats being attacked as they attempt to land an infantry army

caster, John of Gaunt.

By the 1370s the tide of war had changed in France's favour and many, especially the parliamentary commons, began to question the conduct of the war. It was the pressures of war that contributed to making the reigns of Richard II (1377–99) and Henry IV (1399–1413) a period of domestic upheaval, exceptional even by medieval standards. Despite the problems the institution of monarchy

4 Soldiers giving thanks at a shrine for their safe voyage and landing

Comment alexandie paffa en
re . Chapittre.   xx

emerged largely unscathed, but one dynasty of royal advisors was violently replaced by another in quick succession and proposals were even discussed for the dismemberment of the realm. The period also saw the most widespread popular uprising of the Middle Ages – the Peasants' Revolt.

Richard II, aged only 10, succeeded to the throne in 1377. A variety of grievances, including an excessive poll tax in 1381, sparked off the Peasants' Revolt. Agricultural workers from east and southeast England were joined by townsmen and Londoners, but although the grievances were real enough the rebellion soon lost its momentum. Subsequently Richard II became an oppressive king, responsible for exiling or executing the heads of the most powerful families in the land. Much of his reign was dominated by his uncle, John of Gaunt, but after John's death in 1399, Richard confiscated his estates, provoking John's son, Henry Bolingbroke, to invade England while Richard was away in Ireland. The king returned in August and surrendered at Conway, abdicating soon afterwards, only to die a few months later in prison at Pontefract.

The new king, Henry IV (Bolingbroke), also had considerable domestic difficulties which were compounded by the Welsh uprising led by Owen Glendower. Henry eventually overcame these revolts, but died

5 The church of St Magdalene, Battlefield, a few miles to the east of Shrewsbury which was founded by Henry IV as a chantry to pray for the souls of those who died in the Battle of Shrewsbury (1403). The church is now used just once a year – a service is held each 21 July on the anniversary of the battle.

at an early age and was succeeded by his son, Henry
V, in 1413. Henry had ambitions for regaining English
possessions in France and even revived Edward III's claim
to the French crown. He had inherited a realm that was
sufficiently peaceful, loyal and united for him to campaign
extensively in France from 1415 onwards. Large armies
were once again raised and again taxation was voted on a
generous scale. The king's strategy was to ally with French
nobles to undermine French unity. Soon, however, his
ambitions expanded into conquest and colonisation on a
grand scale. His first campaign led to the capture of
Harfleur and the great English victory at Agincourt (1415).
His alliance with Burgundy and with the Emperor Sigis-
mund greatly strengthened his hand in negotiating the
treaty of Troyes (1420) by which the French King Charles
VI made Henry his heir and regent of France and
betrothed him to his daughter Catherine of Valois. Henry
died two months before the death of Charles, leaving his
infant son Henry VI (1422–61, and 1470–1) as heir to his
claims in France. The next thirty years saw a major French
counter-attack and by 1450 the English had again been
removed from Normandy. Just three years later all English
territories in the southwest of France were lost. The Lancastrians, who had regained the northern French empire,
had lost England's entire continental possessions and were
to suffer for it.

Despite his long reign Henry VI has the reputation of
being an ineffective king. He had no military or administrative skills and suffered recurrent bouts of insanity,
which encouraged the feuds between leading magnates
that dominated his reign. The conflict between Gloucester
and Henry Beaufort, Bishop of Winchester, gave way after
their deaths (1447) to the power struggle between the
king's chief minister Edmund Beaufort, Duke of Somerset,
and Richard, Duke of York. In 1453–4, during a phase of
Henry's insanity, York obtained the protectorship, but
after the king's recovery Beaufort again took charge. In
1455 the conflict between the houses of Lancaster and York
erupted into the Wars of the Roses, during which Henry
was dominated by his wife Margaret of Anjou. After
Yorkist victories in 1461 the king was deposed by York's
son Edward and fled to Scotland. He returned in 1464
only to be captured and imprisoned the following year.
In October 1470 Warwick, popularly known as 'the king-
maker', secured Henry's restoration (or readoption),
which lasted until April 1471, at which point Edward
returned to reclaim the throne. Henry was imprisoned in

the Tower where he was eventually murdered. Edward IV became confident enough to involve England once more in continental adventures. After a financially rewarding military campaign in France Edward turned his attention to internal affairs and instituted administrative reforms and more effective enforcement of law and order, notably in the Marches. On his death in 1483 he was succeeded by his brother Richard III, who had imprisoned Edward's two sons in the Tower. Richard was defeated and killed in August 1485 by Henry Tudor, at the battle of Bosworth.

Henry VII (1485–1509) married Elizabeth of York, thus uniting the houses of Lancaster and York. However Yorkist plots, notably those of Lambert Simnel and Perkin Warbeck, continued to threaten his position for most of his reign. In 1489 Henry negotiated the Treaty of Medina del Campo with Spain, which arranged the marriage of his elder son Arthur to Catherine of Aragon, and in 1496 and 1506 the treaties with the Netherlands. He also established peace with Scotland (1499), subsequently marrying his daughter Margaret to James IV. Henry introduced few innovations in government but his shrewd and resolute rule restored order after the Wars of the Roses.

Despite the popular Shakespearean myth to the contrary, the Wars of the Roses had not been nasty, brutish and long. They consisted of short campaigns with intermittent periods of violence in a basically peaceful society. Only in the far north on the Scottish border and in the Calais garrison was there anything approaching a permanent military force. Although the Wars of the Roses nominally lasted for more than thirty years only one year was spent actually fighting. This was not a long drawn-out struggle of attrition, fortification and devastation as was the manner of many medieval wars and generally speaking armies were small and casualties light, but the havoc the wars caused in the aristocratic establishment was real enough, particularly in 1459–61 when a high proportion of the nobility was involved. For the most part economic, social and religious life went on unhindered, and the end result made little difference even to the structure of politics. The Tudors depended on the whole structure of 'bastard feudalism', just as much as their predecessors had done. Henry VII's style of government was not dissimilar to that of King John, except that it was more efficient. There was no significant break with the past and the conventional view that the wars were the last dying convulsion of the Middle Ages, the divide between medieval and modern, is a view which can no longer be sustained in relation to political, or indeed social or economic life.

Taxation and the growth of parliament

Underlying the domestic and foreign policies of the long reigns of Henry III and Edward I it is possible to detect the gradual development of the idea that the crown no longer ruled with the sole help of its own advisors. The 'community of the realm' had to be consulted. Although the 'community of the realm' was an abstract concept which could not be precisely defined, it was clear that if it disliked a king's policy, it was capable of passive resistance. If taxes were to be collected efficiently, the king needed the co-operation of those who paid taxes, and to obtain this he had to consult them or their representatives. From the late twelfth century onwards, the crown had grown accustomed to bargaining with individual shire-communities. It was therefore an obvious step to request these local communities to choose men to speak for them when the king wanted to summon an assembly to represent the community of the whole realm. This is the

1 England and Wales
  during the Wars of
  the Roses (after J. A.
  F. Thomson)

Towns ●
1 Berwick
2 Newcastle
3 Durham
4 Carlisle
5 York
6 Hull
7 Lincoln
8 Chester
9 Newark
10 Shrewsbury
11 Lynn
12 Norwich
13 Coventry
14 Ludlow
15 Warwick
16 Hereford
17 Banbury
18 Milford Haven
19 Gloucester
20 Bristol
21 London
22 Salisbury
23 Canterbury
24 Sandwich
25 Exeter
26 Southampton
27 Weymouth

Battles △
28 Hedgeley Moor 1464
29 Hexham 1464
30 Towton 1461
31 Wakefield 1460
32 Blore Heath 1459
33 Stoke 1487
34 Losecote Field 1470
35 Bosworth 1485
36 Mortimer's Cross 1461
37 Northampton 1460
38 Edgecote 1469
39 Tewkesbury 1471
40 St. Albans 1455, 1461
41 Barnet 1471

Castles □
42 Bamburgh
43 Dunstanburgh
44 Alnwick
45 Warkworth
46 Harlech

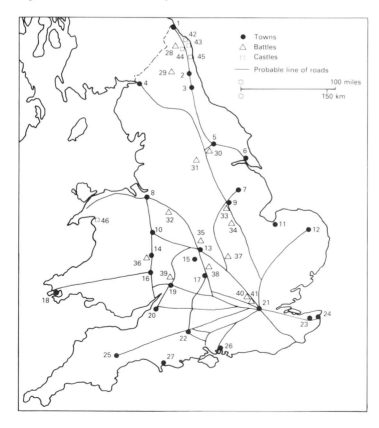

process that has become known as the growth of parliament.

It was the king's continuing financial requirements, more than any other factor, which brought about this development. In Magna Carta it was stated that when a king wanted an aid (a tax) he would have to obtain the consent of 'the common counsel of the realm', but by the second half of the thirteenth century it was no longer taken for granted that a parliament made up of barons always adequately represented the community. In certain circumstances they continued to do so – but not when taxation was being discussed. Under such conditions the close connection between war – the most expensive of royal activities – and the growth of parliament is understandable.

The first crisis in parliamentary history occurred in the late 1290s when Edward I's policies placed him in the position of having to fight wars in Wales, in Scotland and in France at the same time. He therefore had to raise increased finances, and, as a consequence, whereas in the first 90 years of the century the crown had levied nine taxations, the next nine came in just 20 years. With this sharp increase in financial pressure the commons became increasingly important. One of the remedies earlier adopted by Edward was the great recoinage of 1279–80, which had as its purpose the funding of the Welsh campaigns, but it proved to be altogether too successful. Newly minted English coins were in such demand on the Continent that their out-flow created a shortage of coin in England itself and as early as 1283 the king found himself forced to prohibit the export of English money.

The second crisis arose during the early years of Edward III's costly war against France when again substantial funds had to be raised. Thereafter parliament without the commons was inconceivable and by the end of the four-teenth century the commons were devising new parlia-mentary procedures, impeaching ministers and inter-vening in the conduct of foreign policy – though they were only able to do this effectively when royal leadership was weak. Nevertheless, during the Hundred Years' War, taxation levels were considerably higher than in the previous century. The commons normally consented to taxation and as a consequence they survived and flourished; they did not object to taxation on principle, as demonstrated by their support for Henry VI, for, as the commons knew, successful war could be very profitable. The commons did object, however, to unsuccessful wars, as is clear from the stand taken by the 'Good Parliament' of 1376, by the rebels in 1381, and by the low level of support given to Henry VI. After the English had been finally removed from France in the 1450s, taxation once again reverted to a more regular pattern, yet the commons in parliament were so firmly established by that date that no king was able to dispense with them entirely.

Population and economy

Whereas it is possible to spell out in some detail the names and characters of the major figures involved in the government of England during the high Middle Ages, the details of what was happening to the population as a whole are far less precise. The evidence on which our understanding of these areas is based is much more patchy and unreliable, and accordingly no two historians will agree precisely about the number of people living in England and Wales at any one time, or on the dates when different demographic trends emerged. Nevertheless there is general, but not universal, agreement that at the time of the Norman Conquest the population was increasing and that it continued to expand during the early Middle Ages. The continued clearance and enclosure of former woodland, wasteland and marshland are all indicative of land hunger. The creation and growth of new towns together with the expansion of existing urban centres also points to an increasing population up to about 1300. Similarly the fact that rural settlements were being created rather than abandoned up to and until that date, points to population expansion rather than stagnation or contraction.

After 1300 the picture begins to change and evidence for expansion gives way to evidence for stagnation or even shrinkage. Considerable importance is placed upon the agrarian crisis of the early fourteenth century which is seen by many as a watershed in English medieval demographic history. Between 1300 and 1322 there appear to have been a series of harvest failures (1315, 1316 and 1321) and livestock epidemics (1313–17 and 1319–21) resulting in exceptionally high mortality rates. In the following decades there is evidence of a progressive agrarian recession, with the amount of uncultivated land reaching serious dimensions in some counties by the end of the fourteenth century. Opinions still differ as to the real long-term effect of the so-called 'agrarian crisis' of 1315–22. However, it has been described, surely with justice, as the 'worst agrarian crisis faced by England as a whole since the aftermath of the Norman invasion'. All the available evidence would

17

therefore point to a falling population and deteriorating agricultural scene well before the Black Death of 1348–9.

As the rural population rose and the amount of pasture land available receded before the arable, livestock declined in numbers. As a consequence pasture prices rose and meadowland fetched premiums in the late thirteenth century. Without manure, already low levels of productivity on the land fell, and progressive soil-exhaustion was a serious problem on the Winchester manors. For instance, the deterioration in crop yields was especially noticeable in the final decades of the thirteenth century.

2 The extent of abandoned arable land in Buckinghamshire in 1341, based on the *Nonarum Inquisitiones* (after A. R. H. Baker)

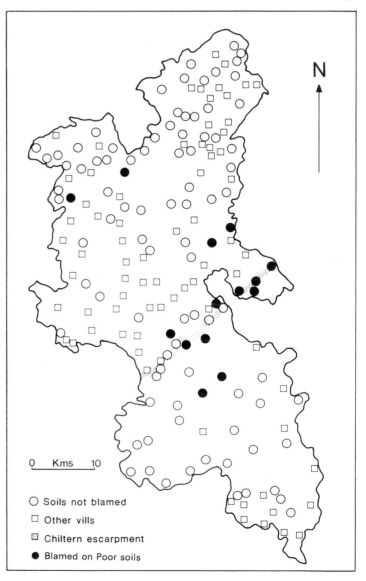

N

0 Kms 10

○ Soils not blamed
□ Other vills
▨ Chiltern escarpment
● Blamed on Poor soils

At Cuxham, in Oxfordshire, the deterioration from the high point reached in the 1290s continued for half a century. Wheat, which had yielded the exceptionally high average of 8.3 quarters for every quarter sown in 1288–99, had declined to barely half as much fifty years later.

Another factor appears to have been a long-term deterioration in the climate. On the Winchester manors a correlation existed between poor yields and land that had been extensively colonised relatively recently, the older and smaller manors escaping the most savage declines. It was just this newly cultivated land, pushed out into the inhospitable margins, that could least endure adverse changes in the climate, whether in the form of a short-term catastrophe like a drought, a flood, a tempest or a frost, or in a longer-term deterioration. It is clear that the relatively warm period of the eleventh and twelfth centuries – the so-called 'Little Optimum' – came to an end in the thirteenth century, the new phase being characterised by unusual climatic instability, bringing droughts, floods and tempests throughout much of the thirteenth and fourteenth centuries, with winters which could be mild, or from time to time exceptionally severe. One of the casualties in English agriculture before 1400, was the decline in the cultivation of the vine. The drop in average temperatures of only a few degrees (which was sufficient to discourage the vine) might not have had much impact on agriculture as a whole had it not been accompanied simultaneously by an appreciable rise in rainfall. A rise in the water-table early on in the fourteenth century, for example at Oakington, on the edge of the Cambridgeshire fens, has been interpreted as the reason for the desertion of the lower part of the village. And the widespread introduction of drainage ditches, cobbled floors and stone-paved paths in many villages in the thirteenth century which had not found them necessary before, also appears to reflect increased precipitation. Raised house-platforms and regularly cleaned-out ditches of the late thirteenth-century village seem to indicate a preoccupation with water disposal which, at the Dorset site of Holworth, near the coast, remained a problem through the fourteenth and into the fifteenth century. In response to problems of flooding, the church floors at Bordesley Abbey in Worcestershire, and at Broadfield in Hertfordshire, were built-up to higher, more secure levels.

The settlers of newly reclaimed land were those most at risk in the wetter conditions and losses were heavy. In coastal areas many of the gains of the early thirteenth century were swept away a century later, for example some 4,000 acres of agricultural land were lost along the length of the Sussex coast. There were similar losses on the Kentish manors of Christ Church Priory, Canterbury, while by 1341 in the Cambridgeshire fenlands over 1,400 acres of former arable land lay inundated and waste. During the fourteenth and fifteenth centuries, the eastern and southern coast lands of England were under attack, while in the East Riding of Yorkshire the monks of Meaux lost much of their land at Salthaugh Grange, together with the whole of their former grange at Tharlesthorpe through flooding. As late as the 1420s flooding on the Pevensey Levels persuaded the monks of Battle finally to abandon arable farming on their formerly profitable manor at Barnhorne, to cut down the acreage in demesne, and to turn over the remainder to cattle.

The Black Death has long been identified as the principle culprit in the change of economic fortunes in England and Europe in the mid-fourteenth century. However there remain considerable differences of opinion about the extent of the damage which it brought about. Estimates of the mortality rate range from 25 per cent to 50 per cent of the whole population, but some authorities argue that although towns would have seen a very high mortality rate, some rural areas were not intensely occupied enough for the plague to have spread at all. Most contemporary and later accounts of the impact of the plague are inevitably anecdotal, such as Wood's record of the Black Death reaching the city of Oxford:

> Those that had places and houses in the country retired (though overtaken there also), and those that were left behind were almost totally swept away. The school doors were shut, colleges and halls relinquished and none scarce left to keep possession, or make up a competent number to bury the dead.

Other chroniclers were universal in their opinion of its immediate consequences. Throughout the land they were writing in the despairing fashion of William of Dene, a monk of Rochester who recorded in 1349:

> In this year, a plague of a kind which had never been met with before ravaged our land of England. The Bishop of Rochester, who maintained only a small household, lost four priests, five esquires, ten attendants, seven young clerics and six pages, so that nobody was left to serve him in any capacity. At Malling he consecrated two abbesses. Both died almost immediately, leaving only four established nuns and four novices. One of these the Bishop put in the charge of the lay members and the other of the religions, for it proved

impossible to find anyone suitable to act as abbess. To our
great grief, the plague carried off so vast a multitude of people
of both sexes that nobody could be found who would bear
the corpses to the grave. Men and women carried their own
children on their shoulders to the church and threw them
into a common pit. From these pits such an appalling stench
was given off that scarcely anyone dared ever to walk beside
the cemeteries.

There was so marked a deficiency of labourers and
workmen of every kind at this period that more than a third
of the land in the whole realm was let lie idle. All the
labourers, skilled or unskilled, were so carried away by the
spirit of revolt that neither King, nor law, nor justice, could
restrain them. . . .

During the whole of that winter and the following spring,
the Bishop of Rochester, aged and infirm, remained at
Trottiscliffe [his country manor between Sevenoaks and
Rochester], bewailing the terrible changes which had
overcome the world. In every manor of his diocese buildings
were falling into decay and there was hardly one manor
which returned as much as £100. In the monastery of
Rochester supplies ran short and the brethren had great
difficulty in getting enough to eat; such a point that the
monks were obliged to either grind their own bread or to
go without. The prior, however, ate everything of the best.

It is possible to measure more precisely the extent of
mortality amongst beneficed clergy in ten of England's
dioceses. The figures are remarkably consistent, ranging
from between just under 39 per cent for York and 39.6 per
cent for Lichfield to 47.6 per cent for Bath and Wells, 48.5
per cent for Ely and 48.8 per cent for Exeter, Winchester
and Norwich. On this basis it is reasonable to assume that
something close to 45 per cent of all parish priests died
during the plague. Similar statistics based on twelve of the
more important monasteries show a surprisingly similar
rate among the monks, 44 per cent of whom perished.
Although these figures are undoubtedly relevant to the
problem of the total casualties caused by the Black Death,
exactly how they should be used to estimate the impact
on the population as a whole is harder to establish. It is,
nevertheless, as certain as any medieval statistics can be
that, for England as a whole, the mortality rate among the
people was between 34 and 45 per cent.

In recent years, however, scholars have been at pains
to point out that the Black Death did not appear in isolation
and that there were other major outbreaks of plague in
1360–1, 1369 and 1379 – plague was, in fact, endemic. The
second of the plague visitations has been identified as a
virulent one which had such a bad effect upon children
that it was called the *pestis puerorum*, the plague of the

children, by contemporary chroniclers. If this was the case
it would explain the permanent fall in population during
the century after the Black Death more effectively than a
single visitation, which would in normal circumstances
have had far less permanent impact than repeated
famines. In any case most authorities are in agreement that
between the 1340s and 1440s the population of England fell
by at least half and that from this stemmed a whole series

3 The population of
England, 1377 (after J.
C. Russell)

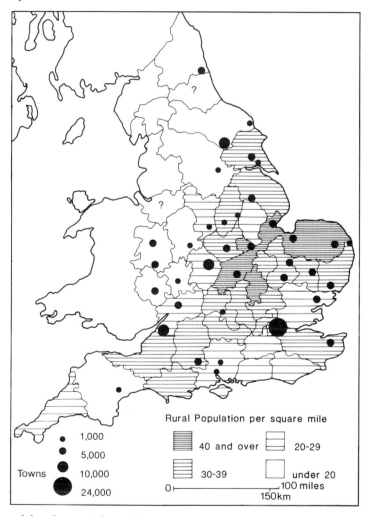

Rural Population per square mile

	1,000
	5,000
Towns	10,000
	24,000

40 and over 20-29

30-39 under 20

0 ⊢————————————, 100 miles
150km

of fundamental social and economic consequences.

The historian Vinogradoff warned that; 'We must really
not raise the plague to the dignity of a constant economic
force.' But equally we should not demote the plague to
the level of an isolated phenomenon having no significant
influence on a wide range of developments in the country.
The Black Death did not initiate any major social or econ-

omic trend but it accelerated and modified – sometimes drastically – those which already existed. The Black Death and the succeeding plagues represented a major catalytic element profoundly modifying the economic and social forces on which they operated. Without them the history of England and of Europe in the second half of the four-teenth and first half of the fifteenth centuries would have been very different.

Just how long the effects of the agrarian recession and the Black Death continued is impossible to say. Certainly references to empty buildings in villages and land still lying waste continue well into the fifteenth century and there appears to have been an impact on urban centres as well. Sections of many towns were said to be empty and derelict during the early fifteenth century when there is a reference to

> diverse and many houses messuages and tenements in the towns of Nottingham, Shrewsbury, Ludlow, Bridgnorth, Queensborough, Northampton and Gloucester now for a long time have been in great ruin and decay and specifically in the principal streets.

Towards the middle of the fifteenth century, however, both agriculture and trade seem to have been well on the way to recovery. The fifteenth century has always been an awkward one for historians, largely because the docu-mentary evidence is far less satisfactory than for the centuries on either side. Partly because of such difficulties the late Middle Ages are often depicted as a period of decline. In the words of Professor J.R. Lander:

> The waning of the Middle Ages is a mesmeric concept which has for long dominated the probes of historians so fascinated by an imagined morphology of decay that one of them has even endowed the century with a collective death wish. At best amid its supposed violent chaos, feeble institutions, economic decline and the macabre details of its *momento mori*, some few hopeful signs can be detected of transition to the modern world and the modern state.

One only has to look at the visual evidence of the land-scape to see that throughout the fifteenth century there was wealth, and wealth to spare above the level of the immediate needs of many parts of England. The extent of building bears ample witness to this prosperity. Although in the Midlands, Leicestershire and Northamptonshire the fourteenth century had been the great age of church building, in other districts, particularly Lincolnshire, East Anglia and the southwest, parish churches now rose to a new magnificence. Between the Black Death and the accession of Henry VII the inhabitants of hundreds of towns and villages rebuilt or enlarged their churches. In the south-western counties and in Lancashire hundreds of little private oratories and chapels appeared during the fifteenth century, a greater number of them attached to remote and lowly houses, some built at crossroads to serve districts far distant from parish churches. Great monasteries made extensive improvements to their buildings, secular lords erected new and elaborate castles, and the lesser nobility comfortable houses.

A Venetian envoy to England in 1497 sent a report on the state of the nation to the Doge which, although it is undoubtedly highly exaggerated, is a far cry from the conventional picture of fifteenth-century England in decay:

> The riches of England are greater than those of any country in Europe as I have been told by the oldest and most experienced merchants and also I myself can vouch for what I have seen. It is owing in the first place to the great fertility in the soil which is such that with the exception of wine they import nothing from abroad for their subsistance . . . and everyone who makes a tour in this island will soon become aware of this great wealth. . . . The population of this island does not appear to me to bear any proportion to its riches.

Kings, castles and houses of the great

Chapter two

The castle during the later Middle Ages

Between 1066 and 1200 many hundreds of castles had been built in England and Wales. They were constructed both in earth and timber and in stone and they formed an important element in both the urban and rural landscape. The majority of castles were built by the crown, barons and other lords as strategic residential, political and administrative centres. Castles also catered for the medieval passion for hunting, as centres from which the lord could ride out and indulge his love of the chase in nearby forests, chases and parks. Indeed, some castles, such as Gillingham in Dorset and Odiham in Hampshire, began as royal hunting lodges, and were subsequently fortified, while many other castles such as Tutbury, Nottingham and Northampton had parks sited immediately adjacent to them.

Of all medieval buildings the castle was the most characteristic of the period to which it uniquely belonged. In the words of R. Allen Brown, the castle was the

> substance of much military and therefore political power, the residence of the great, the cherished symbol of status and often nobility, the hub of administration and the centre in so many ways of public and private life, affecting one way or another most ranks of society through its manifold functions and the labour and service of its maintenance.

6 Portchester castle, Hampshire, a castle that remained important throughout the Middle Ages, because of its strategic siting on the south coast of England. The massive outer defences belong to a Roman and Anglo-Saxon fortification, but were renovated during the early Middle Ages. The most striking military feature of the site is the keep which was erected by Henry I. Amongst the work of later monarchs was the construction of a palace within the inner courtyard by Richard II. Portchester castle was popular with many medieval kings who usually stayed here when visiting Portsmouth. Henry V rested here before embarking for the Battle of Agincourt

Kings, castles and
houses of the great

The history of the castle during the later Middle Ages
faithfully reflects the story of the crown and of the nobility,
in other words those who were responsible for building
them. They reflected the distribution of power in the
kingdom, and on a number of occasions during the Middle
Ages individual barons came close to rivalling the crown
in the number of castles which they held. In the late fourteenth century, for instance, the Duchy of Lancaster held
the major castles of Pevensey, Monmouth, Brecon,
Kidwelly, Kenilworth, Higham Ferrars, Leicester, Castle
Donington, Tutbury, Tickhill, Pontefract, Liverpool,
Knaresborough, Dunstanburgh and Lancaster itself.

By the thirteenth century, however, many castles which
had been built subsequent to the Norman Conquest,
particularly the smaller ones, had fallen into decay and
had been abandoned. Nevertheless, a new generation of
castles was built in the thirteenth and fourteenth centuries,
which often combined impressive fortifications with more
luxurious residential accommodation. There were new
ideas on fortification according to which the concept of
the keep was largely abandoned in favour of greater
emphasis on curtain walls, on a more regular layout, on
wall towers, and on gatehouses which effectively replaced
the keep. The reign of Edward I (1272–1307) marked the
climax of castle-building in Britain. Edward was the last
medieval English king to undertake a major programme
of fortification in stone, and it was through the great
fortresses by which he achieved the conquest of north
Wales that the medieval castle reached the limits of its
capacity as a military structure.

During the early Middle Ages the main bases of attack
against Wales – Chester, Shrewsbury, Montgomery and
Hereford – had been set too far back from Welsh territory,
and the lines of communication had been unduly extended
and were therefore vulnerable. It is true that the English
had penetrated into Wales, and some Marcher lords had
built castles in the hope of holding what territory they had
gained. The siting of these castles, however, had not been
determined by any general strategic plan and most of them
were the private strongholds of independent Marcher
lords. Edward I not only penetrated much deeper into
Wales but he determined to impose English rule on the
Welsh by maintaining permanent royal garrisons on native
soil. In order to house these garrisons new impregnable
castles were required and accordingly new fortresses,
designed to guarantee English supremacy, were built at
strategic points throughout north Wales. Their erection

involved an unprecedented deployment of labour and technical skill and considerable financial cost. The newly-conquered principality was surrounded by a ring of castles which in both size and strength exceeded every existing castle in the British Isles, with the exception of Dover, Caerphilly and the Tower of London. Apart from Builth all were accessible by sea, and could therefore be replenished without mounting a costly campaign such as the one earlier undertaken by Henry III to relieve Dyserth and Deganwy in 1245. Moreover, five of them were built in association with fortified towns similar to the *bastides*, with which the English and French lords of Gascony were accustomed to strengthen their frontiers. A *bastide* was an urban colony whose inhabitants enjoyed economic and other privileges, and who in return were required to contribute to their lord's revenues and to help to defend their particular section of his territories. Edward I had already founded a number of *bastides* in southwestern France, and the new boroughs of Conway, Caernarvon, Aberystwyth, Rhuddlan, Flint and Beaumaris, with their English burgesses and trading privileges, represented the application of the same idea to Wales. The new boroughs represented an integral part of Edward's plan for the subjection of Wales to English rule, and their defences were integrated with the castles to which they were attached.

7 Beaumaris, Anglesey. The town and castle at Beaumaris occupy a dramatic site overlooking the Menai Strait. The castle represents an almost perfect example of symmetrical medieval military architecture. It was established in 1295, soon after the death of the last Llewelyn, by Edward I as one of the main links to his chain of fortifications in north Wales

Edward's conquest of North Wales effectively began in 1277, and in the same year he started work on the building of Flint castle. Flint was one of the most unusual of Welsh castles and although it reflected the changing pattern of thirteenth-century fortification with a regular rectangular plan and boldly projecting corner towers, it also had a circular keep. The keep was separated from the inner bailey by its own moat, and was constructed with a double shell wall 60 feet in diameter. In the same year Edward moved forward from Flint to Rhuddlan on the river Clwyd, where he quickly achieved the surrender of the Welsh leader Llewelyn ap Gruffydd. There was already a timber motte-and-bailey castle at Rhuddlan, which no doubt was used while the new castle was being built. This new castle was designed using the concentric plan which was to dominate later medieval fortifications and consisted of an inner curtain wall, surrounded by an outer curtain wall, surrounded by a ditch, all of which were surrounded by a timber palisade. The master mason and military engineer responsible for the building of both Flint and Rhuddlan, and other Edwardian castles in north Wales, was James of St George, who had worked on the building of many castles in France and Switzerland, including St Georges-d'Espernanche, from which he took his name.

At this stage Edward did not envisage the annexation of the whole of Wales, it was intended that Llewelyn should remain ruler of a small dependent principality, which was to be constricted by lands which had recently been annexed by Edward under the Treaty of Aber-conway. New castles were required to hold those lands and work began at Aberystwyth and Builth. These castles were, however, not complete when David's rebellion in 1282 forced Edward to return and bring the whole of north Wales under his direct control. The castles of 1277 were then repaired and completed, and new and larger ones were begun in the heart of Wales at Conway, Harlech and Caernarvon. In 1294 there was another serious rising in north Wales. Conway held out, but the Welsh attack on Caernarvon inflicted serious damage to the half-built castle there. Edward suppressed the revolt and began a fourth castle at Beaumaris in order to control Anglesey and the Menai Strait, but when he died in 1307 work on Caernarvon and Beaumaris was still in progress. Indeed Beaumaris was never entirely completed although it was capable of being garrisoned.

Castle-building in the second half of the thirteenth century was not confined to north Wales. Many other castles which employed the new defensive principles were built, for example Caerphilly castle was an elaborate structure, the central portion of which used a concentric arrangement similar to that at Harlech and Beaumaris. Caerphilly originally stood on an island, in a lake which was contained by a dam almost 900 feet long, which also acted as a barbican protecting the approach from the east. The inner bailey was rectangular (180 by 120 feet) with

N

Moat

Friary Gate (unfinished)

N. W. Tower

N. E. Tower

Well

Outer Ward

Kitchen

Northern Gatehouse

Apartments (over)

Inner Ward

Chapel Tower

Southern Gatehouse

S. W. Tower

S. E. Tower

Gate next the Sea

Barbican

Dock

Site of bridge

Sluice

Mill

Town wall

0   feet   100

metres

0   20

prominent projecting corner towers and two twin-towered gatehouses in the east and west walls. The curtain wall of the outer bailey was plain, apart from two gatehouses, which lay opposite the inner gatehouses. Edward I was also largely responsible for the work which brought the Tower of London to its present shape.

The Edwardian period marked the climax of medieval military castle-building. Although many castles were built during the fourteenth and even fifteenth centuries there was an increasing interest in, and emphasis on, the more domestic aspects of the accommodation provided. Castles had always been domestic to some degree, but during the early Middle Ages residential considerations came second to those of defence. In the fourteenth century and later, however, the demand for more space and greater comfort becomes increasingly evident in the plan of new castles and in the additions to existing ones. The new structures still looked very much like strongholds, but internally they were houses, and the term fortified house instead of castle becomes more appropriate as the later Middle Ages wore on.

There were many splendid examples dating from this period. They include Tutbury in Staffordshire, mainly rebuilt after 1350; Rockingham in Northamptonshire, dating from the time of Edward I; Dunstanburgh and Alnwick in Northumberland, with their great gatehouses built in the fourteenth century; Bodiam in Sussex built in 1385; and not least the great royal castle at Windsor which was substantially extended after 1350. During the fourteenth century the French sacked Rye, Yarmouth and Newport, and there was consternation along the south coast at the likelihood of their penetrating further inland. The Rother valley, in which Bodiam lies, then contained a larger river which was navigable as far as the castle. Sir Edward Dalyngrigge, a veteran of Edward III's foreign wars, was granted a licence to crenellate the mansion of Bodiam, on the understanding that the castle would protect the immediate countryside from an invading enemy. This important proviso enabled Sir Edward to interpret 'crenellation' in a very broad sense, for the existing manor was abandoned and a new site chosen nearby half-way up the slope of a hill. Although externally Bodiam reflects the style of earlier buildings with its symmetry of walls and towers, the interior was far more sophisticated – a properly designed fortified courtyard house with private suites, separate servants' quarters, chapel and other amenities remarkable for their number and extent. Although Bodiam's defences were never really tested, the castle is today a ruin, but it was not destroyed by siege. It was attacked twice, once in 1484, and again in 1643 by parliamentary troops. It would seem that the castle surrendered with little resistance on both occasions and the walls were not breached. Because its walls were thin and tall the castle was incapable of being defended against the heavy cannon that were then beginning to be used. The only attempt to prepare for the new form of warfare seems to have been the adaptation of existing arrowslits by inserting portholes for guns beneath them.

During the first half of the fifteenth century a small

8 A medieval dovecot at Garway, Herefordshire, Circular dovecots of this type were common features of the manorial complex during the fourteenth and fifteenth centuries. Doves provided an important form of winter protein and in addition their feathers and manure were of use in the medieval economy

number of new castles were built, including the 'tower houses' and fortified manor houses. These were more residential extravagances than true castles and were generally lacking in the defensive strength of their predecessors. In eastern England they were frequently of brick, and include examples such as Tattershall castle in Lincolnshire, built by Ralph Cromwell between 1430 and 1450; Caister-by-Yarmouth in Norfolk, built in the mid-fifteenth century; and the Leicestershire castles of Ashby-de-la-Zouch and Kirby Muxloe built by William Lord Hastings at the end of the fifteenth century.

Ralph Lord Cromwell served with the English army in France and was present at the battle of Agincourt (1415). These years spent in the atmosphere of Franco-Burgundian culture of the time appear have left a deep impression on him. He came into his inheritance in 1419, and from 1422 onwards led an active political life. He received a number of appointments such as Constable of Nottingham Castle and Warden of Sherwood Forest, but the climax of his career was the Treasureship of England which he held from 1433 till 1443. The constant reference to this office in the form of the emblem of the purse in the chimney-pieces of the tower at Tattershall is an indication of the weight that was attached to it. One of the motives for

9 A watercolour of
Tattershall castle by
Thomas Girton (1798).
The immense castle
keep was built in brick
by Ralph Lord
Cromwell in the
middle years of the
fifteenth century. This
fine fortified mansion
served both as a
stronghold and a
residence for Ralph
Cromwell who was
Lord Treasurer to
Henry VI between
1433 and 1443

building was to provide himself with accommodation
commensurate with his new status, while clearly the
perquisites of office contributed something towards the
costs. Several details in the tower, notably the gallery, the
chimney-pieces and the moulded brick vaults are decid-
edly continental, which is not surprising as a German,
Baldwin Doecheman, superintended the brickmaking and
exercised general supervision over the early building work.

Bricks had been employed in the eastern counties in the
thirteenth and fourteenth centuries, but were normally
concealed under rendering or plaster. The possibility of
their use of deliberate display was only appreciated in the
last decades of the fourteenth century, coming into full
flower in the second quarter of the fifteenth century, when

a number of major brick buildings, including Eton College, were erected. Between 1460 and 1480 a crop of towers sprang up about the country, all owing something to Tattershall. The best documented of these is the great brick tower in the castle dominating the town of Farnham, Surrey, erected in 1470–5 by the Bishop of Winchester, William Waynflete. The two towers were rather similar in function, which is understandable since the bishop was Cromwell's executor, responsible over many years for the completion of Cromwell's castle at Tattershall.

The reasons for the decline of the English castle are complex and reflect the political and strategic changes which took place during the Middle Ages. The most popular reason generally advanced for the decline of the castle is the introduction of gunpowder which was first used in England about 1325. However, gunpowder did not really render medieval fortifications obsolete until the sixteenth century, and in any case, fortresses were later designed to resist and to be defended by heavy cannon. Even as late as the Civil War many of the old castles, which had been neglected for two centuries, came suddenly into their own and Corfe castle was able to withstand no less than nine months of battering from Cromwell's artillery. By the fifteenth century their military value had declined largely because of changes in warfare which was being waged by larger, more professional armies who conducted their battles in the field.

It was increasingly recognised that long sieges wasted a great deal of time and effort and could still fail to resolve

10 White castle in the former county of Monmouthshire. This is one of the group of castles which belonged to Hubert de Burgh in this part of Wales during the early thirteenth century. The others were Grosmont and Skenfrith. They were part of the second phase of the English attempt to dominate Wales. Located on a lonely hill, it is one of the most evocative of Welsh castles, built almost entirely in the Edwardian style with a six-sided enclosure within deep walls. There is a drum tower at each angle. There appears to have been a short-lived borough established in the shadow of the castle, but no trace of this now survives.

a conflict. As armies grew larger there was a tendency
towards battles in the open countryside, disregarding
occupied castles, which it was argued would sooner or
later fall when the entire territory was in enemy hands.
Throughout the Wars of the Roses the great castles
continued to be used, but they served largely as safe places
in which to keep important prisoners. When Edward IV
was captured near Coventry in 1469 he was kept first in
Warwick castle, and then moved to Middleham, just as he
himself had earlier placed Henry VI in the Tower of
London. Significantly, on the various occasions when
Henry was taken prisoner, it was not after the loss of a
castle but of a battle – at Northampton in 1460, or St
Albans in the following year. And it was such an open
ground battle at Bosworth which finally settled the affair.

Another factor in the disappearance of the castles was

5 Distribution of royal
castles during the
reign of Henry VI
(after Colvin)

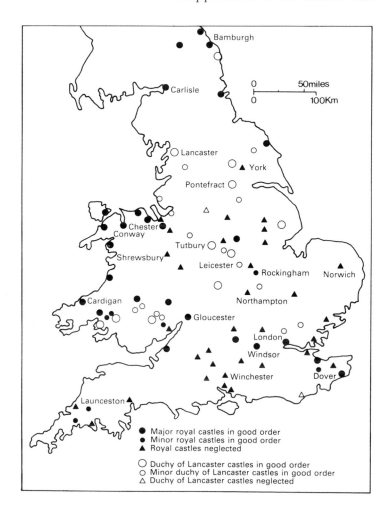

the financial burden they placed upon the crown. The fifteenth century Lancastrian kings owned the majority of castles and their resources were simply inadequate to maintain them all properly. Additionally, as royal administration became increasingly complex and bureaucratic towards the later Middle Ages, so it inevitably became more sedentary. Thus, the king settled down in and around London, the pace and extent of the royal progress through the country declined and there was a corresponding lessening in the need for royal castles. Finally, the gradual development of trade and industry brought into being a middle class which could not afford and did not wish to live in castles, as well as a more sophisticated aristocracy which became accustomed to higher residential standards than those normally available in castles.

Royal houses

Throughout the Middle Ages the king and his court moved about the kingdom. This travelling was in part designed to maintain the peace, but was also necessary in order to spread the burden of sustaining the crown's huge retinue. Each king had his own favourite residences but the pattern of their journeys was also partly dictated by the prevailing political situation. To begin with the king stayed in the great Norman castles, either his own or those of his favourites. Eventually, however, a network of royal houses grew up. Some of these were regular castles or fortified houses, whilst others were relatively modest. Many of the latter started as hunting lodges in the royal forests and finished as the great Tudor royal palaces of Henry VIII.

The history of the king's houses between the thirteenth and fifteenth centuries reflected the fortunes of the castle. Out of approximately twenty houses which Edward I inherited in 1272, only six were still maintained by the crown in 1485. These were Clarendon, Clipstone, Havering, Windsor, Woodstock and Westminster. There were, however, a number of houses which were held intermittently by the king, including Eltham, King's Langley and Sheen. Between 1272 and 1485 there were another twenty-five residences which were held and maintained by the crown for periods ranging from as little as five years to over a century. By the fifteenth century the number of royal houses was appreciably smaller than it had been in the early Middle Ages and their geographical distribution was somewhat different. The houses that Edward I inherited from his father were scattered all over the Midlands and southern England and ministered to the

needs of the itinerant court. In contrast nearly all those
visited by his successors lay within a day's ride of London,
and by the time of the accession of Richard II, Clipstone
was the only royal house remaining north of the Chilterns.
During the Scottish wars of the early fourteenth century
a number of northern houses were acquired, but these
were subsequently granted away. On the accession to the

6 Plan of the king's
house at Clarendon
(Wiltshire) (after
Borenius and Charlton)

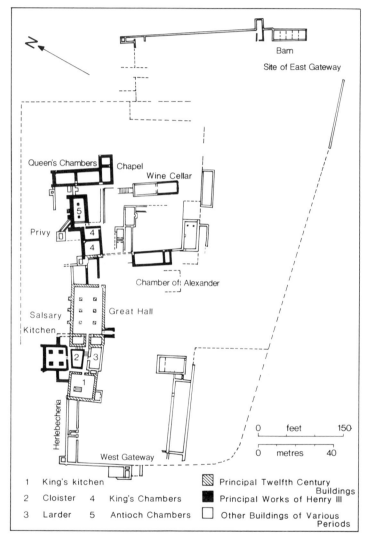

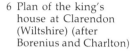

1	King's kitchen	
2	Cloister	4 King's Chambers
3	Larder	5 Antioch Chambers

Principal Twelfth Century Buildings
Principal Works of Henry III
Other Buildings of Various Periods

throne of the Dukes of Lancaster, with their extensive
northern estates, the geographical balance was redressed
somewhat, but little attention was paid to the northern
houses and when the kings of England travelled to the
north in the fifteenth century their usual lodgings were in

castles and religious houses.

The contraction in the number and distribution of royal dwellings in the later Middle Ages was associated with the increasing centralisation of royal government, which made Westminster the administrative capital of Lancastrian and Yorkist England in a way that had not been the case under the Normans and Angevins. It also reflected a decline in royal resources: for during the fourteenth and fifteenth centuries the crown was poorer than it had been in the twelfth and thirteenth centuries. Increasingly the English kings derived their income more from taxation and less from the direct exploitation of the territorial estates with which many of the old royal houses had been associated. Finally, just as castles became less popular for domestic purposes, so too the later medieval kings were accustomed to a higher standard of accommodation than that available in most of the traditional residences. The old Angevin hunting lodges would almost certainly have seemed primitive to the tastes of Edward III or Richard II and by the middle of the fourteenth century only a major reconstruction could have brought such houses as Brigstock, Feckenham, King's Cliffe and Silverstone up to standard. Accordingly they were allowed to fall into decay or were demolished. Freemantle was pulled down in 1276, Feckenham in 1356, Gillingham in 1369, Kempton in 1374. Silverstone was alienated in 1317, Brill in 1337, and Brigstock, Geddington and King's Cliffe had all become uninhabitable by the end of the fourteenth century. In 1310 Edward II gave his house at Oxford to the Carmelite friars, and with the abandonment of the royal house at Bath, and the decay of the 'palace' at Guildford, Coventry was the only provincial town where the king had an unfortified residence.

As the older royal houses in the Midlands and the southwest were being abandoned or demolished, new houses mainly in south-eastern England were being built or acquired. Edward III's principal habitations were concentrated in and around the Thames valley. At Windsor, in particular, he maintained a ring of houses and hunting lodges around the castle so that residences were available throughout the forest. Windsor castle became his normal residence and after 1372 the court remained almost permanently at Windsor or Havering. Richard II also enjoyed the use of the manor house at Kennington, near Lambeth, which he had inherited from his father, the Black Prince. Just before his accession in 1377, the citizens of London staged a torch-light procession for his benefit and were afterwards feasted in the hall. However, Sheen appears to have been Richard's favourite residence and here, on an adjoining island in the Thames, he built a small timber-framed building to which he and his queen could retire from the court. This was apparently the equivalent of the modern summer-house, the first known building of this character to be recorded in England.

Fortified houses

There had always been a conflict in the design of castles, between the demands of military efficiency and the comfort expected by the lord in what was also his residence. With the decline in the military importance of the castle, the emphasis changed. The result in a few cases was a more luxurious castle, as at Bodiam. More often however, the solution was to build a house rather than a castle and to fortify it as required. Fortified houses began to develop in some numbers during the thirteenth century but were mainly built between 1270 and 1370, often in more pleasant and accessible locations than castles.

The licensing and control of fortification was one of the most ancient and jealously guarded prerogatives of the crown. In order to fortify his manor house the lord was required, in theory, to obtain a license to crenellate. In

11 Stokesay castle and church, Shropshire, one of the best known fortified manor houses in Britain. It was built for the prosperous wool merchant Lawrence of Ludlow in the latter part of the thirteenth century and although defence was clearly a consideration, it was designed principally as a residence

the border counties, however, the Marcher lords were empowered to grant licences to fortify houses in the areas they controlled and during the early Middle Ages permission to issue such licenses seems also to have been vested in other territorial lords. By the middle of the thirteenth century these licenses had assumed a standard formula, whereby the licensee was allowed to strengthen his manor house with a moat, and a wall of stone and lime, with crenellations and battlements. Between 1399 and 1470 the need to obtain a royal license to fortify seems to have been less rigidly enforced by the Lancastrian kings, and considerably fewer licenses were granted by the crown, although possibly this also reflects a decline in the extent of building. Fortified houses reached their peak in the first quarter of the fourteenth century, a period of marked civil lawlessness. The reign of Edward II (1307–27) was marked by political unrest and rebellion and it can be no coincidence that the resultant breakdown of law and order was reflected in one of the highest concentrations of licenses taken out in the Middle Ages.

The precise number of medieval fortified houses constructed in England is not known, partly because of the difficulty in classification and partly because they were not all recorded in documentary sources or have not even necessarily been identified on the ground. There were at least 450 licenses to crenellate granted in the Middle Ages, but there were probably many more fortified houses in existence for which licenses were never obtained or recorded. They were to be found not only along the Scottish borders and along the Welsh Marches, where there were external enemies, but also far away from national boundaries where no such outside threat existed. There were approximately 30 in Staffordshire, for example, 20 in Leicestershire and 22 in Bedfordshire. It is therefore fair to assume that the siting and distribution of the fortified houses tended to reflect local and regional patterns of land ownership rather than any national plan.

Among the earliest and most striking examples were Stokesay and Acton Burnell in Shropshire. Stokesay Castle, probably the best known fortified medieval manor house in England, was built by a prosperous Shropshire wool merchant, Laurence of Ludlow. In 1294 it was recorded that 'certain English merchants, licensed by the King, crossed the sea with their wool; these ought to have been led by Laurence of Ludlow . . .', but Laurence had been drowned at sea. Laurence received a license to crenellate Stokesay in 1291 when he probably added another

tower. Its great hall, whose substantial windows make it
scarcely defensible, was probably built in the 1270s. A
major boost to the fashion for building fortified manor
houses appears to have followed on from Edward I's
conquest of Wales. In 1280 Robert Burnell rebuilt the castle
at Holdgate (Salop). As Chancellor of England he was well
aware of the castles being built in north Wales and the
remarkable surviving tower of this structure, now sitting
behind a sixteenth-century farmhouse, illustrates the
extent of his wealth and importance. But perhaps more
representative of this movement was the castle at Acton
Burnell (Salop) which was built after the conclusion of the
wars in 1284. It is a large rectangular house with square
towers projecting at each corner, it is moatless and the
doorways are sited at ground level. Despite its outward
appearance Acton Burnell castle had a thoroughly
domestic function. The castle sits next to the ruins of a
structure which carries the grand title of the 'Parliament
Barn', so called as a result of the first representative parliament being held here on the occasion of a visit from
Edward I.

At Bolton castle (Yorks), built almost a century later,
considerable emphasis was placed on the domestic facilities. The plan is compact with high rectangular corner
towers, projecting only slightly, and no gatehouse. The

12 The sombre ruins of
the fortified manor
house at Acton
Burnell, Shropshire.
This castle was built
by Robert Burnell,
Bishop of Bath and
Wells, and also
Chancellor of England
at the end of the
thirteenth century.
Although it adopts
some of the styles of
the Edwardian
castles, the absence of
a moat and outer
defences indicate that
it too was designed
primarily as a
residence.

main accommodation was at first-floor level where the great hall, the kitchen, the chapel and the private family quarters occupy much of the north, west and south ranges. The east range, incorporating the entrance passage, was primarily geared towards defence. In spite of its impressive height Bolton castle is far less military-looking externally than Bodiam, and certainly a long way removed from any of the great Edwardian castles. Its relatively plain external walls were simply a secure cladding for a large domestic establishment.

By the end of the Middle Ages the creation of new wealth from sheep farming and commercial activities enabled local gentry to build new houses on a larger, more grandiose scale, and to forsake what one observer called 'the damp, insanitary sites of former ages'. However, not all moated sites were unhealthy and damp, as Lord Hastings's fortified house at Kirby Muxloe in Leicestershire testifies. To create the great rectangular pool many hundred cubic yards of soil were removed and a stream dammed and diverted. An older manor house at Kirby was partly incorporated in the new building but the much more ambitious scale of the new moated house took in

13 Old Bolingbroke, Lincolnshire. The recently uncovered remains of John of Gaunt's hexagonal castle at Old Bolingbroke lie within a massive perimeter boundary. This also incorporates a substantial pond or small lake used certainly for fish breeding, but also perhaps for pleasure purposes as well. Henry IV, son of John of Gaunt, was born here in 1367. In 1643 the castle was captured by the Parliamentarians and destroyed immediately afterwards

41

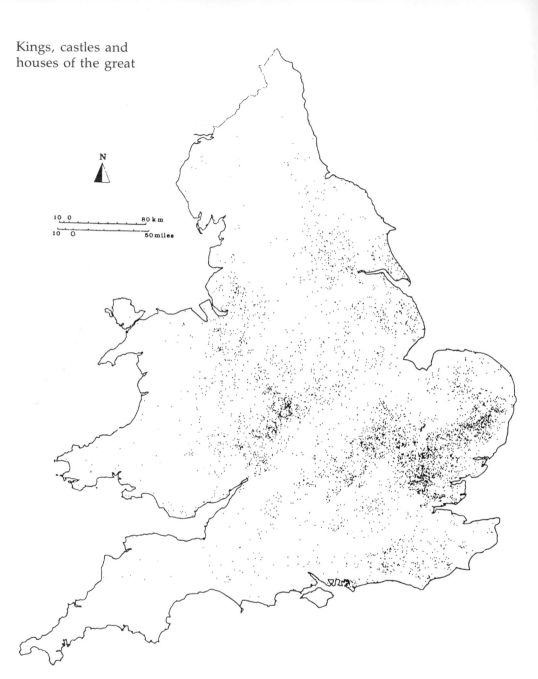

N

10 0 _____ 80 km
10 0 _____ 50 miles

7 Distribution map of
moated sites in
England and Wales
(after Aberg)

former orchards and gardens, from which it is recorded
labourers had to remove trees: oaks, ashes and elms. By
the spring of 1481 eleven ditchers were working four days
a week on the moat. The type of manor house which Lord
Hastings built bore only a superficial resemblance to the
solid castles of the earlier Middle Ages. Although
defensive needs were considered, the house being

equipped with gunports, as so often was the case, the defences would only have withstood a moderate assault. A relatively new element in the design of the house was the amount of careful attention given to decoration and display. The house was set back from the village with an open approach, across which its proportions could be admired. Brick was the principal building material used and courses of brickwork were made into patterned decor-

ations culminating in an heraldic design over the main gate. The manor at Kirby was intended primarily as a country gentleman's house and not a fortress. The same principle can be seen at another of Lord Hastings's castles built at Ashby-de-la-Zouch. Within a few years Thomas Grey built another brick house at Bradgate Park four miles away, and this had no fortifications at all.

Such grand fortified houses were largely or entirely new foundations of the fourteenth and fifteenth centuries, and as such reflected contemporary attitudes to domestic comfort in fortified premises. Such new houses were, however, still greatly outnumbered by existing castles. For simple economic reasons it was not possible to build entirely afresh. In such cases the demand for greater domestic space and comfort was met by additions to the

14 Kirby Muxloe, Leicestershire. The remains of a fine but unfinished house at Kirby Muxloe, built by Lord Hastings in the early 1480s. Hastings was executed in 1484. The house is particularly important as it was intended to incorporate a considerable number of luxury features which became commonplace in the country houses of the sixteenth century as defensive considerations were gradually dropped altogether

existing fabric, and this practice goes a long way to explain
the great variety in the appearance of British castles as we
see them now. Most frequently the additions took the
form of new towers which, with their many floor levels,
added greatly to the volume of accommodation available.
An excellent example of this is provided by the late fourteenth-century developments at Warwick castle. Gradually
defensive considerations were completely abandoned and

15 Moat and outer
courtyard wall of
Pembridge castle,
Welsh Newton,
Herefordshire. The
castle served as a
dwelling house
throughout the
Middle Ages

by the second half of the sixteenth century, although a
considerable number of medieval fortified houses were
still occupied, the new country houses which were being
built incorporated only the most perfunctory architectural
defences.

Moated manors and farmsteads

As we have seen, some fortified houses used moats as a
means of protection but there was another category of
moated sites, lower down the social scale. These lesser
moated sites were a common feature of the medieval landscape, numbering well over 5,000 and located in every
county in the country. The definition of the term 'moated
site' is a complex one thus the simplicity of the term is
deceptive, in so far as the only unifying feature was the
moat itself. In the broadest sense, the term includes a wide

range of sites from castles with moats, through the great moated fortified houses such as Kirby Muxloe, to much more modest moated farmsteads. It is normally taken to mean a manor house or farmstead which was surrounded by a wide ditch usually containing water. Indeed, it was only the presence of such an encircling ditch which distinguished these dwellings from the normal manor house. Their owners tended to be the smaller landowners

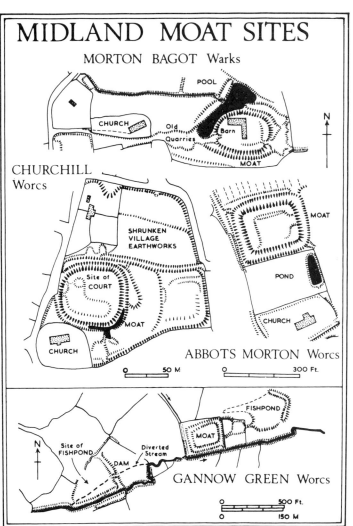

and their moated homesteads represented working units in the land-use pattern of the period up to about 1400.

The typical moated site consisted of a roughly rectangular 'island' surrounded by a ditch, which could be oval, circular, triangular, pentagonal or quite irregular

in shape. They also consisted of 'double' or even triple
moats normally lying adjacent to each other – in such cases
each of the islands appears to have performed a separate
function, one occupied by the house, the others by various
outbuildings and gardens. The enclosing ditches were
usually between 3 and 6 yards across. The 'island' aver-
aged 4,000 square yards in size and was usually located
on flat land or on land level with the surrounding countryside. The size of the dwelling built on the site varied
considerably, from a quite small, simple house to a much
larger complex one with yard, barns, stables and gardens.
Access to the moated homesteads was provided by a
causeway, drawbridge or permanent bridge. The function
of the moats has in recent years been the subject of
considerable speculation. Reasons put forward for moat
construction have included defence, drainage and fashion,
added to which moats clearly had an economic function
and could be stocked with fish and used by ducks and
swans.

During the twelfth century only a small number of
moated sites were constructed and the majority came into
being between about 1200 and 1325, with perhaps as many
as 70 per cent of known sites dating from this period.
Following the economic recession of the fourteenth
century fewer were built, although there was still a tendency for the grander aristocratic dwellings to be moated.
Three areas in particular had considerable concentration
of sites: the tract of country between Chelmsford and
Harlow in Essex and Bishop's Stortford in Hertfordshire;
an area extending from Suffolk into north Essex, with a
particular concentration north of Framlingham; and the
Birmingham area extending south into Warwickshire and
Worcestershire. Northern and southwestern England
contained virtually no moated sites, nor did the areas of
higher inhospitable ground such as the Pennines and
Exmoor.

From an examination of the distribution of moats within
individual counties, it is clear that surface geology, soils
and drainage played an important part in their location
although a number of other local factors also contributed.
Moated sites were frequently associated with medieval
land reclamation, and were particularly common in areas
of former wood, waste and marsh. Many moats carry place
names which incorporate elements associated with late
secondary medieval settlement, such as 'green', 'field',
'wood', 'ash', 'oak' or 'marsh'. In some counties moated
sites tended to be thickly clustered in areas of former royal

forest, being founded as the land was taken out of royal
control and brought under cultivation. This is well illustrated in Worcestershire, where there was a particularly
dense concentration of moats in the former areas of Feckenham Forest and Malvern Chase, where much assarting
took place during the twelfth and thirteenth centuries. On
the other hand, moats are markedly absent from the
forests of Wyre and Kinver in the northern part of the
county. These areas remained as royal forests throughout
the Middle Ages and were thus in theory protected from
assarting. A similar pattern can be observed in the adjacent
county of Warwickshire, with its twofold division into
Arden and Fielden, which lay respectively north and south
of the river Avon. The former was poor and infertile, well
wooded and settled relatively late, while the latter was
prosperous with fertile soils and little woodland and
settled at a much earlier date. It is significant therefore
that to the north and east of the Avon moated sites are
plentiful, while to the south they are rare.

In Lincolnshire, where moated homesteads were
common, much of the land was held by socage, that is
by freemen in exchange for fixed services to the lord.
Accordingly large manors centred on a single village were
rare. As a result, the tenurial framework of land-holding
was such that moated settlements could easily develop.
Rapid growth in population in the mid-thirteenth century
led to a demand for land by the large class of freeholders
which had recently emerged. The larger landowners,
impoverished by the Barons' Wars, met these demands
by subdividing their manors and granting lands to the
freeholders. Members of this new class of sub-tenants
appear then to have improved an existing hall or built a
new house with a moat, perhaps as a safety insurance, or
possibly to herald their new status and relative prosperity.

Moated sites were rarely integrated into the medieval
village layout and were often located just outside the
ancient village core. In the Welsh Marches during the later
Middle Ages there was a tendency to build new moated
manor houses sited well away from the main village settlement, replacing earlier manor houses which had lain
within the village. When manors were divided into two
or more portions, new moated manor houses were often
created and sited away from the village. In Leicestershire,
however, the earthworks of former moated manor houses
can be seen sitting in the middle of the earthworks of
deserted medieval villages. Although it is not unknown to
find moats actually wi.hin the village fabric, the stra-

tigraphy of these earthworks would suggest that in these cases the moat was dug either after the village had been abandoned or while it was in the process of decay.

The pattern of distribution of moated sites can therefore be seen as a product of a complex pattern of a wide range of social, economic, historical and geographical factors. The most plausible explanation of the chronology and distribution of moated sites makes them a passing seigneurial fashion among the ranks of society below the contemporary castle builders. Moat building, whether as a defensive device or a status symbol, largely died out during the later Middle Ages. As the pressure on land eased, the marginal areas where many moated farmsteads had been built became economically less important and by 1500 many moated farmsteads had already been abandoned.

Water, fishponds and mills

Throughout the Middle Ages water management was of considerable importance. An efficient system of running water was an obvious advantage to keep moats clean but effective water control was required for a wide range of other activities, such as milling and to replenish fish ponds. In Castle Rising (Norfolk) the parish boundary has a long narrow projecting tongue following one bank of a stream, at the end of which projection stands a mill. It appears that when the parish boundaries were established, it was considered important enough to guarantee that a strip of land should be retained for a path and millrace to serve the mill.

Fishponds were often found attached to castles, moated manors and monasteries. During the thirteenth century royal ponds were producing large quantities of fish for the king's table and for stocking the ponds of favoured subjects. Research in Warwickshire and elsewhere has shown that fishponds were not a seigneurial monopoly; villagers as well as manorial households drew fish from them. Pike was the most popular fish, but eels, tench, bream, perch and roach were all common. During the early sixteenth century Prior Morton of Worcester produced fish on a commercial scale, as well as experimenting with carp. Chub do not feature unless they happened to be accidentally present, while trout were a post-medieval introduction.

River valleys throughout the country were intensively occupied and exploited and many isolated valleys still contain a wealth of earthworks and relict features. Many

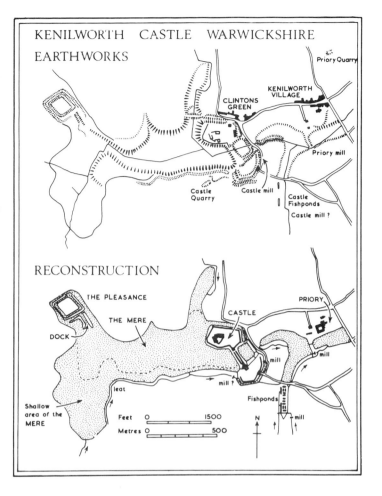

of the valleys which in the Middle Ages would have been full of activity are today largely empty and overgrown. In many cases the dams of medieval fishponds have been breached and are today dry, but the surviving earthworks are often distinctive. A regular unexplained break of slope across the valley floor will frequently mark the site of an old dam. In many cases there will have been a series of linked ponds, leaving a string of valley earthwork remains. They were normally rectangular excavations beside a small stream or spring and are not generally found in close proximity to large streams or rivers. Other examples have embankments to maintain a pool of moderate depth, with either a gentle flow of water through the pool or a system of sluices to isolate the pond's water completely.

The pond was frequently made by building an earthen bank across the line of a watercourse. One side of this bank might be stone-revetted for strength, while a sluice

49

served to let excess water escape. Where possible, the
shape of the valley retained the pond, but if the valley
sides themselves were not sufficiently steep, two further
embankments were often built parallel to the stream. A
fourth bank upstream was sometimes constructed to
complete the rectangle. In their developed form fishponds
had auxiliary breeding tanks linked to them by a maze of
channels and sluices, with different chambers for different

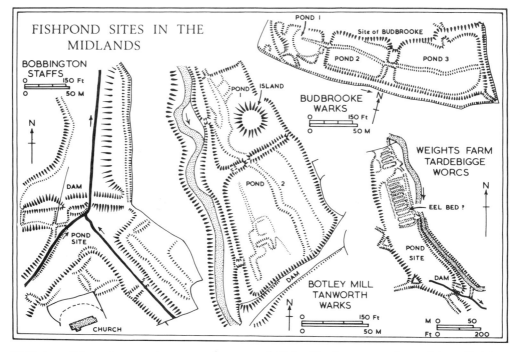

10 Various fishpond
earthworks in the
Midlands

types and ages of fish. Such a complex of interlinking
ponds was identified at Bordesley Abbey, Worcestershire,
where an intricate system of water management operated.
Not far away at Washford Mill, a Knights Templar establishment, the excavation of another fishpond complex
revealed traces of timber buildings, together with a woven
straw pannier used to transfer the fish from breeding tanks
to the larger ponds.

Islands in the ponds were common and are thought to
have been used for growing reeds and rushes and serving
as a home for waterfowl. The most fully developed
complexes were like those at Harrington in Northamptonshire, close to another preceptory of the Knights Templar.
This consisted of a battery of different shaped embanked
ponds, lying in a shallow valley, with deep supply channels and linked by a complex system of waterways. A
mighty dam at the royal fishpond site at Silverstone

created what was the largest lake in Northamptonshire until the late eighteenth century. The parish boundary at Silverstone appears to have been altered to follow the stream which no longer runs down the valley but is carried round the pond by a high-level leat.

Often it is only the mute record of earthworks which survives to tell of the enormous effort which went into the construction of these integral elements of the medieval

economy. Occasionally, however, there are hints in the documents of the activities of the silent armies of engineers and labourers who constructed the castles, moats, fishponds and watermills. There is a casual reference to the repair of a dam at one of the king's fishponds at Woodstock in 1249. Also there is, for example, a reference to *fossatores* and other workmen digging trenches, excavating the moat and putting up a new barricade round the site of Beaumaris castle. The thirteenth-century *Red Book of Worcester* tells of islands in fishponds at Alvechurch (Worcs) which can still be recognised on the ground today. Late thirteenth and early fourteenth-century documents mention a moat (literally 'dug out waters'), a fishery, two

11 An early fourteenth-century sketch of digging out water works (B.M.M.S. Egerton 1984 f. 14a)

51

islands in that fishery, a mill pool and two mills. One mill
survives and a house has been built on the site of the
Bishop of Worcester's Palace but the other features survive
only in earthwork form. In 1312 a mill was built for the
Earl of Arundel at Acton Round (Salop). The following
account gives a good idea of the landscape implications of
creating such water works:

For making the walls	14s 3d
For the mason for building the walls and digging the stone	33s 3d
For Rich. Crumpe for the same	5s 8d
For making 430 laths for the same mill	10s 3d
For buying iron and making russes for mill wheel	9s 7d
For buying two mill stones	24s
For carriage	6d
For cord	1½d
For wax	1d
For thatch covering	1s 6d
For a basket	3d
For 1 plate	3d
For digging the pond for 4 days	2s 2d
By way of payment for digging the mill ditch to the pond for 14 days	16s ½d
Labour for 5 hours for 18 days	9s 4d
For 42 hours labour at the same place	9s
For 2 carpenters for 3 days to cart way timber	12d
Stipend for carpenters for 8 days	16d
	£6 18s 7d

Excavating and building probably represented the most
important non-agrarian activity in medieval England.
Throughout the country there remains evidence of this
industry; medieval energy created a deeply engrained
landscape which, in rural areas at least, survived with
little alteration into the nineteenth century. Traces of the
buildings and landscape of the Middle Ages still provide
us with a rich historical document, as the photographs
and plans in this book clearly demonstrate. It is, however,
a record which is diminishing each year and if the pace of
destruction continues at its present rate, ours will be the
last generation privileged to see these works except in
isolated pockets.

Villages in the late Middle Ages

Chapter three

The countryside fills up

The Domesday Book (1086) clearly demonstrates that by
the late eleventh century England was a much occupied
country. Throughout the folios of the Domesday survey
we are able to detect a countryside in the process of filling
up, a process that was to continue for a further two
centuries, so that by 1300 it is estimated that the level of
population could have been as high as 5 million. The
population was not, however, uniformly distributed, the
highest density being in East Anglia and gradually thin-
ning out towards the west where there were considerable
areas of woodland and marshland remaining to be brought
into cultivation. Nevertheless by 1086 it would appear that
almost all the potentially good agricultural land was under
cultivation. There were still some notably blank areas, such
as the forest lands of north Warwickshire, which were
colonised during the following two centuries, and the dry
sandy soil belt of Surrey, Berkshire and Hampshire. These
were not to be brought into cultivation until the seventeenth and eighteenth centuries, but in England as a whole
there were not the large expanses of 'wilderness' available
for systematic colonisation which were still to be found in
continental Europe at this time. All that remained for the
increasing population of the early Middle Ages to colonise
was land which was essentially marginal, at least for arable
farming. The settlement history of the early Middle Ages
should therefore be seen against a background of dwindling land resources.

The precise effects of these developments on the settlement pattern are difficult to gauge, but by 1300, when we
have a reasonably complete archaeological record as well
as a daunting body of documentary evidence, the pattern
is fairly clear. In some places these sources enable all
aspects of village life to be reconstructed – the seigneurial
and ecclesiastic administration, the commercial, economic
and social life, and occasionally even the detailed pattern
of the evolving village morphology. In 1300 nucleated
settlement was to be found over much of the country.
Compact and often well regulated villages with dependent

vills or townships all sitting within their own open fields distributed at roughly one-mile intervals was the normal pattern over most of lowland England. Naturally the details varied considerably from village to village and from one region to another; but in general terms each village had its church, manor house and more humble tenements sited close to each other, surrounded by a considerable acreage of arable land, normally divided up into strips. A mass of tracks and ways serviced the fields and eventually led to common meadows, pasture, waste and woodland. The lord would have reserved a certain area of 'demesne' or land for his own cultivation. Where seigneurial control was strong the lord also reserved other areas for his exclusive hunting activities in the form of deer parks.

The large nucleated village was of course not universal. Many dependent townships often occupying the less attractive land were by their very nature quite small, and in areas where pastoral farming continued to dominate, the need for regulation was less and the dispersed hamlet and isolated farm continued to exist. In medieval Wales for instance, the ideal bond hamlet legally consisted of only nine houses. In such areas it was often the 'infield-outfield' system which persisted, with animals grazing on the extensive common pastures, parts of which were subject only to intermittent cultivation. Whatever the detailed arrangements, however, the picture that emerges over much of the country is of a tightly managed landscape. The manorial court was responsible for the regulation of internal field boundaries, the precise amount of grazing and rights of gathering on the common waste, and it also supervised trackways, protecting free passage, and the streams, ensuring that they were not illegally disturbed. The manor court collectively administered rules of husbandry, watched over the local customs of tenure and inheritance, and enforced local peace and order.

By 1300 it is possible to identify a series of English landscapes which were being fully used at a subsistence level. A glance at an aerial photograph of the countryside of central England will reveal the intensity of medieval cultivation. Ridge and furrow is to be found over considerable areas of the Midlands, in some places appearing to cover individual parishes completely. Terracing was even introduced in some places in order to exploit steep ground and valley slopes which had not previously been cultivated. Additionally traces of medieval field cultivation are to be found at heights of over 1,000 feet on moorland and hillside in places such as Dartmoor, indicating that great pressure was being exerted on limited land resources, so much so that Professor Postan concludes:

> In the older parts of England the lands taken up for the first time by the arable farmers in the 13th century were as a rule of the lowest possible quality; too forbidding to have tempted the settlers of earlier centuries, and some of them too unremunerative to have been maintained in cultivation by farmers of a later age.

The countryside was already too full to enable the plantation of a rash of new villages; the equivalent of the French *villeneuve* were the new urban centres which sprang up throughout the country in the twelfth and thirteenth centuries and which were able to absorb some of the surplus population. It is difficult to overestimate the scale of medieval urban plantation, places such as Salisbury, which were created as administrative and ecclesiastical centres, but above all designed to attract, develop and monopolise trade. At a more modest level there is ample evidence to show that many hamlets were being created or expanded in the twelfth and thirteenth centuries. In some cases it is possible to detect village expansion on to areas of former arable, where new tenements were carved

16 The deserted medieval village of Onley, Northamptonshire, shows the remains of the village enclosures and high street lying on top of ridge and furrow. This would indicate that the village was laid out over the top of arable land, probably at a time of land hunger in the twelfth or thirteenth century

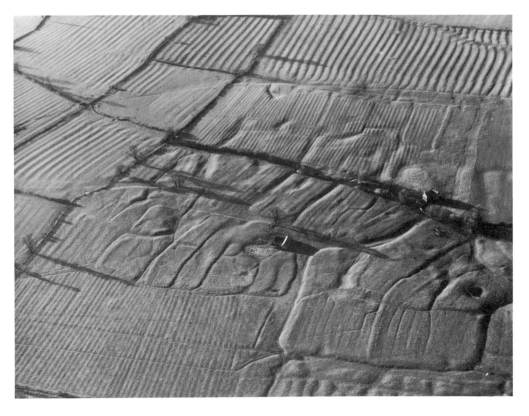

out of the open-field system. Aerial photographs of deserted village earthworks frequently demonstrate this phenomenon. At Cestersover, Warwickshire, the southern part of the deserted village earthworks extend over the top of an area of ridge and furrow, while at Newbold Grounds in the parish of Catesby, Northants, the entire village earthworks sit on top of ridge and furrow. These villages were often based on isolated farms, or in the case

12 Outline plan of the deserted village of Cestersover (Warwickshire), showing village earthworks extending over areas of former ridge and furrow

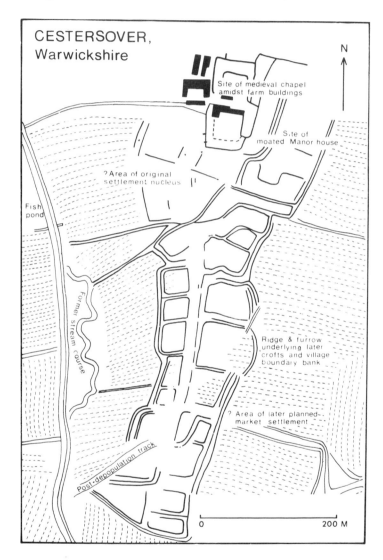

CESTERSOVER, Warwickshire

N

Site of medieval chapel amidst farm buildings

Site of moated Manor house

? Area of original settlement nucleus

Fish pond

Former stream course

Ridge & furrow underlying later crofts and village boundary bank

? Area of later planned-market settlement

Post-depopulation track

0   200 M

of Lychett Minster (Dorset), field chapels; here the chapel lay on the edge of Wareham Forest and was first recorded in 1244, when marginal land was being developed. The records of 'assarting' (land colonisation) everywhere tell a story of land, often of a very inferior quality, being brought into cultivation. In parts of the country assarting was associated not so much with the creation of new villages or even hamlets, but with the establishment of isolated farmsteads, operating from within newly won agricultural land. Frequently, as we have seen, such farmsteads were surrounded by a simple moat, dug partially for reasons of rudimentary safety and partially for reasons of status. As one might expect moated sites are often found on marginal ground and were frequently abandoned during the later Middle Ages. There is an unusual group of such moated sites on top of the Chiltern hills in Buckinghamshire, now hidden under extensive beech woods, these sometimes formidable earthworks providing us with convincing reminders of medieval land hunger.

There were a few areas where more ambitious village colonisation took place. In a 1251 survey of Downham in the Cambridgeshire fens there were 13 new free tenants holding 69 acres of reclaimed land at a place called *Apesholte*, while in the adjacent parish and manor of Littleport 60 new tenants were holding nearly 500 acres of similarly reclaimed land in the same area. Further northwest at Doddington, which then included the present parishes of March, Wimblington and Benwick, many new assarts were recorded in 1251 as well as 111 new tenants. All these areas of reclamation lay on the lands of the Bishop of Ely, a prolific land reclaimer during the early Middle Ages. Certain large-scale drainage enterprises in the fens created completely new villages. For example, in Elloe Wapentake, Holland (Lincs) some 30 square miles of fenland was reclaimed and settled between 1170 and 1240. Fleet (Lincs), one of the new villages, was composed of a regular row of homesteads sited next to their portions of the newly reclaimed fields, each of which stretched into the fen. Today many fenland 'villages' have been all but abandoned in favour of earlier established, less exposed settlements.

The nucleated village
One of the problems involved in writing about a national phenomenon such as the village is that local and regional differences are so marked that generalisation is often invalid. Settlement patterns and the shapes of individual settlements have never been absolutely static and there are numerous examples of changes even during the thirteenth and fourteenth centuries. Some scholars of settlement history now go as far as to maintain that the volatility

of settlements was such that no firm rules can be laid
down about settlement dynamics, apart from the fact that
there has always been change.

The nucleated village which is such a familiar element
in the landscape today was a factor not of ethnic or cultural
origin, as earlier generations of scholars maintained, but
of economic and social forces. Nucleation appears to have
been brought about by a combination of increasing population and increasing authoritarian control through the
manorial and parochial systems. The need to maximise
food production was matched by increased control by the
owners of land, and, as it happened, the church tightened
its control at the same time. Many communities which
had previously possessed dependent chapels or had been
served from a central minster-church gained parochial
independence in the twelfth and thirteenth centuries. The
creation of new churches and parishes, an important
development of the early medieval period, appears to have
reinforced the emphasis on nodal settlement. For a time
the very presence of a large, imposing stone building in
the village appears to have had a stabilising effect upon
the geography of the settlement and the psychology of the
community. The overall rigidity of land tenure that had
developed by the thirteenth century appears for a short
while to have brought about a slowing down in settlement
mobility. By 1200 the basic pattern of village distribution
was established and to some extent fossilised, the
constraints imposed by a strictly disciplined communal
agrarian system being such that it required the very
erosion of that system to enable settlement mobility to
operate once more on a large scale.

Open-field agriculture and village nucleation can now be
demonstrated as a widespread feature of the high Middle
Ages. Writers such as H.L. Gray in his book *English Field
Systems* (1915) claimed that the distribution of open-field
arable was limited primarily to the Midlands. However,
later scholars using a wider range of sources, including
field evidence, have come to the conclusion that open-
field agriculture in one form or another was to be found
in every English county. Even in the lowland areas of
central and southern Wales open-field strip farming
appears to have been introduced where circumstances
were favourable, and in the southwest of England, areas
such as northwestern Somerset and Devon provide
evidence of open-field agriculture in the lower, flatter,
more fertile coastal plains. In reality Gray's map of the
Midland field system more accurately presents the areas of

open-field which survived into the post-medieval period, rather than the full extent of medieval open-field farming.

We can perhaps take the argument a little further; in the southwest, the Welsh border and the northwest there appears to have been an uneven move towards open-field farming accompanied by settlement nucleation in the early Middle Ages. Often land which in the long run was totally unsuitable for arable farming had been brought into cultivation, but as soon as local pressure for land was eased, it reverted to its traditional use as pasture or rough grazing. Thus in some parts of the country open-field agriculture with its associated system of strip farming was apparently a short-lived feature of the landscape, surviving for less than two or three centuries. The archaeological record of ridge and furrow in these areas tends to be correspondingly slight compared to areas such as the Midlands where the system survived for almost a thousand years.

After the open-field system decayed, nucleation was no longer a pre-requisite of the agrarian regime and once bundles of strips had been enclosed into hedged fields centralised communities could even be a positive disadvantage. It is therefore hardly surprising that it was precisely in those areas where open-field agriculture was abandoned first that the village fabric crumbled earliest of all. We then see a reversion to a mixed pattern of scattered farmsteads and hamlets. Conversely nucleated villages survived best in those areas – namely the Midland counties – where regulated open-field agriculture continued to operate into the eighteenth and even the nineteenth century.

We know about almost all the English villages which were in existence by 1316 from a document known as the *Nomina Villarum*, added to which there is the almost complete coverage of the lay subsidy of 1334, with its extensive lists of settlements. Between them these documents name over 14,000 villages and additionally include many unspecified hamlets and places. However, the documents reveal relatively little about village topography or about the nature of the dwellings which lay within the villages. Medieval records are generally silent about the shape and form of the settlements they assess or tax, for that was not the purpose when they were made. A few rare surveys include topographical information, such as the rentals of the Peterborough Abbey manors (*c*.1400) which describe the tenants' houses as they lay along the village streets. More common are indirect references, such

as those included in a mid-fourteenth century rental for
Sherborne (Glos), which located the tenements in the 'East
End' and 'West End' of the village. The division between
the two ends survives today, with the church and manor
lying at either extreme. In many cases later layouts have
replaced medieval ones, and new houses have obliterated
traces of their predecessors. Even the shape of a village in
the fifteenth or sixteenth century may be no guide to its

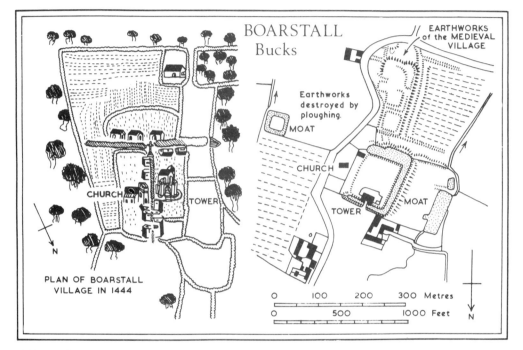

13 Boarstall,
Buckinghamshire.
Comparison of the
mid-fifteenth-century
map (*left*) compared
with the earthworks
of today

plan two or three centuries earlier. If we compare the plan
of the village of Boarstall (Bucks) as it appears on one of
the very earliest maps, dated 1444, with the remains of
the settlement as it is today we can see that there is very
little correlation between the two (Fig. 13).

As we shall see, excavation on deserted medieval village
sites has warned us about the dangers of taking later
village plans too literally. We must be wary of discussing
medieval villages in terms of their present form or from
their form as seen on the first maps. In much the same
way as many place-names have changed beyond recognition, so too have the villages to which they are attached.

Planned villages
The work of Dr Brian Roberts and others has indicated
that the early medieval period witnessed a major redesign
of villages in northern England with tofts being laid out

on regular lines, using standardised measures. Manorial documents attest to the existence of two-row, and in some cases three– and four-row settlements on the estates of the Bishops of Durham, where new settlements were laid out using uniform units of measurement. In some cases the documents provide a clue to the location of the rows by the inclusion of a compass point, such as 'West Row' and 'East Row'. Through a combination of documentary

research and an examination of existing boundaries on the ground Roberts has convincingly suggested that many Durham villages were replanned in the twelfth and thirteenth centuries as a necessity, following the devastation of the northern borders – the 'Harrying of the North' by William the Conqueror. In some areas villages would have been rebuilt, but in others new sites were chosen and the planned village appears to have grown at the expense of smaller hamlets located nearby. Aycliffe, a large multiple-row green village, was listed in a gilly-corn schedule along with the villages of Newton Ketton, Chilton, Woodham and the hamlet of Woodhouses. Gilly-corn rents were paid by all bond and free tenants of the monks of Durham as a contribution to the provision of alms and were levied on lands brought into production before 1200. Significantly, Newton Ketton was already mentioned as early as 1235 as having 'formerly' sixteen tenants and the settlement had

17 The regulated medieval village at Appleton-le-Moors in Yorkshire. The common characteristics of such settlements take the form of a central axial road, regular property boundaries running off at right angles from the main street and regular back lanes on either side. The church occupies a prominent position at the apex of the village and there is little evidence of the village expanding outside its original core. Such symmetrical villages are particularly common in the north-east of England, but are found in other parts of the country.

completely disappeared by the early fifteenth century. Woodham suffered a similar fate, Woodhouses can no longer be traced in the landscape, and although Chilton still survives aerial photographs have revealed evidence of considerable shrinkage. It seems likely that the new village of Aycliffe had absorbed some of the population from the other communities. In the same way the two-row green settlements of Middridge, Cowpen Bewley and Bolam

18 The deserted medieval village at Walworth, County Durham. The earthworks of the former village here can be seen arranged around what was formerly a square green. The green is now occupied by a farmstead and the presence of a large house and garden on the left hand side suggests that the village was removed as a result of emparking, probably in the sixteenth century. If the village had survived in its original form it would have provided a remarkable example of a planned square medieval rural settlement

show evidence of an 'Old Town' site lying amidst the fields.

In the case of East Witton (Fig. 14), a village in the Pennine dales, it is possible to trace the replanning of the settlement in the early fourteenth century. The original community was in the form of a hamlet straggling from the ancient church of St Ella northwest towards a once extensive marginal green near Scane Sike. In 1086 there were just 13 tenants in the township, but by 1627 in addition to the hamlet which then had 17 houses, there was a well defined street green with 22 houses on the northern side and 25 on the southern. Jervaulx Abbey appears to have been responsible for the development of the new green village designed to provide a setting for the Monday market and Michaelmas fair first held here in 1307.

A somewhat later and unusual example of village replanning comes from the delightful village of Mells in

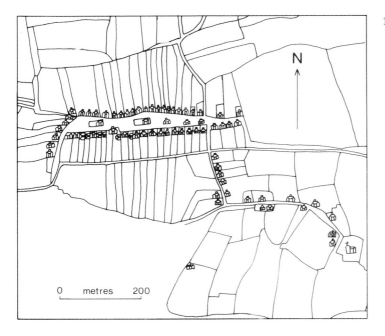

14 East Witton, North Yorkshire. A plan of 1627 shows that the original village nucleus lay to the south-east of the village which appears to have been replanned by the monks of nearby Jervaulx Abbey in the early fourteenth century. The village plan appears to conform to the arrangements by sun division of *solskifte*

Somerset, called by Leland 'a praty townelet of clothing'. It has indeed many pretty cottages, especially by the Green near the stream, but its main interest is in New Street running at right angles to the High Street towards the church, though not aligned on either porch or vestry. It was built by Abbot Selwood *c.*1470 as part of an incompleted plan to rebuild Mells with four straight streets meeting in the Roman fashion. The terraces consist of houses each with one room on each side of the entrance and a spiral staircase in a polygonal annexe by the back door.

19 Mells, Somerset. Mells was redesigned by Abbot Selwood in the late fifteenth century in an unusual attempt to create a village in the shape of a cross. It has some of the characteristics of the Vicar's Walk at Wells, which lies close by

63

Regularly planned medieval villages were frequently associated with colonisation, but in some instances they were brought about by deliberate redesign. In certain areas the impact of new planned towns appears to have filtered down to the village level. Olney in Buckinghamshire is a well known example of a medieval planned settlement with its broad main street, triangular market area and regular parallel burgage tenements. Close by is the village

20 Braunston, Northants. Braunston provides a fine example of a planned medieval village, which could well have developed into a town, with its long high street and triangular green or market area at the far end. The regular parallel property boundaries and back lane clearly indicate its planned origin, as does the central point occupied by its church. There is also evidence at Braunston that the village was laid out or expanded on to existing arable land. The tower sitting next to the church formed part of a windmill

of Hanslope, which, although it may have shared Olney's urban aspirations, remained a village. Hanslope's plan, however, incorporates a number of 'urban' features which are identical to those found in its more successful neighbour.

The anatomy of the village

Despite such clear examples of medieval village design, attempts at classifying village plans are generally fraught with difficulties, though it is possible to indicate certain common types. Villages are either regular or irregular – some so irregular that it is difficult to imagine how they evolved; others regular enough to have been drawn up with ruler and graph paper. Compare, for example, the adjacent villages of Nuneham Courtenay and Marsh Baldon in Oxfordshire (Fig. 15). The former was moved from its Thames-side site to its present position along the Oxford-Henley road in 1760. Its creation is well docu-

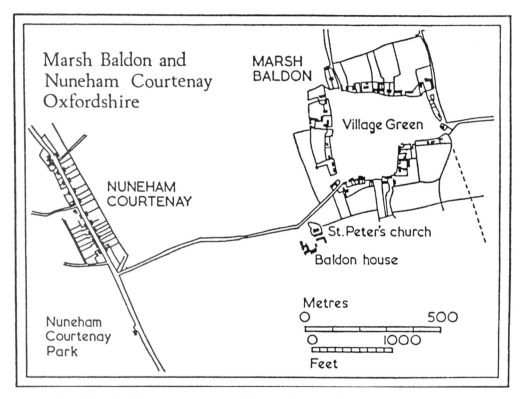

Marsh Baldon and Nuneham Courtenay Oxfordshire

MARSH BALDON

Village Green

NUNEHAM COURTENAY

St. Peter's church

Baldon house

Nuneham Courtenay Park

Metres

0   500

0   1000

Feet

mented, while the latter has no surviving evidence for its foundation apart from its regular layout which strongly indicates plantation in marshy ground, as its name suggests. The large regular green at Marsh Baldon, around which the village houses lie, is some way from the church and manor house and was most probably a secondary undocumented plantation of the early Middle Ages.

15 Nuneham Courtenay and Marsh Baldon, two adjacent planned villages of different dates in Oxfordshire

Within the broad division of regular and irregular layouts there are three basic types of village – those with a linear plan, those centred around a green or open space, and those with a compact plan. The village can be broken up into a number of constituent elements – church, road pattern, land parcels, and greens and open spaces. The church, as the centre of village life in the Middle Ages, should logically be in the centre of the village but there are very many examples where this is not the case. Some churches were established in isolated positions in order to serve a scattered community of farmsteads or small hamlets, and hence may bear little relation to any one settlement. Later settlements which are divorced from the church are often quite regular, sometimes dating from a deliberate attempt to refound or develop a more rationally planned settlement away from an original nucleus of which the church was part. In some cases parish churches were simply left behind as the settlements they served migrated to a more advantageous position, by a crossroads or a more sheltered site. Sometimes the village has disintegrated altogether leaving the church as the sole surviving building.

If the church (or chapel in a hamlet) occupies a croft in the main street, or if it is sited at the end of a main street, in the centre of the village or in some otherwise prominent position it may well be contemporary with the design of the village. If it occupies an unaligned position at the end of the settlement as an awkward feature in the village plan, or is unrelated to the pattern of other closes, it may well be a relict feature surviving in a later village plan. There are a few settlements, such as the Aldwincles (Northants), the Barfords (Oxon) and Swaffham Prior (Cambridge), which possess two medieval parish churches. The reason for such an apparently illogical state of affairs may arise from the fact that there were originally two settlements sited near each other which eventually grew together – the term polyfocal has been applied to such settlements, which have evolved from two or more quite independent nuclei. Some villages were divided between two or more manors, resulting in two manor houses and occasionally in a second church as well.

Church buildings frequently reflect demographic trends in the communities they serve: additions and extensions usually indicate population expansion, while demolished aisles, filled arch-aisles or even the complete demolition of parts of the body of the church may indicate substantial population decline (plate 28b). Similarly the simplicity or grandeur of the decoration in a church will often reflect the level of wealth of the lord or the community at particular stages in its history. The best known and most ostentatious examples are those churches which were elaborately rebuilt on the proceeds of the wool trade. Although in many places the evidence is of a more subtle variety, it is nevertheless still sometimes possible to deduce the story of prosperity, demographic pattern and philanthropic phases evident in a settlement's history. The survival of Saxon or Norman architecture is in fact often evidence of *lack* of improvement, money or development. The apparently late medieval church may have had all its earlier features buried, encased, destroyed or removed.

The village road pattern, like the overall plan, may be regular or irregular. The regularly attended village roads

21 The twin parish churches at Swaffham Prior, Cambridge. They appear to have been the result of pious manorial rivalry during the Middle Ages. One is now derelict and largely ruinous

of today with specific widths and cambers are clearly not original features. Previously trackways wandered over the available public open spaces and frequently altered course in bad weather to avoid mud and potholes. The main road through the village may have been the only true thoroughfare, the others being merely lanes or open spaces between plots. At all periods, there have been encroachments on to central open spaces, side lanes or back lanes that will inevitably have blurred the original regularity of some village plans. *Culs-de-sac* may have been merely access roads to fields, waste or meadow land, or they could indicate roads terminated or diverted for the creation of a park or as a result of enclosure. Other apparently dead-end roads found on early maps may in fact continue on the ground as abandoned trackways in the form of field boundaries, earthworks or hollow-ways.

There has been relatively little analysis of the form and disposition of land parcels in surviving settlements, although the croft, toft or earthwork house-platform is recognised as an important element in deserted medieval villages. Normally there will have been considerable amalgamation, sub-division or alteration of sizes and shapes of land parcels, so that it may be difficult to distinguish original arrangements. However, old internal divisions and small linear earthworks may provide clues. Some land parcels within the village can be identified as special units. The churchyard is an obvious case in point, but there may be others formerly occupied by the sites of castles, monastic houses, or rectories and manor houses. In most villages the land of the manor house or demesne will have been larger than the normal croft, and there may have been various adjacent closes and one or more moats. In some instances the allocation of such an area as a 'precinct' may have brought about the diversion or blocking of roads and the annexation or alteration of adjoining properties.

The green was a feature of many English medieval villages. Before metalled roads were introduced, most villages had their house frontages set far enough back to permit an open grassy space in the centre of the settlement which was used for rough grazing, fairs and markets. There are a number of villages, however, where the green plays a particularly important part in the village plan. Much has been written about villages with greens, and it has sometimes been assumed that 'green' villages date from the Saxon foundation of the settlement. However, it is clear that such greens are often divorced from the church, and the more ancient centre of the village, and that they frequently date from the period of medieval village reorganisation which has already been discussed. In some cases village greens represent a very late development and were created by communities of smallholders or squatters, who enclosed areas of former open common land around which they had settled. This category of green village could date from the fifteenth or even the post-medieval period and tends to be characterised by the absence of a parochial church. Paradoxically there was an influx of landless peasants, onto the edge of commonland areas in the fifteenth century. They were there because the process of enclosure of arable for pasture, which followed the economic recession in the fourteenth century, was followed through a century later by lords taking advantage of high wool prices and evicting their tenants, and thus continuing the depopulation.

Village buildings

The only village buildings of the fourteenth century which
normally survive today in a recognisable form are those
which were built of stone, namely churches, manor houses
and occasionally barns. While the churches survive in
considerable numbers, there are relatively few medieval
manor houses. Indeed most surviving manor houses in
villages are not medieval at all but date from the seventeenth, eighteenth or even nineteenth centuries. There
are, however, enough surviving examples to show that
medieval manor houses were either of the simple,
rectangular, first-floor hall type dating from the twelfth to
the thirteenth centuries, or of the later end-hall type. In
all manor houses the emphasis was on the hall, the home
of the lord and the place of the manorial court, where
accounts were audited and records kept. As the nearest
equivalent to a public building the manor often warranted
the use of stone. Despite its unquestioned importance in
the village hierarchy, the manor house often appears to
have consisted of a group of buildings performing separate
functions, for instance at Cuxham (Oxon), a manor
belonging to Merton college, the early fourteenth-century
manor complex consisted of quite separate units of hall
attached to the lord's room, kitchen, bakehouse, oven,
gatehouse and latrine. Additionally there were a number
of barns and animal byres, a granary, and two dovecotes.

In the context of the medieval village and manor the
term 'lord' is a generic one, referring to the landlord, be
it an individual, or more frequently an estate belonging to
an abbey, a cathedral, a magnate or the crown. Where the
lord was not a resident individual there would still have
been a manor house, manorial demesne, and other lordly
elements such as the deer parks. These would have served
a representative of the land-owning institution in the same
way as they would a resident lord. In many villages there
is no surviving medieval manor house, but buildings
which were the prerogative of manorial or rectorial owners
may stand in the shape of dovecotes and tithe barns.
Such buildings could also have been attached to monastic
granges which had been sited in the village. It is difficult
to date dovecotes, although generally speaking the circular
examples are medieval. They were certainly built and used
for pigeon breeding from the twelfth century onwards.
Sometimes they are obscured by other farm buildings, or
they may survive as low earthen or circular hollow
mounds. Tithe barns are generally recognisable by their
size, or by elaborate timber roofing structures, but, like

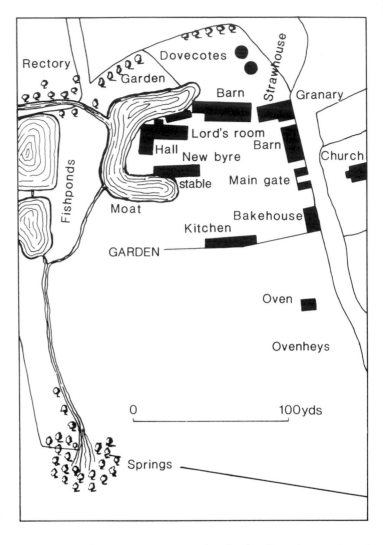

16 Reconstruction of
manorial complex at
Cuxham,
Oxfordshire c. 1315
(after P. D. A. Harvey
and James Bond)

dovecotes, large barns were also built after the medieval
period.

The evidence for peasant houses is best examined under
deserted villages, references such as that to 'old hovels,
decayed beams and half-destroyed walls' at Wittam (Lincs)
in the thirteenth century are rare. The surviving evidence
on the ground of medieval peasant housing is clearly
biased towards the dwellings of the richer villagers, but
these were a minority and the majority lived a precarious
existence. It seems likely that the most common houses
were crude and flimsy structures, generally erected by the
inhabitants themselves from the cheapest of local materials
– mud, wood and thatch. Normally they consisted of one
room only, for returns from Colchester and the

surrounding villages around 1300 show that even among
taxpayers only a minority of families had more. Most of
them, too, were exceedingly small. One cottage excavated
at Seacourt (Berks) had internal dimensions of 10 by 12
feet and another at Wharram Percy (Yorks) measured 10
by 20 feet. The room or rooms were usually open to the
roof; and there was a central hearth but no chimney.

17 Medieval house-types

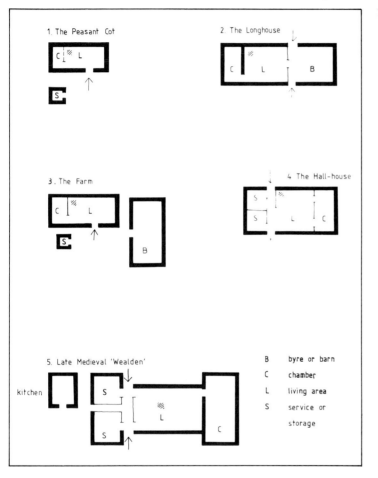

1. The Peasant Cot

2. The Longhouse

3. The Farm

4 The Hall-house

5. Late Medieval 'Wealden'

kitchen

B   byre or barn
C   chamber
L   living area
S   service or
      storage

Towards the end of the Middle Ages, particularly in the
well wooded areas of southeast England and the west
Midlands, vernacular houses of sufficient substance to
have survived appear in the countryside in large numbers.
The earliest form of domestic dwelling which survives in
any quantity in western Britain is the one-storey cruck
house. This consists of pairs of curved timbers propped
together to make a series of bays of which the simplest
form is the single-bay cruck. As the impact of the agrarian
depression began to abate and as agriculture was reorgan-

22 The cruck gable end of a late medieval house at Weobley, Herefordshire. Such buildings reflected the development of a class of more prosperous yeoman farmers emerging out of the agricultural depression of the late fourteenth and early fifteenth centuries

ised on fewer but larger and generally more prosperous units during the fifteenth century, more elaborate rural dwellings began to appear. These were timber-framed, sometimes with projecting upper storeys known as jetties, and close-studded walling. The numbers of such houses indicate that they were probably the homes of prosperous yeoman, and their design seems to have originated at a higher social level in towns. They vary greatly in size from two to six rooms implying a considerable differentiation of wealth among the farming communities of England. Most of them had a central lofty open hall with two two-storeyed ends. Their chief characteristic was that by the fifteenth century they had become completely detached from their farm buildings. The process by which this detachment took place has been well demonstrated from a number of deserted village excavations.

In the southwest, Wales and the north the earliest houses which have survived date from the late Middle

23 A longhouse in Brittany which still has animals at one end and human habitation at the other. Unlike a true longhouse, this is not entered by a central door leading into both portions. Such houses were in common use in western England and Wales right up until this century.

Ages and are derivatives from the long house where
animals and men were housed under the same roof. A
cross passage, which was a feature of the early long
houses, instead of leading into the pantry and buttery was
used for access to the byre by the cattle, and for feeding
the cattle once they were tethered. Contemporary references to men and animals living in the close proximity of
long houses are rare, but in 1340 at Hallow (Worcs) we
hear that William de Hampton surrendered his holding,
curtilage and long house to his daughter and son-in-law.
They were to pay a rent of 6s yearly and perform some
small services on William's behalf; but William reserved a
right for his oxen to have their stalls in the house whenever
he wished. The presence of such byres can often be
detected after they have been transformed into a parlour
or kitchens when the house was later upgraded. In
particular the beam containing slots designed to take the
tethering posts has survived in a number of former long
houses. Otherwise these long houses usually conceal their
diagnostic features. Open hearths have been replaced by
chimney stacks, either inserted centrally or at the gable-
end; and the halls have been split at first-floor level,
making them warmer and more comfortable with greater
privacy. Differences in their size and plan appear to reflect
social or economic status. For example, a survey made in
1600 of Settrington in Yorkshire describes the housing of
villagers, e.g. husbandmen, grassmen and cottagers, in
descending order of prosperity; with four-bay houses for
husbandmen, and three-bay houses for grassmen and two
bays for cottagers.

Some of the best assemblages of late medieval houses
survive in the Welsh Marches where there is a wealth of
half-timbered buildings. These can be seen both in towns
and villages and as isolated farms; Weobley in Herefordshire is basically a fossilised medieval town, with a broad
central green around which are sited streets containing a
wide range of remarkably well preserved half-timbered
buildings dating from the fourteenth to the seventeenth
centuries. However, because reasonable supplies of timber
were still available in the west Midlands the half-timbered
building tradition continued well into the post-medieval
period and has led to many fine structures built between
1500 and 1700 being erroneously labelled as medieval.

The deserted medieval village

The closest we are able to approach most medieval villages
is through the investigation of deserted villages. Over the

18 Deserted medieval
villages: sites
recognised by the
Medieval Village
Research Group up to
1977. (Map revision,
from M. V. R. G. lists
by Robin Glassock with
assistance from Alan
Nash; cartography by
Michael Young and
Pamela Lucas,
Department of
Geography,
University of
Cambridge)

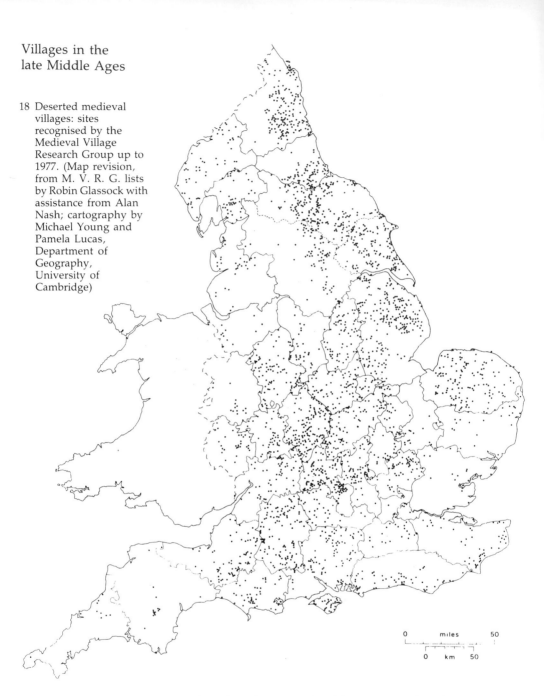

past few decades considerable attention has been paid to
abandoned medieval settlements in this country. Whereas
35 years ago only a handful of such sites had been identified, we now know that there are perhaps as many as
3,000 deserted villages in England alone, and as work
progresses each year new sites are located (fig. 18). Over

220 sites have been identified in Lincolnshire, 165 in
Northumberland and well over 400 in Yorkshire. Even in
those parts of the country, such as the southwest and
northwest, where such villages were initially not recognised, examples of abandoned sites are now to be found in
abundance. Although quite insignificant totals of deserted
villages have been identified in counties such as Herefordshire and Cumbria, there is no doubt that this reflects the
lack of detailed fieldwork rather than the absence of such
sites. In Shropshire, for instance, only a handful of sites
was known when a national distribution map was drawn
up in 1966; since then well over 100 sites have been located
and the picture is still far from complete. The subject has
been reviewed in an important book edited by Maurice
Beresford and John Hurst entitled *Deserted Medieval Villages*
(1971). This deals in detail with the development of the
study of abandoned medieval settlements from both the
historical and archaeological viewpoints, and provides a
wealth of information concerning medieval occupation.

Table 1 Local intensity of depopulation per 10,000 acres
(after Beresford and Hurst)

County	Number of known deserted villages per 10,000 acres (15 sq. miles)
Isle of Wight	3.1
Warwickshire	2.3
Oxfordshire	2.1
Yorkshire, E.R.	1.7
Leicestershire	1.4
Northamptonshire	1.4
Nottinghamshire	1.4
Lincolnshire	1.3
Northumberland	1.3
Rutland	1.3
Buckinghamshire	1.2
Wiltshire	1.2
Yorkshire, N.R.	1.2
Norfolk	1.0
Hampshire	0.9
Hertfordshire	0.9
Berkshire	0.8
Gloucestershire	0.8
Huntingdonshire	0.8
Dorset	0.7
Bedfordshire	0.6
Derbyshire	0.5
Durham	0.5
Kent	0.5
Yorkshire, W.R.	0.5

Before we move on to the examination of the physical
remains from deserted villages some attention should be
paid to the causes of village abandonment during the
Middle Ages. The fortunes of rural settlement tend to
reflect national economic and demographic trends, and
therefore only a few settlement desertions can be attributed to the twelfth or thirteenth centuries as this was
generally speaking a period of village expansion. In Leice-

24 The earthworks of a well preserved deserted medieval village at Argam in Yorkshire. The village, much of which was built of stone, has left substantial remains of house footings still visible. The enclosure on the left hand side of the holloway may belong to a post-desertion enclosure on the site

stershire, for instance, only four villages disappeared
between 1086 and the early fourteenth century. These
desertions were almost certainly the result of operations
by Cistercian abbeys who, in obtaining the solitude which
was required of them, were responsible for the extinction
of a number of villages during the early Middle Ages. The
Cistercians at Combe in Warwickshire, for example, were
given land within the parish of Upper and Lower Smite.
These two villages have disappeared, and the former
church of St Peter at Lower Smite is now built into a
farmhouse. The earthworks at Upper Smite are faintly
discernible near a farmhouse at Nobbs Wood. The parish
name is now preserved only in Smite Brook, Smeeton
Lane and Smite Hill. The antiquarian Dugdale described

how the foundation of the Abbey in 1130 had created 'pasture ground where anciently two villages stood, the depopulation whereof hath bene ancient, for the vestiges are scarce to be discerned.' The Cistercians at Stoneleigh (Warwickshire) similarly recorded in their Leger Book that the monks 'settled in the place where Crulefeld Grange now is, having moved away those who lived there to the village now called Hurst.' In the mid-twelfth century Revesby Abbey offered land in outlying villages to those of its tenants who would leave the villages of Stichesby and Thoresby which adjoined the monastery. They all accepted and 13 families left Stichesby and 11 went from Thoresby; neither village was ever repopulated.

Elsewhere changes in physical geography brought about the demise of a number of villages in the early Middle Ages, coastal erosion being the most common cause. On the east coast of Yorkshire, a strip of land up to a mile wide in the area of Holderness was removed by coastal erosion in the thirteenth century, with the result that an estimated 20 villages simply disappeared. Storms are recorded as having removed thousands of acres of agricultural land in Cambridgeshire, Kent and Sussex; while in the north the Scots periodically raided deep into Yorkshire, destroying perhaps as many as 140 villages in 1218 alone. Some of these settlements, such as Mortham (north Yorkshire), were burnt and were never rebuilt.

The great wave of village abandonment, however, began after 1300, and continued at an accelerated pace during the fifteenth century. Various, sometimes very complex, explanations have been offered for later desertions, the most plausible being that the population had simply passed the limit to which it could grow, given the economy, technology and agriculture of the time. Disease and soil exhaustion then became factors in reducing population. Decline had already set in when at the end of June 1348 a ship docked at Melcombe Regis (Dorset) bringing with it the 'Black Death'. The great bubonic plague of 1348–9 is the most common scapegoat chosen as the cause of village abandonment. At Hale in Apeforth parish (Northants), for example, in 1356 we hear 'the premises are worth nothing now because no one dwells or has dwelt in Hale since the pestilence', and later in the same century Hale was still recorded as worth nothing 'because the messuages are wasted'. The marginal siting of this particular township probably made it more vulnerable to permanent devastation than larger villages. At Tusmore in Oxfordshire the lord appears to have transformed his empty holdings into a deer park during the decade following the Black Death, and at Bolton near Bradford (north Yorks) the tax collectors of 1379 found 'not a sole remaining'. The village of Tilgarsley in Oxfordshire which formed part of the Eynsham Abbey estates was abandoned at the time of the Black Death and never resettled. In 1359 the collectors of the lay subsidy reported to the Exchequer that no one had lived there since 1350 and they could not collect the 94s 9d tax. The status of the village was considered *De Banco* by the judges in 1370 and again in 1378 and 1383. The Exchequer was loth to give up the hope that villagers would be persuaded to resettle, but by 1422 the village was divided into closes and leased out. Even when a village was not completely depopulated shrinkage could occur and there were many villages which were considerably smaller in the latter part of the four-teenth century as a result of the plague. The village fabric had been dealt a severe blow, but nevertheless most of them continued to operate with a smaller population working an increased area of pasture and a smaller arable area.

In addition to the Black Death all over Europe natural disasters such as poor harvests, soil exhaustion and pesti-lence took their toll on population and on settlements during the fourteenth and fifteenth centuries. This decline was not to be arrested until the sixteenth century, and in some rural areas not until the mid-eighteenth century was there any marked reversal of this trend. The Black Death, devastating though it was, simply contributed to an already deteriorating situation. In the Cambridge area, for instance, it is estimated that the population was nearly halved between the late thirteenth and early sixteenth centuries. The population had been so dense in East Anglia that the effects of the decline were particularly spectacular. The depopulation of the Norfolk countryside can be measured through the number of ruined churches. Of about 900 medieval churches nearly 250 are in ruins. Between 1300 and 1600 there was a steady process of settlement decay and abandonment accompanying the decline in population. Up until the mid-fifteenth century this was a relatively gradual process, but from 1450 onwards there was a massive and rapid change in land-use from arable to grass. The form of agriculture which required a substantial number of husbandmen in the village changed to a pastoral form with a much smaller labour force. The stimulus to this change in land-use came from a significant and continuing expansion in the demand for wool coupled with the fall in population. It would appear that the earlier stages of this demand had been met by using the post-plague surplus arable land for grazing and that the continuing pressure for wool had even been accommodated in part by overstocking the commons with sheep, but eventually the demand could only be catered for by landlords deciding to make the complete transition from arable to pastoral husbandry.

The late medieval swing from corn to grass sometimes involved the total area of a township's fields and was an almost irreversible action resulting in the end of arable husbandry. Agricultural workers were superfluous and their houses simply fell into decay; without villagers there was no village. From the late fourteenth to the late eighteenth centuries there was little incentive to change back to cereal production and when corn was eventually sown again over the sheep pastures there was no significant return of population to the village. A new arable landscape was managed from a small number of farmsteads located conveniently throughout the township, and there was no need for villagers to return with their ploughs.

During the fifteenth century all sections of society, even prosperous peasants, were turning to sheep farming, and in the process depopulating villages. Hailes Abbey had extensive pastoral estates in the Cotswolds and a Chancery petition of the mid-fifteenth century demonstrates that they were in part achieved by harrying villagers. Referring to Longborough (Gloucs) it states that the Abbot of Hailes

> dayly stodyth to foll) hys cruell intentys to decaye
> mynyche and distroye the tyllage of the said lordship which
> is the livyng of the kings subjects and the destruction of
> youre power oratours.
>   He hath [900 sheep] and dayly exacteth requreth and
> oppresith with divers exaction to the intent too dryve them
> oute of the said lyvingys because he wolde have the said
> manor holy decayed and convertid into pasture contrary to
> the kyngs lawes and statutys.

While a statute of 1402 declared that the monks and other subjects of the king should not be insulted by being called *'depopulatores agrum'* (depopulators of the fields), an act of 1489 made it an offence to convert open fields to pasture if it involved the removal of smallholdings over 20 acres. Overlords were expected to take action to ensure that, in proven cases, arable holdings were reinstated. The preamble to the 1489 Act describes why the crown was concerned:

> Great inconveniences daily doth increase by desolation and
> pulling down and wilfull waste of houses and Towns within

25a Late sixteenth century All Souls plan of the village of Whatborough (1586) in Leicestershire showing newly enclosed pastoral fields created from former arable strip farming. The descriptions of the newly enclosed fields include the following comments: 'theise grounds doe also lye in ridge and forrow' and 'theise groundes have likewise bene arable'

that his [i.e. the king's] realm, and laying to pasture lands which customarily have been used in tillage, whereby idleness – ground and beginning of all mischiefs – daily doth increase, for where in some Towns two hundred persons were occupied and lived by their lawful labours, now be there occupied 2 or 3 herdmen and the residue fallen in idleness; the husbandry, which is one of the greatest commodities of the realm, is greatly decayed; churches destroyed; the service of God withdrawn; the bodies there buried not prayed for; the patron and curate wronged; the defence of this land against our enemies outwards feebled and impaired; to the great displeasure of God, to the subversion of the policy and good rule of this land.

This polemic probably overstates the extent of the problem, but it was no accident that, during the sixteenth century, the landless peasant or vagrant was a common figure in political tracts and even in poetry. In a late

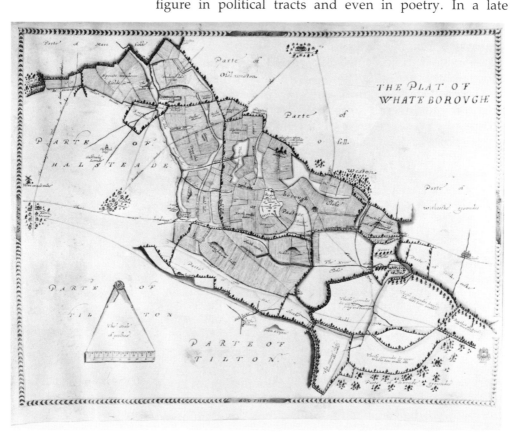

sixteenth century *Epigram* offered to Queen Elizabeth, Thomas Bastard voiced a familiar complaint:

Sheep have eaten up our meadows and our downs
Our corn, our wood, whole villages and towns.
Yea, they have eaten up many wealthy men

Besides widows and orphan children
Besides our statutes and our iron laws
Which they have swallowed down into their maws.
Till now I thought the proverb did but jest
Which said a black sheep was a biting beast.

The same century also saw the development of 'squatting'
by landless peasants on the edges of common waste and
marshland on a large scale. In some areas sizeable squatter
communities developed. The squatters were normally
present on the sufferance of the lord of the manor,
although in some cases, as on the Clee hills and the Stiper-
stones in Shropshire, cottagers were enticed on to common
land by lords who needed labour for their nearby quarries
and mines. Cottages were therefore often built near to
extractive industries and many of the squatters were part-
time coal-miners, lead-miners or quarrymen. Usually they

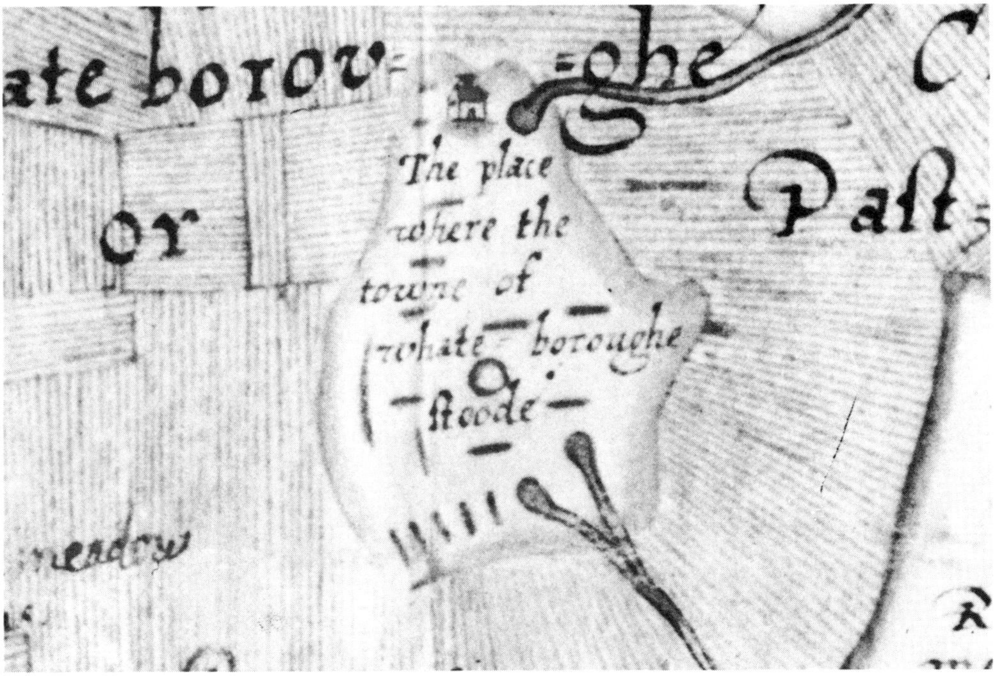

were required to pay an annual rent of 6d or 1s. A number
of squatter cottages have survived and can be seen ringing
the areas of enclosed common or encircling a surviving
common.

Contemporary writers make it clear that this was a
conflict between private profit and social welfare. A new
Act designed to stop or slow down village depopulation
was passed in 1515 followed in 1517 and 1518 by Cardinal
Wolsey's Commissions of Inquiry to enforce the legis-

25b Detail of the All
Souls map of
Whatborough
showing the site of
the deserted
medieval village
with a single
shepherd's
farmhouse still
standing. The
description of the
field poignantly reads
'the place where the
towne of
Whateboroughe
stoode'

lation. Although we cannot take all the evidence literally, these inquiries provide us with interesting insights into the depopulating process. For instance, it was reported that the Prior of Bicester had held five houses with 30 acres attached to each and 200 acres of his own at Wretchwick (Oxfordshire):

> He held this land on the second of March 1489 when those messuages were laid waste and thrown down, and lands formerly used for arable he turned over to pasture for animals, so three ploughs are now out of use there, and eighteen people who used to work on that land and earn their living there and who dwelled in the houses have gone away to take to the roads in their misery, and to seek their bread elsewhere and so are led into idleness.

26 The earthworks of a deserted medieval village of Wretchwick, Oxfordshire surrounded by ridge and furrow (see also fig. 19)

Not all those who lived in the houses can have been as poor as this statement would suggest. Wretchwick rentals for 1432–7 give the tenants' names, their holdings, as well as those holdings which were vacant. About a dozen families lived there, several of whom farmed additional holdings for which the priory could not find tenants, and some of these families, at least, are likely to have accumulated enough movable capital and expertise to start again elsewhere. The abandoned village site can be clearly seen today in the form of earthworks and banks surrounding Middle Wretchwork Farm (plate 26 and fig. 19).

The changing demographic and economic pattern of the late Middle Ages brought about the elimination of nearly one quarter of the village settlements of medieval England, and seriously weakened the structure of many more. The reasons why some villages were lost and others survived is still a matter of debate. Obviously a proportion of those abandoned were marginal; those settlements that had been pushed towards and beyond the margin of cultivation were naturally more vulnerable and many of them succumbed. Those settlements occupying difficult or unpleasant sites were also obvious candidates for destruction. The appropriately named medieval settlement of Cold Weston which lay at 900 feet above sea level on a north-facing slope in Shropshire was deserted in the fourteenth century and it was recorded in 1300 that the living had been presented to four parsons 'but none of them would stay'. There were, however, many other villages in Midland England that appear to have suffered because of the opportunism of the local lord rather than any inherent weakness in their ability to survive. Whole groups of villages on the Warwickshire/Oxfordshire border were wiped off the map by landlords taking advantage of high wool prices, leaving a landscape unnaturally empty of nucleated settlements. It is an intriguing exercise to examine a modern Ordnance Survey map and see the substantial gaps left where there were once villages and to speculate about the reasons for the continued existence of the survivors – a busy road, a bridge or even an unworldly lord, who failed to see the financial advantages of conversion from arable to pasture.

Hundreds of deserted village sites have received archaeological attention in recent years but, because of the nature of the archaeological record, the progress of excavation is slow. Unlike urban sites deeply stratified deposits do not normally develop under rural conditions and excavation on such sites has to be particularly meticulous. One of the features to emerge from excavation is that during the late twelfth and thirteenth centuries, over much of the country, where stone is to be found there was a change from constructing peasant houses in wood and turf to stone. This trend appears to have started in the south and southwest and then moved northwards. The change may possibly be accounted for by the diminution of timber supplies through the clearing of woodland for agriculture

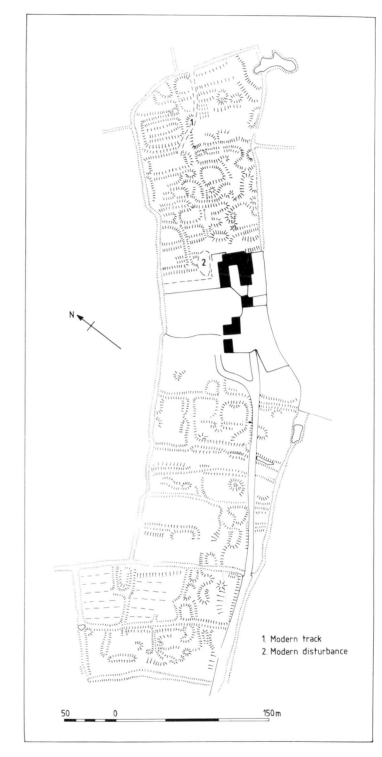

N

1. Modern track
2. Modern disturbance

50   0   150m

19 The earthworks of
Wretchwick deserted
village, Oxfordshire
(see Plate 26)

and for industrial purposes. The stone used was normally available locally, but occasionally more exotic stone, re-used from a manor house or church, was incorporated into the base of domestic buildings. Only buildings of this nature would normally have had well-cut stone and similarly they would have been the only buildings using mortar, although clay bonding was fairly common. In some areas where stone was not readily accessible, stone from the abandoned houses of the deserted village has been subsequently robbed out.

Another feature to emerge from recent excavation is the fact that vernacular building traditions are of the same antiquity. For example, in the chalklands of Yorkshire and Lincolnshire the buildings were frequently of chalk, while in the southern chalk areas the buildings were mainly of flint. During the later Middle Ages in parts of the country some buildings were again constructed of timber, in many cases sitting on a low stone sill. It is not quite clear what initiated this change, but it may be related to the greater availability of timber due to the economic decline of the fourteenth and fifteenth centuries.

In the clay areas to the southeast and northwest of the stone belt the change from timber to stone construction was not possible. Fieldwork on these sites provides evidence of flat tofts with no sign of solid house foun-dations. Excavation has demonstrated the existence of cob and timber structures which leave very little trace apart from soils of different colours and textures. For example,

27 The extended earthworks of the deserted medieval village at Barton Blount, Derbyshire. This village which was abandoned like so many others in the later Middle Ages, has recently been subject to excavation

85

at Barton Blount (Derby) a complex sequence of timber buildings has been uncovered, but these were never replaced by stone or stone-based structures. On the other hand at Faxton (Northants) and a number of other Midland sites crude stone sills were introduced after 1300.

It has been possible to recover a considerable amount of information about peasant dwellings from several sites. Floors were either of clay, stone cobbles or covered with stone flags; on a few sites evidence of floor boards has been found. In many peasant houses the floor surfaces have been removed mainly as a result of constant clearing, which also meant that stratified deposits have disappeared. Most roofs were constructed of perishable material such as turf, reeds, straw, or wooden shingles and in consequence little roofing evidence has survived. The principal cause for the constant rebuilding of houses during the medieval period may well have been the poor roofing, which enabled dampness to penetrate the walls, causing the need for frequent rebuilding, although fire was also a constant threat.

Quite apart from the main dwellings, barns and byres,

20 Caldecote, Hertfordshire. The excavated remains of an early farmyard complex (after G. Beresford)

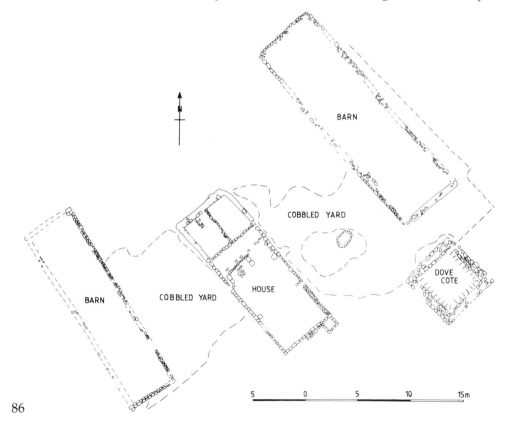

BARN

COBBLED YARD

DOVE COTE

BARN

COBBLED YARD

HOUSE

5   0   5   10   15m

there were usually other outbuildings in the back yard. These were often short-lived structures leaving little trace, and as excavation has tended to concentrate upon the more obvious buildings, little is known about them. The corn-drying kiln is a commonly found feature in the form of a circular oven with a long flue leading to a stoke hole. Ovens and rubbish pits have also been found quite close to the main building complex and indeed the former were rarely built within the dwelling house until substantial stone chimneys were introduced in the later Middle Ages.

On those sites where there has been extensive excavation it has proved possible to trace the development and decline of houses, enclosures and outbuildings over a considerable period of time. At Upton (Glos), for instance, one dwelling started as a long house with animals and humans sharing the same roof and entrance. To this

28a An isolated Herefordshire church surrounded by the earthworks of a deserted village, now rather symbolically being grazed by sheep

28b The parish church at Merton, Oxfordshire, showing the blocked-up arches of a south aisle. Such infilling and contraction was common in parish churches during the later Middle Ages as the population served by the parish church declined

building was added a barn extension entered through a separate door, and finally a completely separate outbuilding for animals was constructed, giving the basis of the later farm, farmyard and subsidiary farm buildings (Fig. 21). A similar pattern of farmhouse development was traced at Gombeldon (Wilts). Interesting evidence of climatic deterioration has come from the excavation of a number of buildings at Hound Tor in Devon, an abandoned settlement high up on the Dartmoor. Towards the end of their lives, c.1300, corn-drying kilns appear to have been inserted in a number of long houses, indicating the onset of damper conditions. At Wharram Percy (north Yorks) where the most extensive excavations on any deserted village site in Britain have taken place, numerous dwellings were built on top of one another, indicating a rebuilding approximately every thirty years. Elsewhere too this pattern of continuity and change can be traced over many years. One of the extraordinary features of this rebuilding was that the houses were not reconstructed on exactly the same alignment each time; they were often rebuilt at an angle to the original site and in some cases over a long period of time have turned a complete circle.

Such changes in alignment were not confined to actual house sites, but often affected the whole toft pattern and fundamental layout of the village. This evidence is consistent both with the documentary and topographical record, which point to a large-scale programme of village rebuilding and redesign in the Middle Ages. At Wawne (Humberside), for example, there were about twelve peasant houses set in a rectangular area in one part of the village in the twelfth and thirteenth centuries. These were arranged in a piecemeal fashion as though they had been built and added to over the years as the village gradually expanded. In the fourteenth century, however, all these houses were destroyed and a completely new layout was constructed some distance to the south, with sixteen houses all laid out in a row parallel to the street. Similar examples of village redesign have been observed at Wharram Percy and at Seacourt (Oxon), where a completely new street of stone-based houses was constructed in the thirteenth century.

The investigation of deserted villages has transformed our understanding of medieval rural settlement. However, settlement shift, shrinkage and abandonment continued into the post-medieval period, indeed the sixteenth century was a particularly active period for depopulators. Deserted or 'lost' villages have always been an evocative

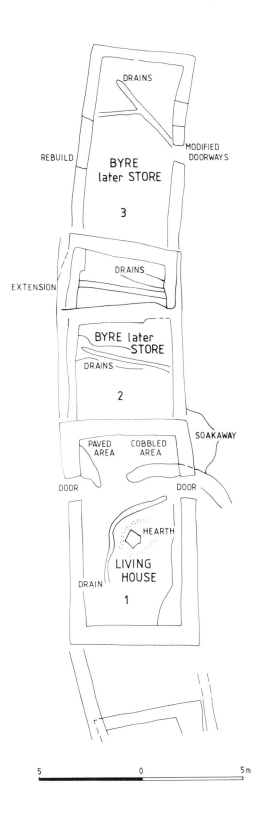

DRAINS

REBUILD

BYRE
later STORE

3

MODIFIED
DOORWAYS

EXTENSION

DRAINS

BYRE later
STORE

DRAINS

2

SOAKAWAY

PAVED
AREA

COBBLED
AREA

DOOR

DOOR

HEARTH

LIVING
HOUSE

DRAIN

1

5   0   5 m

21 Upton, Gloucestershire. The phases of development from a long house (1), to a building where the animals are segregated (2), to a separate farm house, yard and byre (3) (after P. Rahtz)

topic and later poets and writers such as Thomas Bastard
were frequently concerned with the plight of those who
had lost their homes in dramatic circumstances. Although
in truth settlement abandonment involving such evictions
formed only a small percentage of all desertions, nevertheless it was the pathos of such settlement mortality that
inspired Oliver Goldsmith to write his *Deserted Village*,
when he appears to have been describing the later forcible
movement of Nuneham Courtenay by the Earl of
Harcourt. In the dedicatory letter which prefaces the poem
the experience prompted him to remark astutely

> I have taken all possible pains in my country excursions for
> these four or five years to be certain of what I allege. Some
> of my friends think that the depopulation of villages does not
> exist, but I am myself satisfied.

Later scholars were not so certain and lost sight of the
abandoned settlements which must have been common-
place in the later Middle Ages. It was not until historians
took to the fields and located the traces of the former
habitations on the ground that the 'deserted village' rightly
re-entered the vocabulary of medieval scholars.

Medieval agriculture

As England was essentially a rural country throughout the Middle Ages, subsistence and wealth were fundamentally derived from the countryside. Much of the available landscape was in some form of agricultural use by about 1300, at which stage there was extensive arable cultivation in the countryside reaching up to 1000 feet in remote hillier areas. There was, however, considerable regional variation with stock-breeding and sheep-rearing forming an important element in the farming regime, particularly in the western parts of the kingdom. On the Pennine slopes of Lancashire, for example, around 1300, it is recorded

29 Sheep shearing from a thirteenth-century calendar, Bodleian Library

that one farmer kept a number of vaccaries stocked with some 1,200 breeding cows. After about 1350 the picture began to change with a far greater emphasis upon animal husbandry and a dramatic diminution in the area of arable farming in the country as a whole. The other major trend to emerge was in the form of a marked decline in the area of demesne farming, associated with the move away from obligatory services towards paid agricultural labourers. As noted in the previous chapter, this agricultural activity took place largely within a framework of field systems which have been the object of considerable scholarly analysis over the past one hundred years.

91

Open-field systems

Over many parts of England the field system of regular
hedged and fenced fields that we see today is the result
of relatively recent developments dating from the period of
parliamentary enclosure in the eighteenth and nineteenth
centuries. It is a landscape associated with straight roads,
wide verges and large isolated brick-built farm complexes.
This landscape sits upon an earlier one, with which it
only occasionally coincides. Even the casual observer will
readily recognise extensive earthwork traces of an earlier
agrarian system, a system that is most commonly associated with the Middle Ages – open-field agriculture. Its
most frequent physical manifestation is in the form of
fossilised ridges and furrows which, when they were
ploughed, often formed the basic unit of medieval cultivation. Each strip was normally ploughed consistently as
a discrete unit towards its centre. This resulted in the
creation of high-backed ridges with intervening furrows.
The pattern of ploughing employed by the communal
plough-teams frequently resulted in giving them a characteristic reversed S or C shape, known as the *aratral*
(plough) curve. There has been much discussion about the
connection between ridge and furrow and strip-farming
and naturally there has been a tendency to link the two
together, but this is not universally true. Certainly ridged
fields were created outside open-field regimes and open-
field systems frequently operated without ridging. Each
ridge was not necessarily co-extensive with each strip or
unit of landholding, but where detailed studies have been
carried out by comparing the distribution of ridge and
furrow with the strips marked on early estate maps, as at
Padbury in Buckinghamshire, for instance, it can be seen
that there was often a high degree of correlation.

The open-field system developed, in part, within an
existing agrarian framework which may well have originated before the Roman conquest of Britain. Aerial photographs of recently ploughed-out ridge and furrow on the
chalklands of southern England have revealed former
blocks of ridges sitting neatly within what appear to have
been 'Celtic' fields. The detailed analysis of ridge and
furrow in other areas has also shown that they were laid
out within a pre-existing framework, which was almost
certainly created in prehistoric or Romano-British times.
Traces of open-field agriculture in the form of earthwork
ridge and furrow, soil-marks and crop-marks of ridge and
furrow are ubiquitous in central England and surprisingly
common in other parts of the country. As the enclosure

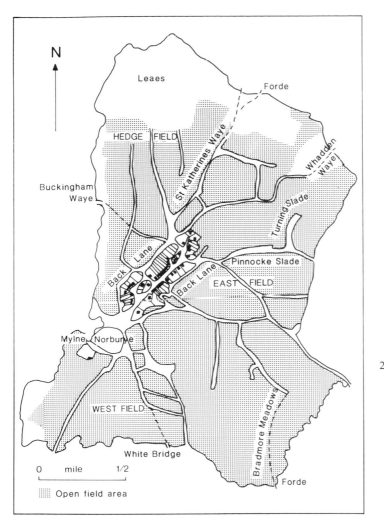

N

Leaes

Forde

HEDGE | FIELD

St Katherines Waye

Whadden Waye

Buckingham Waye

Turning Slade

Back Lane

Pinnocke Slade

Back Lane

EAST FIELD

Mylne Norburye

WEST FIELD

Bradmore Meadows

White Bridge

0   mile   1/2

Forde

Open field area

22 Padbury,
Buckinghamshire, a
typical Midland open-
field parish taken from
an estate map of 1591.
An examination of
ridge and furrow in
Padbury showed a
close coincidence with
the strips recorded on
the original map (after
M. W. Beresford and
J. K. S. St Joseph)

of open fields was frequently associated with a change in
land use from arable to pasture both in the Middle Ages
and later, the relics of former ploughing activity were
effectively frozen. It takes many years of determined cross-
ploughing to eradicate ridge and furrow completely, and it
is still so widespread that it constitutes the most extensive
surviving category of archaeological earthwork in the
country, providing us with blueprints of the design of
former agrarian systems.

There has been considerable controversy over the reason
why strips were ridged. One argument for ridging is that it
increased the land area, another is that it provided readily
identifiable property boundaries and a third common argument was that it helped drainage. For example, the manor
court at Shipton (Salop) in the mid-sixteenth century

93

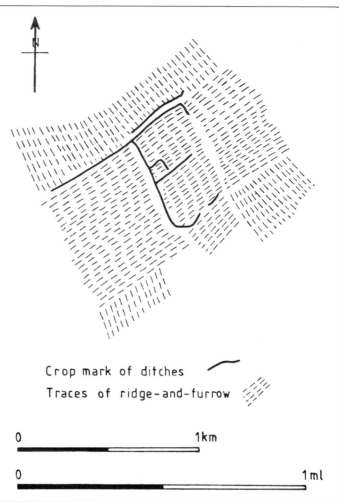

Crop mark of ditches

Traces of ridge-and-furrow

0   1km

0   1ml

23 Medieval ridge and
furrow overlying a
'Celtic' field system
(after C. C. Taylor)

ordered that 'everyone doe plow the land so that the rain-
water may run thereof'. Probably there were different
reasons for ridging in particular areas, but it may have
survived for so long as a common technique simply due
to agrarian conservatism. Nevertheless despite its widespread occurrence, ridge and furrow is not and never was
universal even in parts of the country where a form of
open field agriculture was being practised. For example,
documentary evidence indicates that it was rarely created
in areas such as south Devon and the East Anglian Breck-
lands. In such areas it seems that the strips were ploughed
flat without furrows in order to retain moisture, using
grass banks to define the strips. Such baulks still exist in
the surviving open fields at Braunton in Devon (known
locally as *landsherd,* derived from Old English *landesearu,*

meaning boundary), although even here they are rapidly disappearing through strip amalgamation.

'Open-field agriculture' is not necessarily synonymous with medieval agriculture although much, if not most, English medieval agriculture operated on an open-field basis. Difficulties arise in our understanding for two reasons. First, the physical appearance of different agrarian systems was often very similar, despite fundamental

differences in land tenure and rotational systems. Second, the system which reached its zenith in the Middle Ages persisted in some areas for several centuries afterwards. Indeed in Midland England it was not until parliamentary enclosure in the period 1750–1850 that many open-field systems were ultimately eclipsed. Modified open fields can still be found, most notably at Laxton (Nottinghamshire), on the Isle of Portland (Dorset), at Braunton, at Eakring in Nottinghamshire and on the Isle of Axeholme. The dilemma which is created by such striking regional differences and the survival of elements of the open-field system has made medieval agriculture difficult to analyse and a topic of considerable controversy.

The economic historian M.M. Postan wisely warned that: 'It is even more dangerous to generalise about the

30 Abberwick, Northumberland. A shrunken village surrounded by extensive traces of ridge and furrow. Unlike much Midland ridge and furrow these furrows are of an irregular width and shape as they have been altered to accommodate local marshy conditions

organisation of medieval agriculture than its physical and demographic background.' There is a great temptation for scholars analysing medieval agriculture to draw too heavily upon the extensive body of post-medieval evidence in order to reconstruct agrarian systems of the Middle Ages. The intrinsic dangers inherent in this approach are that topography and field systems which can be identified from post-medieval documents and maps cannot automatically be assumed to be medieval. There are rare examples of medieval maps which in general terms indicate the form of the contemporary field systems, shown on the fifteenth century Boarstall map (Fig. 13). Nevertheless, there is little authentic cartographic information available before 1580. There are, of course, a range of other sources such as terriers, rentals and manorial court rolls which enable the reconstruction of some systems, but at least on a regional basis the pattern that emerges is partial. Where estate accounts survive it is often easier to reconstruct the agricultural regime and economy than the physical characteristics of a field system.

The problems of examining and identifying traces of true medieval agriculture are not made any easier by using surviving field evidence, as unadulterated traces of medieval field systems are rare. Most of the archaeological remains of open-field agriculture date from the last occasion on which the fields were ploughed. In some cases this was in the fourteenth or fifteenth centuries, when arable land was turned over to pasture or went out of agricultural use altogether, but in other areas strip-ploughing went on as late as the eighteenth or nineteenth centuries. Therefore although the surviving physical traces may provide an accurate facsimile of earlier systems, they are not actually medieval. The excavation of ridge and furrow rarely provides conclusive dating evidence and only in rare circumstances is it possible to identify any relationship between ridge and furrow and other dateable features. There is, however, substantial evidence to suggest that during the period of population expansion, new settlements were not only being created in remote areas close to the margin of population, but in some cases were actually being laid out over areas of former arable land. For instance at Braham Farm, Cambridgeshire, a medieval enclosure clearly overlies ridge and furrow. As already noted aerial photographs of deserted medieval villages sometimes show how, during a period of settlement expansion, existing tofts were extended onto, or new tofts created over, ridge and furrow. In the case of Barton

Blount in Derbyshire, aerial photographs show clearly that the village has expanded northwards over areas of earlier ridge and furrow. Indeed, in a number of cases it appears as if a whole medieval settlement has been superimposed on a ridge-field system. Such settlement expansion onto open-fields appears to date from the twelfth and thirteenth centuries, and is contemporary with the most extensive phase of medieval arable farming. In parts of the Midlands

31 Kington, Herefordshire. Even when ploughed out traces of ridge and furrow are identifiable as crop marks. On this photograph the crop markings of former medieval agricultural fields overlie markings of an Iron Age enclosure. In the top left there are two sets of crop marks of ridges suggesting that the open field system was reorganised here at some stage.

complete parishes are covered with ridge and furrow, and even steep hillsides were brought into cultivation through the use of lynchets or terraces. Strip lynchets were formerly believed to be prehistoric in origin, but have now been identified as integral parts of open-field systems (plate 31).

Open-field agriculture is alternatively known as the 'common-field system', 'the two– or three-field system', 'strip-farming' or the 'Midland system'. The authentic medieval open-field system consisted of four elements. First, the arable land was divided into long narrow strips or *selions*, which were owned or tenanted by a number of people normally occupying a central village settlement. Each landholder had scattered parcels or strips of land distributed throughout the arable fields, intermingled with those of his neighbours. The strips of the open fields were

grouped into furlongs (*cultura*), 'flatts', 'shotts' or 'wongs'
as they were known in some parts of the country. Contrary
to popular opinion, strips were not a standard length,
neither were the furlongs. Furlongs varied considerably
in size even within a single manor. Groups of furlongs
cumulatively formed fields (*campi*), of which there were
often three named fields of roughly equal size. In theory
this arrangement suited the rotational agrarian practice
best, that is two-thirds arable, one-third fallow each year.
It was not essential to have three fields for this agricultural
system to operate. In some instances there were only two
fields or in some cases four, five or even more fields. The
essence of the system was the rotation operating within
the field framework. This did not have to be dictated by
the number of named fields. Indeed even where there
were three fields operating, the rotational system did not
necessarily follow the field system – the furlong, not the
field, was the rotational unit. In Clapham's words, 'crop
rotation is independent of the lay-out of the fields'. On a
Corpus Christi estate at Whitehill, Tackley (Oxon), a four-
field system operated on perfectly regular rotational lines,
with the furlongs acting as the unit of rotation. However,
in some places such as southern Warwickshire and Worcestershire a four-field system does actually seem to have
operated in association with a four-course rotation of
fallow, barley, legumes and wheat.

Second, both arable and meadow land were pastured
by the stock of the farmers between harvest time and
when the seed was sown. In most years approximately a
third of the arable land within the open fields lay fallow
in order to allow it to rest and be manured by the grazing
animals (also providing the animals with feed). This meant
that on arable lands and, to a lesser extent, pasture and
meadow, strict rules governing the nature of crop cultivation and the control of animals were necessary. Third,
where there was pasture, waste or common land this was
used for stock-raising, again often involving regulation of
the number and type of animals allowed to graze there.
Finally, the administration and implementation of this
agricultural system had to be organised by a formal
meeting of the farmers, normally in the form of a manorial
court or a village assembly.

One village which has been studied in some detail is
Cuxham in Oxfordshire, where a regular open-field system
operated in the later Middle Ages. The arable lay in three
large fields containing respectively 121, 126 and 127 acres.
This division into fields was related to a scheme of crop

rotation: each field in turn was under a winter crop such
as wheat, and then a spring crop, such as oats or barley;
each was finally fallowed for a year to recover fertility, so
that one-third of the village arable was rested each year.
Each of the fields was divided into furlongs and each of
the furlongs into strips. The holdings of individual tenants
consisted of scattered strips intermixed with those of their
neighbours, although the demense land had been partially

consolidated by the purchases and exchanges in the thirteenth century. The meadowland was similarly divided
and ownership was dispersed. Finally lord and tenants
had rights of common pasture on the moor, and certainly
on the arable fields when fallowed or after harvest.
Cuxham was a 'common field' village in the sense that
the villagers enjoyed common rights on the arable after
harvest, on the fallow, and on the uncultivated 'waste'.

One misconception about the open-field system is the
belief that the strips were periodically re-allocated among
the landholders in order to ensure that each had a fair
distribution of land of different quality within the
community. Although there are many instances of redistribution of meadow land, and some cases of pasture, there
is little evidence for the re-allocation of arable land on a
regular basis. An exception appears to be have been in
Northumberland, where in the sixteenth century re-allot-

32 A scene from medieval
life showing a horse-
drawn plough at the
top with a beggar and
the stocks below (late
fifteenth century)

Quoniam tu dominus alti
super omnem terram: nimie
tus es super omnes deos

33 Harvesting cereal
crops from a
fourteenth-century
manuscript

ment of arable land was common, but even this did not take place on an annual basis. It was customary in parts of the northern counties to change the arable fields at intervals by putting old plough land back to common pasture and taking a new field from the common.

In the purest form the strips represented the individual units of one man's holding. Although the system was not universally one of subsistence, it is clear that up until the thirteenth century at least there was a considerable subsistence element involved in medieval agriculture over large parts of the country. It therefore follows that each farmer should have had a relatively evenly distributed land allotment, and not have had a disproportionate share of his strip under fallow in any one year. Also, each farmer should have had a share of ground on soils of varying quality. However even though such equality of land holding may have existed at different points in time, over the centuries strip amalgamation and swapping eventually resulted in considerable variations in the size of holdings (see Table 2). Open-field maps of the late sixteenth century show a pattern of land ownership and tenancy in which something of the medieval complexity had been simplified in the interest of convenience and economical working. From the fourteenth century onwards landlord concessions had enabled some villagers to make exchanges and sales so as to bring together the scattered strips of a holding. Not many tenants succeeded in bringing all their land into two or three large parcels, but almost everyone had moved in this direction. Both voluntary and involuntary changes of ownership worked to modify the basic simple pattern

Table 2 Approximate land divisions of Lower Heyford, 1604

	No. of Strips	Acres	Roods	Perches	Percentage of total
Lampland	3	2	2	32	0.35
Thomas Guy	2	0	2	32	0.07
William Endall	4	3	2	19	0.48
Roger Wighton	5	2	0	18	0.28
Thomas Bruce	199	125	3	25	17.43
Barth Tipping	184	104	3	32	14.52
James Mynne	92	37	0	37	5.12
William Tredwell	162	45	0	27	6.22
Thomas King(e)	156	57	2	37	7.88
John Sheres	144	66	0	30	9.13
John Green	19	15	2	36	2.21
Richard Elkins	78	30	0	20	4.15
George Merry	126	60	2	35	8.44
John Merry	89	43	2	3	6.02
Gabriel Merry	119	104	1	21	14.38
Norton	92	22	2	9	3.11
Thomas Faulkoner	53	31	0	33	4.29
Simon Elfret	58	7	1	0	0.97
Parsonage	76	21	1	8	2.90

Source: Thomas Langdon, map of Lower Heyford, Corpus Christi College, Oxford (1604)

Yet the system was stubborn. To change it, as potential enclosers found, the agreement of almost everyone else working the fields was required. Quite apart from the natural conservatism of the countryside, the system did ensure a rough justice in the distribution of both good and bad land. The evidence for an original equitable allocation of strips is clearest for the glebe land whose rectorial ownership frequently remained consistent over the centuries, with the original parish church endowment identifiable on the ground. When glebe strips were surveyed even as late as the eighteenth century it was sometimes found that they still occupied a standard position in each furlong throughout the field system. At Langtoft, East Riding, the glebe strips were the 11th, 12th, 26th, 27th, 30th and 31st in each furlong, while at Great Givendale, East Riding in 1784, the parson's strip was always the end one in a furlong, with that of the lord of the manor next to it. Such a distribution must reflect a former regular division of strips amongst the community at one stage. It is just possible in certain instances that this division dates back to the creation of the strips from the clearance of former wood or waste land, but more likely it reflects a redistribution of strips at a particular point in time, perhaps when a village was being reorganized.

Emphasis has already been placed upon the extent of regional variety to be found in open-field farming. In some parts of the country different inheritance customs helped to create different field systems. In south-east England, for example, there was a system of land transfer known as partible inheritance, under which custom the land was divided equally between all male heirs. This resulted in a curious pattern of small blocks of open or strip fields not always cultivated or grazed in common, mixed up with areas of enclosed fields. Some of the latter were cultivated in strips for cropping purposes and later sold, leased or inherited as individual strip holdings. Another variation was to be found in the Holderness area in the low-lying region to the east of the Yorkshire Wolds. The townships normally had only two arable fields. Many strips within the fields were of great length, often extending from one field boundary to another, a distance of over a mile in some townships. Strips lay parallel throughout the greater part of a field and where furlongs did occur, they were few in number within any one field, and usually acted as functional rather than physical divisions. Similar examples of very long parallel strips were to be found in Lincolnshire and on areas of the Wessex chalklands.

In east Devon many of the vills were surrounded by extensive tracts of arable land, but the diagnostic attributes of the Midland communal rotation system were missing. The arable land of each settlement comprised a multiplicity of units, some called fields, some furlongs. There was no fallow field, and the practice of village-wide common

34 Medieval market scene showing a sheep and cattle auction

pasturing on the uncropped arable was absent. The fields were adapted to the system of convertible husbandry which was prevalent in medieval Devon and which required arable to be broken up into many parts, each at a different stage in the long-term cycle of crops and grass. In east Devon there was enclosure as early as the 1250s and it was well under way by the mid-fourteenth century. Most of the holdings here were fragmented and their scattered fenced or hedged closes were relatively small and elongated in shape, fossilizing the pre-enclosure pattern of strips. As textile manufacturing became more important, pasture became increasingly dominant and the buoyancy of demand for land led to small bundles of strips which were ideal for pasturing livestock being enclosed. Regions such as this were much more flexible than the Midland belt, and could therefore be converted to severalty when the occasion demanded. The subdivided units were small, numerous, irregularly arranged – quite unlike the patterns of furlongs in the roughly equally sized fields in the Midlands with their accompanying communal rights and regulations. The agrarian history of the Devon region is therefore not one of decay of the two– or three-field systems, but the transformation of an indigenous and flexible multi-field arrangement.

Further west in Cornwall, the investigation of a small abandoned settlement called Garrow on Bodmin Moor revealed a system of hand cultivation which had been created, in highly marginal conditions, apparently in response to land pressure. The medieval farmers were obliged to set out their field systems in the form of large beds on top of prehistoric systems. The strips or beds ran lengthways up and down the hillside, and were approximately 220 yards long, with straight sides and a fairly constant width of 2 yards. They lay in groups separated by baulks of granite boulders and stones gathered from field-clearings. The furrows were approximately 20 inches wide and the number of ridges on a group varies from 7 to 50. The fields reached the very limits of the rivers and used up all available areas where bedrock was not showing. Measures adopted within the fields also indicate efforts to avoid wasting land, for instance prehistoric huts standing in the way of the run of a field were enclosed to form a paddock, and two of them even had their floors paved and the entrance widened to serve as pens.

Another important variation was the 'runrig' or 'infield-outfield' system which operated on poorer ground in northern and western England. This consisted of the 'infield' which was closest to the vill or farmstead, and which was cultivated every year and a second field, the 'outfield', which was divided into two, one part being cultivated for several years and then grassed for a few years, the other part being very largely uncultivated. The 'infield-outfield' system itself operated in a wide variety of different ways and some scholars have argued that the 'infield-outfield' system was the foundation from which the two– and three-field system evolved. In some cases the 'infield-outfield' system survived without substantial change throughout the Middle Ages. At Carburton in the forest area of Nottinghamshire an infield-outfield system survived into the early seventeenth century, when it was recorded in cartographic form. In the area immediately adjacent to the town there were regular openfield strips. There is, however, a large area known as the Brecks which was common land, available when required for cultivation but not a permanent part of the ploughlands (fig. 24).

Not only were there marked regional differences in field systems and in their operation. During the Middle Ages field systems proved themselves to be surprisingly adaptable to changing economic conditions. The movement from two to three fields is well documented in some places. In Wiltshire, for example, two fields were

24 The early seventeenth-century infield-outfield system at Carburton, Nottinghamshire (Notts County Record Office SP 14/83/80). Church field, Tenter field and Water Breck field operated as permanent open fields (or the infield), and much of the remainder of the parish formed the 'outfield'

converted into three at Poulton and Heytesbury during
the century after 1250; and at South Stoke in Oxfordshire,
the Abbot of Eynsham 'partitioned into three parts his
lands which previously were partitioned into two parts'.
Sometimes the object of converting two fields into three
may have been to adjust the layout of the village arable to
a pre-existing three-course rotation; sometimes to increase
the amount of land under crops by decreasing from one-
half to one-third the arable area fallowed each year; and
sometimes it was simply to accommodate new land which
had been assarted. Later, during the fourteenth and
fifteenth centuries, some field systems were able to adapt
to a significant reduction in the amount of arable which
was required. A study of demesne lands at Bourchier Hall
in Essex in the fourteenth century indicates that changing
techniques of cultivation accompanied a decline in the
extent of the arable area after 1349. Even without a contraction in demand for grain and the subsequent rise in labour
costs after the Black Death, the arable component of the
demesne appears to have been shrinking. A regular
3–course division extended over almost all the cultivated
lands of the demesne. There were, however, some
outfields where oats were grown, the cultivation of this
hardier crop suggesting that the 3–course regime had been
stretched to the limits of its wheat-growing capacity. Culti-

25 The abandonment of
open-field agriculture
in western Shropshire
resulted in the
widespread desertion
and shrinkage of
dependent
townships during the
later Middle Ages
(after V. C. H.
Shropshire)

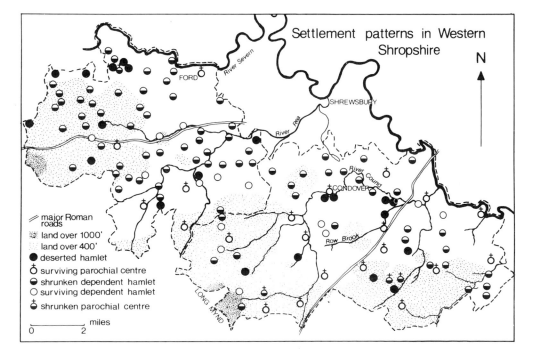

Settlement patterns in Western
Shropshire

N

FORD

River Severn

SHREWSBURY

River Rea

River Cound

CONDOVER

Row Brook

LONG MYND

major Roman
roads
land over 1000'
land over 400'
● deserted hamlet
☉ surviving parochial centre
◕ shrunken dependent hamlet
○ surviving dependent hamlet
☺ shrunken parochial centre

miles
0   2

vation at this margin proved to be more than the soil could sustain and it began to show signs of exhaustion. By the late 1330s wheat cultivation was barely paying its way and by the 1350s grain had to be bought in from outside. In response the better land was allowed to lie fallow in order to give it time to recover and oats were sown extensively, mostly on land that had previously been pasture. By 1356–7 the old 3–course rotation pattern had been totally abandoned. This had been made possible by the severe reduction in the area under arable cultivation and a reduction of the sown acreage from 253 acres in the late 1330s to 137 acres in the early 1350s.

Enclosed fields

There were sections of the country where strip fields never existed and agriculture was based entirely on enclosed fields bounded by permanent hedges, walls or banks. These fields varied greatly in shape, size and purpose but generally they developed in localities with a relatively low population, where the isolated farmstead or hamlet was more common than the village, and where pastoral farming was more important than arable. In parts of the West Country the patchwork of enclosed fields that operated during the Middle Ages was directly descended from prehistoric field systems. In these areas there had been no need to change tenurial organisation or farming practice. Recent work by Professor Glanville Jones has demonstrated clearly the survival of Celtic agrarian practice in parts of western Britain into the Middle Ages as well as the physical field systems.

Throughout the Middle Ages there were manors, even in central England, where all or sections of the fields were hedged. In the west, particularly as the population fell dramatically during the later fourteenth and fifteenth centuries, former open fields were turned over to pasture. In counties such as Herefordshire and Shropshire by the time the first cartographic surveys were made only very small areas of open fields survived. From about 1300 onwards the process of enclosure by the exchange of strips by tenants and the amalgamation in small fields became a regular feature of the landscape. Much of this enclosure was undertaken by private agreement, often without any documentation or any record being made. But in 1321, for example, there is reference to an enclosed croft called 'oldrugges' in Stoke St Milborough (Salop). In other cases, the repeated stricture of the manor courts to tenants telling them to pull down fences or newly planted hedges attests to the gradual attrition of open-field systems. Often small bundles of strips were enclosed together in irregularly shaped fields, frequently in the immediate vicinity of the settlement.

In the early fourteenth century the deeds of Tavistock Abbey in Devon record the process of enclosing open field strips. It began with the consolidation of holdings, brought about by purchase and exchange. Then a trench was dug to mark the limits of the holder's land, and the soil removed from it was thrown up into a mound on the inner side of the ditch. (A lease of Furze Close at Woodovis in 1465 specified that the ditch should be 4 feet wide and 4 feet deep; and the same dimensions were given at Leigh in 1398.) The mound was then planted with a quickset hedge, and grew in the course of time by the addition of soil thrown up whenever the ditch was cleared. No feature of the Devon landscape is more characteristic than these vast banks, crowned with oak, ash, hazel, or other coppice wood growing to a height of 18 feet or more and forming an impenetrable screen. It is possible that such coppice fences may have been designed at first to make good the loss of fuel resulting from forest clearance. 'Many farms have no other woodland, nor supply of fuel, than what their fences furnish; yet are amply supplied with this; besides, perhaps an overplus of poles, cord wood, faggots, and the bark of oak, for sale.'

The enclosed area was locally termed a *park*. In size it could be anything from an acre upwards but parks of 25, 34 and 40 acres were not uncommon. One of the features of this type of early enclosure is that the field boundaries often respect the boundaries within the former open fields. They tended to conform to former furlong boundaries, unlike later parliamentary enclosure where the enclosure commissioners completely ignored former land units and created their own new field patterns. In 1306 Robert Davy, acting on behalf of the abbot of Tavistock, bought up several parcels of land in Ogbear-ham, 'both enclosed and unenclosed'. Another document of the same period mentions 'all the parks of Ogbear situated between Ogbear and Ottery'. The 1387 Extent of Hurdwick refers to eight 'parcels' of land in Bowrish and Downhouse, occupied by as many tenants; but over 'parcel' a later hand written 'close' in each case. After the first quarter of the fourteenth century we hear no more of selions and furlongs in the vicinity of Tavistock; and though in some parishes the open field survived for another century or two, by 1549 the arable lands of Devon were reported to be among the most completely enclosed in England.

After the middle years of the fourteenth century, enclosure of arable open fields for pasture gathered momentum in other western counties, often resulting in the abandonment or shrinkage of the associated village. However, in the Vale of Blackmoor in Dorset, enclosure did not result in deserted villages. At Purse Caundle, the common-fields disappeared in the early fifteenth century,

35 Early enclosure of open field strips at Brassington, Derbyshire. The small size of the fields and the adherence of the hedges to the line of the ridge and furrow is indicative of late medieval or immediate post-medieval enclosure

at Marnhull between 1361 and 1410 and at Hazelbury Bryan by 1434, certainly in the latter case to be replaced by large enclosed fields of permanent pasture.

The clearance of areas of former waste and woodland and their enclosure into fields was associated with the growing population and a need to increase the area of agricultural production. From the documentary evidence it appears to have reached its height in the thirteenth century, when it is clear that there was extensive assarting. Enclosures were prominent in those districts where land was being taken from the woodland: in Essex and Hertfordshire; in the wooded uplands of the West Midlands; in Sherwood, Charnwood and Rockingham forests in the East Midlands; and in the Kent and Sussex Weald. In the parish of Whiteparish in south Wiltshire where there were relatively small areas of old forest, the fields are today highly irregular and have obviously been cut out of the former woodland, but the much straighter farm boundaries are still traceable. It is therefore possible to reconstruct the process by which each farmstead was established upon the forest edge and the land behind it cleared

piecemeal into long strips up to the cleared land of
adjacent farms. Some of the actual clearances are recorded
in documents as in one of 1270 when 14 acres of assarts
were enclosed by 'a dyke and a hedge'. In the Forest of
Arden in Warwickshire there was a vigorous colonising
movement in the early Middle Ages. As elsewhere in the
country this was partly stimulated by peasant land hunger
in the old settled lands to the south of Arden and partly by
seigneurial encouragement, based on the desire to increase
income from rents and dues. The colonising process here
involved the piecemeal reclamation of woodland, leading
to the creation of new farms and fields. The resulting
landscape consisted of enclosed fields or closes, on average
about five acres in area.

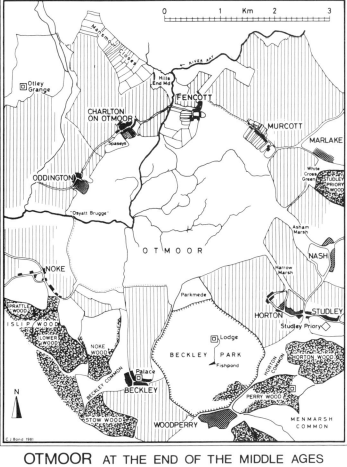

OTMOOR AT THE END OF THE MIDDLE AGES

26 Medieval settlements
and their open fields
ringing Otmoor,
Oxfordshire. All but
the wettest land was
put to some form of
economic use by the
end of the Middle
Ages. The Mansmoor
Closes were late
medieval enclosures
taken out of Charlton
on Otmoor's open
fields. Attempts to
enclose Otmoor in the
eighteenth century
led to riots. (Compiled
by J. Bond)

109

The process of woodland clearance did not always result
in the creation of new enclosed fields; sometimes the
newly won land was added to existing open fields, a
particularly common practice in northern England. It has
been demonstrated how northern villages of the twelfth
and thirteenth centuries were frequently marrying newly
cleared land to an older core of open-field land. Even in
the north, however, such assimilation of the new to the
old was not universal. Some Elizabethan maps show
villages with a large inner block of open-field furlongs but
an outer ring of hedged fields. This double landscape was,
however, quite compatible with the maintenance of open-
field farming. Alternatively assarted land could be used for
a non-agrarian function. For example, when new burgage
plots were being created at Clun in Shropshire they were
said to lie on assart land.

The reclamation of marsh and fen

In the west, on the Somerset Levels, work continued on
the reclamation of fen and marshland, but drainage was
mostly piecemeal in character. In eastern England landowners were engaged in the extension of arable across the
level silt-lands around the Wash. Some of the new land
was incorporated into the existing strip fields, but much
was enclosed directly into small fields. This process
certainly started before the eleventh century and

27 Sawtry All Saints and
Sawtry St Andrews,
Huntingdonshire,
from a map of 1612
showing enclosed
fields taken from
fenland

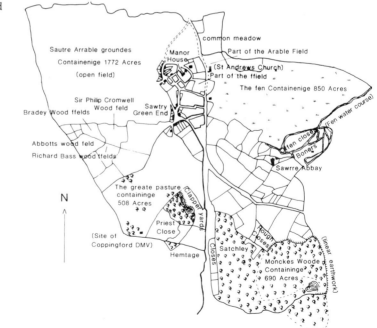

continued throughout the next two centuries. Co-operation by groups of villagers was required to carry out
this work, the basic requirement being the construction of
massive banks running parallel to the sea. Behind these a
new area or level was drained, turned over to pasture and
in some cases cultivated. In a survey of 1251 at Little Port,
Cambridge, 60 new tenants were holding nearly 495 acres
of new land and these holdings are still reflected in the
field pattern on the ground today.

Agricultural technique in the Fenland reflected the
movement for the reclamation and helped it develop. In
the siltland in particular orthodox open-field husbandry
gave way to enclosed fields, but there is some evidence to
demonstrate that two-course and three-course husbandry
was still being practised. Flexibility and the power to
respond to the various agricultural and pastoral opportunities offered by fen and marsh were characteristic of fenland
agriculture, with its hundreds of small holdings and its
extensive monastic granges. The pattern of crops grown
illustrates this flexibility in the restricted growth of wheat,
which was mainly found on the drier siltlands, especially
where there were monastic estates, and the preference of
the Fenlanders for growing flax and hemp. Pastoral
farming was very important at all times in Fenland,
especially cattle-farming in Spalding and the Precinct of
Crowland, but sheep-farming was also significant even in
the middle of the twelfth century. Indeed the name Shepea
in the Precinct of Crowland is at least as old as this and
may even date from the tenth century. During the thirteenth and fourteenth centuries conditions in the fens
seem to have deteriorated partly as a result of change
linked to a change in sea level. For instance, it was said
in 1251 that the Bishop of Ely's demesne at Elm 'sometimes
decreases and sometimes increases on account of the sea'.
The response of farming techniques to the decline in the
condition of the fens and marshes appears very strikingly
in the change from an economy which was nearly 70 per
cent arable and only 30 per cent meadow and pasture late
in the thirteenth century to one which, at most was only
40 per cent arable, and in Elloe much less than this, by
the end of the Middle Ages.

The immense reclamations and the largely arable
farming of the period which ended in 1307, were the
outcome of the great pressure of population which created
some of the largest villages in England. The villages of
Elloe increased their arable, pasture and meadow by
reclaiming land from the fen to the south and the sea to

the north. On the seaward side reclamation began with accretions in the estuaries of the South Holland rivers between the villages, and led to the creation of a great sea-bank, which was to remain the final bulwark of defence until the reign of Charles II. Accretion occurred rapidly between 1100 and 1300, and consisted of 'newlands' enclosed by groups of landholders, who were frequently poor freemen and villeins and often the tenants of manorial lords, who on occasion took part in the process themselves. The land enclosed in this way was put to every kind of use, and often lay in small precisely measured strips, sometimes called *offoldfal*. There is one instance of a large area enclosed in common by the communities of Whaplode and Holbeach.

On the fenward side the process was much more extensive, and was the result of communal effort. There were four fen-banks in Spalding, Weston and Moulton: Austendyke, the settlement bank made before the Conquest; Old Fendyke, made at an unknown date after this, but probably early in the twelfth century; New Fendyke, made before 1189; and Goldyke, made in 1205. In Whaplode, Holbeach and Fleet there were five fen-banks; Hurdletree Bank, associated with the earliest settlement; Saturday Dyke, made about 1160–70; Hassock Dyke, made in 1190–5 or 1186–8; Asgardyke or Lord's Dyke, made in 1205, and Common Dyke made in 1241. In Sutton, Gedney and Tydd St Mary, Raven's Dyke, Old Fendyke and New Fendyke corresponded with the second, third and fourth banks in Holbeach, and there was a further section of bank made south of Sutton St Edmund after 1229. After 1205 the fen-hamlets of Cowbit and Moulton Chapel grew up in the course of the century, and the priory of Spalding established its grange at Goll soon after 1294. In the 1241 enclosure the fen-hamlets of Whaplode Drove, Holbeach Drove, Gedney Hill and Sutton St Edmund grew up, as also did the Crowland Abbey granges of Aswick and Fenhall, and Spalding Priory's grange at Gannock.

These numerous enclosures from sea and fen indicate a period of immense activity between the Conquest and the end of the thirteenth century. The greatest work was undoubtedly the reclamation of the fens, and although an exact estimate is difficult, topographical study shows about 50 square miles reclaimed from the fen alone between about 1170 and 1241. To this must be added a large, but indefinite, amount of land acquired from the sea during the same period.

Woodland, forests and parks

Chapter five

The diminishing woodland

By the early Middle Ages only parts of England were still well wooded. There was little primeval woodland left, and even some of those areas generally associated with a heavy woodland cover such as the Midland claylands had been partially recolonised by trees since the end of the Roman era. In areas of marginal agricultural activity, particularly in the north and west and in the Weald, there were still plentiful supplies of timber, but increasingly during the twelfth and thirteenth centuries there was pressure on the diminishing areas of woodland.

Nevertheless many manors still possessed some woodland, which was in common use by manorial tenants for collecting dead wood and grazing animals. One thirteenth century Yorkshire document makes reference to common pasture *in bosco et plano* at Holme on Spalding Moor, 'and timber in the wood to make their [tenants] houses and fences and to burn', together with the right to feed pigs in the wood. Another specifies the amount of timber to be taken yearly from the woods as well as the number of pigs to be fed there. 'Outwoods', woodland usually reserved for the lord's use, were also to be found in many manors. Naturally enough woodland in otherwise heavily cultivated areas tended to be in remote places on parish boundaries and well away from settlement. Woods also tended to be limited to areas of poorer land, on very steep and damp slopes and also on flat clay hilltops which were difficult to drain. Occasionally such ancient enclaves of woodland were bounded with linear earthworks in order to define their limits clearly. One such area which has been studied in detail is Hayley Wood (Cambridgeshire) which belonged to the Bishops of Ely. Its shape, like that of many medieval woods, was irregular in outline and it was surrounded by a formidable bank and ditch. Dr Oliver Rackham has demonstrated that it is possible to trace the changing shape of the wood over the centuries by plotting the boundaries from different dates.

It is now recognised that coppicing was an important element in the medieval rural economy. Rackham has

113

demonstrated that within Hayley Wood there were
internal earthworks to keep out deer and other animals
from the coppiced areas. It seems probable that the boundaries of some coppiceland units have survived in the shape
of later parks and other discrete parcels of land usage.
Surveys and accounts of the great religious houses show
that coppice cycles were well understood. The abbey at
Bury St Edmunds, for example, had an impressive
network of well managed woods; these included Monks'
Park, where coppicing records date back to 1252.

Medieval woods produced three types of product which
were distinguished by the terms 'timber' (*maeremium*),
'wood' (*subboscus*), and 'firewood' (*robora*). 'Timber' was
used for making structures, posts, beams and planks and
it was cut from trees called standards, or from maidens
grown from seed or suckers. 'Underwood' was taken in
the form of poles, produced by cutting coppices, pollards
or young suckers. Maple, wych-elm and hazel were all cut
at intervals, and the resulting stumps produced further
shoots. When these were protected from the browsing
habits of deer and other animals they grew rapidly to
produce a crop of poles. The third commodity, fuel, was
normally produced from dead or dying trees. The wood-

36 Cottingham Woods in
the forest of
Rockingham,
Northamptonshire, in
1580 showing the
woodland divided up
between hunting areas
in the form of
Rockingham Park, the
Laund of Benefeelde
and a series of
coppices surrounding
them

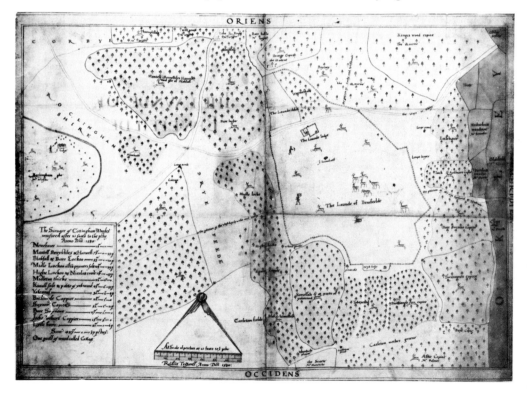

land economy is well illustrated in a survey of the Bishop of Ely's estate at Long Melford (Suffolk) dated 1386 which under 'woods' includes the following entries:

> In the great wood 260 acres by estimate in which can be made every year 600 faggots, worth 8s (at 16d the hundred).
> The agistment in the same is worth £2 per annum.
> In the wood called lenyng 90 acres, one-sixth part of which each year is 15 acres which are worth £2 12s 6d at 3s 6d per acre.
> Le Speltne is 80 acres by estimate, one-sixth part of which each year is worth £2 7s 10d at 3s 6d per acre.
> In the little park 60 acres and the wood is worth £1 10s per annum at 3s per acre (sic)
> Cutting thorns in various places is worth 12d a year.
> Pannage of pigs worth 6s 8d a year.
> Total £9 6s 0d a year.

As pressures both on coppice and woodland remained considerable in parts of the country there were many accounts of timber shortages. An indignant protest by a chronicler of Pipewell Abbey (Northants), writing soon after 1320 asks: why is the forest being denuded of trees on all sides? The first culprits he claimed were the hearths which used up the oaks as fuel, then the grants of timber for windmill sails: 'How many windmill sails they have in different abbots' times no one knows, except God to whom all things are known!' The worst grievance was the process of assarting. 'It is well known that the furlong of arable called Coleshawe by East Grange once had a wood on it, as indeed the foundation charter shows. Now it is all arable, the monks having permitted the men of Barford to assart it and bring it under cultivation.' Accounts of clearance come from almost all the woodland areas of England and of Wales, but they are frequently laconic or uninformative. The place-name record, however, clearly recounts the toll on woodland. 'Woodhouse' and other names with wood elements are common, 'assart' is sometimes shortened to 'sart', 'stocking' means 'piece of land cleared of stumps'. 'Field' and 'green' are other common clearing names and the cleared woodland 'parks' of Devon have already been mentioned. Areas with such medieval names were often settled with moated farmsteads, particularly in Midland England.

Alongside the process of coppicing erratic conservation measures were introduced. As early as 1179 the Exchequer had imposed 'a common and fixed penalty' on those who made assarts in forest land, 'to wit a perpetual rent of one shilling for each acre sown with wheat and expence for each sown with oats', although this measure should

perhaps be interpreted more in terms of realising revenue
than conserving woodland. The Statute of Merton in 1236
attempted to protect the rights of those landowners whose
grazing-rights were being diminished by the enclosure of
grassland and woodland. Bishop Herbert de Losinga left
detailed orders concerning the conservation of woodland
at Thorpe Wood near Norwich *c.*1100. From the thirteenth
century the crown intermittently recorded its anxiety about
the timber shortage and felling for crown gifts of timber
was stopped in 1257.

In addition to regular manorial woodland, substantial
areas were devoted to hunting. Tracts of land which were
devoted to hunting were often well wooded, and were
categorised as *forest, chase, park* and *warren*. The *forest* was
a large area of country belonging to the crown and subject
to forest law: the *chases* were effectively private forests,
which a few great nobles and ecclesiastical lords were
allowed to create on their estates; the *park* was a relatively
small secure area enclosed for hunting and part of the
demesne land of the lord of the manor. An additional sub-
category was the royal park, a number of which were
subject to forest law because they lay within or adjacent
to a forest area. In certain instances such as at Gillingham
Park in Dorset a royal park formed the original nucleus
from which a royal forest was created. Sometimes the park
was broken down as a preliminary to the afforestation
of the surrounding district. There is, however, no clear
evidence that isolated royal parks were subject to the full
rigour of forest law. Finally the *warren* was a game area
allotted principally to hare and rabbits. In addition, there
was the much more common legal right of *free warren*
granted by the crown to lords of the manor, entitling them
to hunt the smaller game over their own estates.

Forests
The Normans had introduced the continental concept of
the 'forest' into England. Forests consisted of an area of
land outside the common law, which operated under
special laws and regulations designed to protect the king's
hunting. In those areas subject to forest law which were
well wooded, woodland was incidentally preserved, as the
vert or green food on which deer fed was also protected.
The main purpose of the royal forest was to protect the
fallow deer, the red deer, the roe deer (until a judicial
decision in 1339 removed it from the list because it was
supposed to drive away other deer), and the wild boar,
though the latter was hunted to extinction by the middle

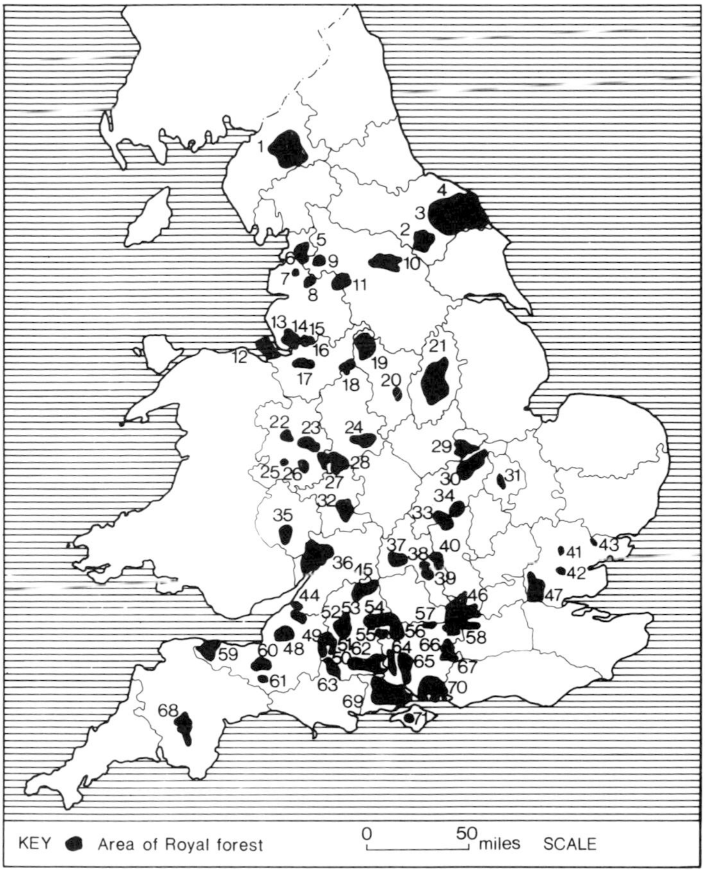
KEY Area of Royal forest
0 50 miles SCALE

28 The royal forests 1327–36 (after L. Cantor)

1 Inglewood
2 Galtres
3 Spaunton
4 Pickering
5 Quernmore
6 Bleasdale
7 Myerscough
8 Fulwood
9 Bowland
10 Knaresborough
11 Blackburn
12 Wirral
13 West Derby
14 Simonswood
15 Toxteth
16 Croxteth
17 Delamare
18 Macclesfield
19 High Peak
20 Duffield
21 Sherwood
22 Lythwood
23 Wellington
24 Cannock
25 Stretton
26 Shirlett
27 Morfe
28 Kinver
29 Rutland (or Leighfield)
30 Rockingham
31 Wauberghe
32 Feckenham
33 Whittlewood
34 Salcey
35 Hereford Hay
36 Dean
37 Wychwood
38 Shotover
39 Stowood
40 Bernwood
41 Hatfield
42 Writtle
43 Kingswood, Essex
44 Kingswood, Somerset
45 Braden
46 Windsor
47 Essex
48 Mendip
49 Selwood, Somerset
50 Selwood, Wiltshire
51 Melksham
52 Pewsham
53 Chippenham
54 Savernake
55 Chute, Wiltshire
56 Chute, Hampshire
57 Pamber
58 Bagshot
59 Exmoor
60 North Petherton
61 Neroche
62 Clarendon
63 Gillingham
64 Buckholt
65 Bere by Winchester
66 Alice Holt
67 Woolmer
68 Dartmoor
69 New Forest
70 Bere by Porchester
71 Isle of Wight

of the thirteenth century. The principal beast of the chase was indisputedly the fallow deer which was introducted to Britain after the Norman Conquest. In order to render the forest law effective over large areas, an elaborate administrative machinery developed alongside, but separately from, the common law. The hierarchy of forest officials included two justices of the forest – one for those north of the Trent and one for those to the south – wardens in charge of individual forests and subordinate foresters, usually local landowners who served as foresters over particular parts of the forest. The wardens often possessed considerable holdings within the forests, as in the case of the Warden of Savernake Forest in Wiltshire, an office that for most of the Middle Ages was in the hands of the Esturmy family.

Although the chief function of the royal forest was the preservation of game, it is clear that some of the remoter forests were actually being regularly used as a major source of timber, and that game were a secondary

consideration. Shirlett forest in Shropshire was originally
of considerable extent, and remained partly under royal
control until the sixteenth century. It appears to have been
the original *shire forest* representing the residue of the early
Shropshire forests – Shirlett in fact means a *'share of the
shire'*. In 1233 two of the king's carpenters were sent to
Shirlett to make bottices to fortify Montgomery castle
'when the need arises'. Ten years later oak trees were sent

throughout the county as 'the men of Llewelyn were in many places rising'. Wood from Shirlett was consistently sent to Shrewsbury castle and jail. A survey of Shirlett in 1235 noted a great amount of recent timber felling and recorded 'the custody is good as regards oak trees and underwood, except that great deliveries had been made by order of the king to the Abbeys of Shropshire, Buildwas and Wenlock. . . . There is small abiding of beasts excepting coming and going from other forests.'

At times unauthorized asserts within forests were accepted when they were duly reported, but other asserts were made only after application to royal officials for permission and with prior approval from the king. In these cases, the procedure was for inquests to be held to determine whether the proposed assarts would be to the damage of the king or his forest, and the permission was granted only when no damage was expected. There were occasional instances of assarting on a larger scale that were due to the initiative of manorial lords, and the forest records show that monasteries were usually involved when large areas were newly placed under cultivation. At Windsor the king, as manorial lord, was involved in extensive assarting, after he had determined that no damage to the forest would result from clearance. Numerous references confirm that the criterion in deciding whether to grant a license for an assart in the forest was whether the king's profit from the assart would be greater than any damage to the forest. The only other consideration was whether a proposed assart would infringe upon the common rights held by other men in the forest. The right to license an assart was in itself an economic factor of considerable value as shown by the gifts to the crown for these licenses and the king's granting of licenses to men whom he wished to reward for their services to him.

In addition to exploiting the woods on the royal demesne lands for the timber, the prohibition against cutting woods within the royal forest was turned into another source of revenue for the crown by granting licenses allowing individuals to cut their woods within the forest. Before a license was granted, the king would order an inquest to determine how much cutting could be done without damage to the royal forest. Such inquests were even held to examine emergency appeals, such as that of the nuns of Romsey who needed the money from sales of wood in order to finance the rebuilding of their abbey. Other nuns in similar financial difficulties obtained licenses to sell underwood up to 40 acres and to sell 40

37 Wenlock Edge, Shropshire, which formed the core of the Long Forest during the early Middle Ages. The forest extended along the ridge and on either side of it joining up the forests of Shirlett in eastern Shropshire and Longmynd and Clun Forest in the west. At one stage half of the county of Shropshire was designated royal forest, but the process of deforestation had already begun by the late twelfth century

oaks from their woods. In addition to placing a limitation on the amount of woods that could be sold, licenses of this type usually required the owner to construct a low hedge around the cleared area that would allow the deer to enter and leave but would protect new growth from cattle, horses, or pigs foraging in the forest. The usual punishment for men who cut woods without license, including foresters, was through the forest courts, which assessed fines or confiscated the lands from their owners until adequate payment was made to the king to redeem them.

The forest had probably reached its widest extent by the end of Henry II's reign when up to a third of the whole country was deemed to be under forest law, but it proved impossible to maintain such vast areas. Quite apart from the problems of administering large royal forests the implementation of forest law was liable to be abused by local forest officials and its enforcement aroused bitter resentment among the populace. The royal forests came to be identified with the arbitrary authority of the king and this identification led the barons to use the forest as an issue in their struggle to restrict royal power, added to which the relatively meagre revenues obtained from the forests by the licensing of assarts and purprestures (enclosures), and from the fines levied by the forest courts, became increasingly irrelevant. During the fourteenth century the system of public finances which developed was based upon taxes levied on the growing wealth of the nation, and eventually completely eclipsed revenues, potential and real, obtained from the royal forest.

Large districts in Devon, Staffordshire and Shropshire, Yorkshire and Essex were disafforested in 1204, and in the same year the men of Cornwall paid for the disafforestation of their whole county for the considerable sum of 2,200 marks and 20 palfreys. The removal of forest jurisdiction from such an extensive area enabled hundreds of new farms to be created in Cornwall during the following 150 years, as former wood and wasteland was brought into private agricultural use. The reduction of the royal forests was therefore already well under way by the time of Magna Carta (1215) and the Forest Charter (1217), both of which incorporated concessions which are normally identified as marking the beginning of the long procedure of dismantling the royal forests. Nevertheless the process by which the crown relinquished its control over large tracts of forest was not a smooth one. Intermittently various monarchs tried to re-establish forest law over former forest areas, and forest perambulations, particularly during the thirteenth and fourteenth centuries, display a considerable degree of confusion over what was actually inside and what was outside forest boundaries.

Henry III re-established various areas of forest, but he granted away others as well as loosening the constraints of forest law in certain areas. Later Edward I tried to tighten up the control of forest areas, but there is little evidence of large-scale reafforestation in the last quarter of the thirteenth century. Indeed Edward made some concessions in the 1270s, when for example he released the Forest of Blackmore (the largest of the Dorset forests). However by this date the clearance of woodland and the establishment of new settlements here was already well advanced as many farms lying in parishes within the forest are first recorded in the thirteenth century. Edward also disafforested the county of Northumberland for the modest yearly payment of 40 marks. Despite such concessions hostility to the forest system grew rapidly in the next twenty years, and was an important contributory factor in the political crisis of the late thirteenth century. Some orders for disafforestation were made under strong pressure at the Parliament of Lincoln (1301), but these were revoked as soon as possible, and the final surrender was averted until the early years of Edward III's reign.

By about 1334 the area of royal forest in the country had

38 Medieval hunting lodge now used as a private residence at Upper Millichope on Wenlock Edge. This building appears to date from the thirteenth century when it lay within the Long Forest

shrunk to about two-thirds of what it had been in 1250.
During this period, most of the individual forests had
diminished in extent and some, like the Forest of
Northumberland and Allerdale Forest in Cumberland, had
disappeared completely. The largest forests still in existence were the New Forest, the Forest of Dean, Sherwood
Forest, Windsor Forest, Inglewood in Cumberland and
Pickering in Yorkshire. During the early Middle Ages the
crown had relied upon its forests in southern England to
feed its itinerant court, whose size and appetite meant that
enormous quantities of venison and game were regularly
required. An account of King John's petty expenses on the
occasion of a short visit to Bath in 1212 underlines the
former importance of hunting to the court. Besides 114
warreners, there were 25 dogs in the care of huntsmen,
and 24 keepers. In March the following year John was
again at Bath, 5s was paid for fowl for the falcons, and 5s
was given between the head falconer and his associates.
The falconers were also paid ten marks for flying their
birds. The size of the court on the move can also be
assessed from these accounts as there were 55 stable boys,
62 horses, 6 carters divided 12 pence per day between
them, and a further 15 horses consumed 16 bushels of
oats, the charge for a night's livery, hay, oats, forage,
lights and litter being 3s 2d.

By the first half of the fourteenth century the size of the
immediate court had diminished and the king spent far
longer periods of time in London. The need to maintain
the southern circuit of royal forests therefore decreased in
the same way that the national network of royal houses
declined. The crown came to value areas of woodland for
entirely different reasons, that is for the timber required for
ships and fortifications and for the fuel for manufacturing
industry. The history of the royal forests in England during
the later Middle Ages is that of a long, slow decline with
no special crises to measure the stages of that decline. It
was not so much that there was a substantial decrease in
the actual area to which the forest law was nominally
applied, but rather that its application became less and
less effective so that increasingly areas were 'forests' in
name only. The change in the status of the forests was
that they no longer commanded the serious attention of
the crown, sufficient to ensure the enforcement of the
forest law, because the contribution they made to the royal
revenues had become increasingly insignificant. However,
the basic administrative structure of the forests persisted
throughout the Middle Ages, and the main uses to which

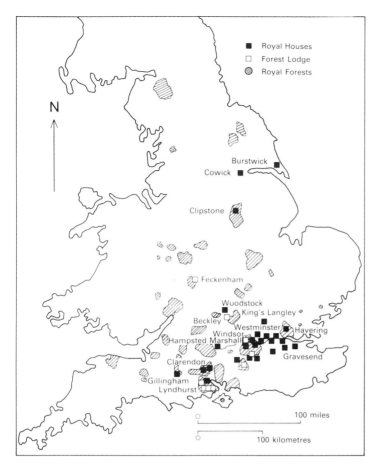

Royal Houses
Forest Lodge
Royal Forests

N

Burstwick
Cowick
Clipstone
Feckenham
Woodstock
King's Langley
Beckley
Westminster
Windsor
Havering
Hampsted Marshall
Gravesend
Clarendon
Gillingham
Lyndhurst

100 miles

100 kilometres

29 The relationship between royal houses and royal forests in the reign of Edward II (after Colvin)

the forests had always been put continued as before, but on a smaller scale: farms and wastes were rented and timber and underwood were sold. Hunting within the forests was still restricted to the king and to his ensigns, though the enforcement of this restriction became increasingly difficult, especially after the mid-fourteenth century.

These late medieval trends led directly to the lament of John Manwood, who wrote in 1598 in a time when 'the Forrest Lawes are growen clean out of knowledge in most places in this Land, partly for want of use':

> I do not speak this to that end, that I would haue Forrest Lawes rigorously executed upon offenders in Forrestes, but to haue them so executed, that Forrests may be still knowen for Forrestes, and the game preserved for her Maiestie; for otherwise, it was better to disafforest them altogether, and then her Maiestie shal be discharged of the great fees that are yeerely payed to Officers of the Forrest, out of her Maiesties Court of Exchequer.

123

Chases

During the Middle Ages the terms 'chase' and 'forest' were often used synonymously. The chase was for all practical purposes a forest in private hands, areas over which local magnates, usually nobles or great ecclesiastics, were given exclusive hunting rights by the king. As in the case of the forests, not only the deer but also a variety of other smaller animals were reserved for the holder of the royal franchise. Chases were normally subject to common and not forest law, and the rights of the chase varied in different parts of the country. In some cases the owners exercised limited rights of protection, while more often restrictions similar to those operating in royal forests were imposed upon people living within the chase. During the fourteenth century the Earls of Lancaster owned extensive chases at Blackburn, and Bowland in Lancashire, Duffield Frith in Derbyshire, Leicester and Needwood in Staffordshire, and they exerted a degree of supervision and control over these

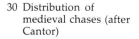

30 Distribution of medieval chases (after Cantor)

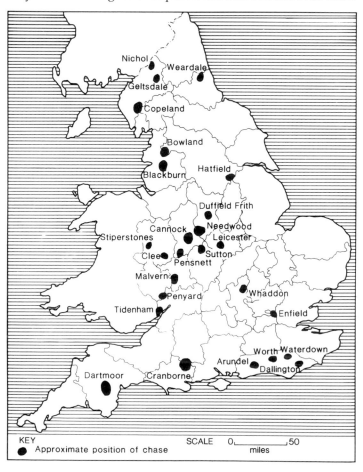

KEY
● Approximate position of chase

SCALE 0 � 50
miles

areas which was at least as complete as that imposed by the crown over royal forests. Indeed in the case of Leicester chase the earls were empowered by the king to enforce the whole body of forest law through the stewardship of their own officials. The earls appointed a master forester, a forest receiver who was responsible for the financial administration of the chase, three foresters and a variety of other officials. There were similar appointments in the other Lancastrian chases. When a Lancastrian king – Henry IV – came to the throne, the Duchy of Lancaster became crown land, and the Lancastrian chases became royal forests.

Other chases were, for various periods, in the hands of landed magnates, both lay and ecclesiastic. For instance in the twelfth century Sutton Chase in Warwickshire was taken from Cannock Forest by the Earl of Warwick. Tidenham Chase in Gloucestershire, which was at one time in the Forest of Dean, was in the hands of the Earl of Pembroke by the early thirteenth century, and was also taken out of royal forest. At the end of the thirteenth century Cannock Chase, which belonged to the Bishop of Coventry and Lichfield, covered an area of about 40 square miles and it too had originally been part of a larger forest. Unlike most other chases, part of the western edge of Cannock was defined by a boundary bank. Such perimeter banks were created when there were no other obvious topographical features available. The chase remained in the bishop's hands throughout the Middle Ages but reverted to the crown at the time of the dissolution.

The history of Cranborne Chase is more complex, as it passed in and out of royal hands, including those of King John who hunted there frequently, but the chase remained with the de Clare Earls of Gloucester for much of the Middle Ages. It was given to Robert Earl of Gloucester by William Rufus at the end of the eleventh century, at which time it appears to have encompassed several hundred square miles extending from Dorset into Wiltshire. Cranborne Chase consisted largely of a chalk plateau, which was never very heavily wooded and contained both open rolling downland and also numerous woods and copses as well as incorporating a scatter of villages surrounded by their arable fields. Some idea of the extent of the medieval woodlands on the chase is given in a survey of 1296 which demonstrates that there were 1,433 acres of woodland, and the pasture, which was worth 100 shillings a year, could not be sold because of the deer. Cranborne gradually shrank in size but continued to be used as a hunting

31 Plan of Morfe forest,
1582. Copy of map of
Morfe forest in 1582
(PRO E. 178/4428)
drawn as evidence in
an enquiry about
grazing rights. The
map shows that little
woodland remained in
the forest by this date.
The original is very
faded and the names of
Gattacre are illegible
and consequently are
not shown on this
copy. The original is
coloured and
measures 25 by 27
inches. There is no
scale on the original
map

ground until as recently as 1828.

In the Welsh Marches the Brown Clee hill had originally formed part of the massive Forest of Shropshire, but as early as 1155 it had been granted, with an area of surrounding land, as a private chase to the Cliffords at Corfham castle (not far from Ludlow). Gradually the restrictions on activities within Clee Chase eased, but there was an interesting legacy of common rights, both on the hill and in the surrounding area. A document of 1612 called 'A Description of Clee' demonstrates the persistence of the common rights of all the townships that had lain within the ancient forest and chase. Common rights on Brown Clee included agistment and pannage (grazing rights for livestock), turbary (right to cut and collect turfs), and estovers (right to take wood for repairs and fuel). These rights, however, were reserved for those townships that actually lay on Brown Clee. The inhabitants of the old chase area away from the hill were allowed common rights

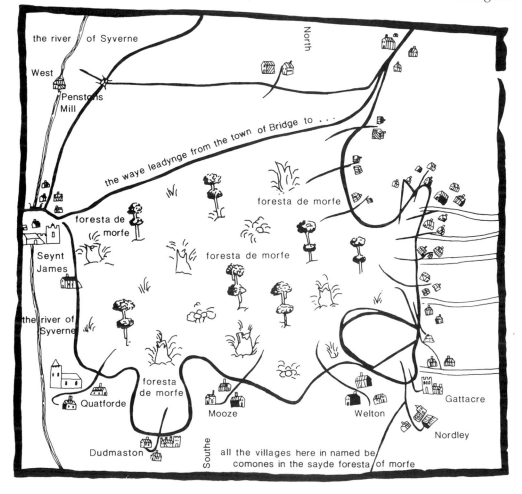

of considerably less importance. In return for these privileges, the 'out-commoners' were subject to a modified
form of forest law and in particular they had to refrain
from disturbing deer found amongst their crops. The out-
commoners had to follow very precise routes from their
townships to the grazing areas on the Clee. These roads
were known as 'driftways', 'straker' ways or 'outracks'.
Because of the sandy nature of the subsoil in this area
many of these tracks were deeply entrenched into the
foothills of the Brown Clee and can still be traced as
sunken or 'hollow'-ways. The routes were still in use in
the seventeenth century when it was claimed 'the driftways are long and tedious because the strakers were to
drive the lands and commons belonging to other lordships
before they could reach Clee soil.' The name 'outrack' is
still given to a number of roads leading to the Clee hills
and other outracks survive on the Long Mynd and in other
hilly parts of the Marches. An interesting footnote to this
story was that at the time of parliamentary enclosure
(1809), Thomas Mytton, lord of one of the Clee manors,
Earnstrey, tried to claim extensive allotments on Brown
Clee as 'lord of the Clee Chace'.

Similar intercommoning rights operated on other areas
of former forest and chase. Around Dartmoor, for
instance, inhabitants of the former forest (chase after 1239)
possessed rights known as 'venville', a corruption of *fines
villarum* (the rents of the vills). There were various categ-
ories of Dartmoor commoner each of whom enjoyed
different rights. Least privileged were the householders of
the whole of Devon, who were classed as 'strangers' or
'foreigners' and were allowed to depasture beasts on the
commons of Devon surrounding the forest without
payment, and upon the forest itself only on payment of
certain small fees. Next were the venville tenants who
paid a small fixed rent to the king or duchy and were
allowed free pasture on the commons and forest by day
but had to pay extra if they remained in the forest by night.
The numbers of animals they turned out were supposed to
be limited to the number their farms would support in
winter (a restriction known as levancy and couchancy),
but extra beasts could be grazed if they paid for them as
'strangers'. They could also take from the forest all they
needed for fuel, building, and hedging, 'save green oak
and venison'. Lastly there were the ancient tenement
holders who had free rights in the forest only and who
owed certain services such as the obligation to form manor
court juries and assist in the cattle drifts. A number of

39 Stylised hunting scene
from a fourteenth-
century manuscript
showing dogs killing a
wild boar.
Immediately behind
the hunt are some
coppice trees

other rights appear to have existed, such as that enjoyed
by the *carbonarii*, the diggers of peat used for making charcoal for smelting tin-ore.

Parks

One of the most important elements in the medieval rural
landscape was the deer park. The primary purpose of the
medieval park was to keep deer for hunting, but other
animals were sometimes kept including semi-wild white
cattle. The park differed from the forest, chase and warren
in that it was completely enclosed, and by the late thirteenth century most wealthy lords aspired to a park, which

was normally located some distance from their manor house. The origins of a few such parks, such as that at Woodstock, can be traced back before the Norman Conquest, but the vast majority were created in the early Middle Ages. During that period the crown issued hundreds of 'grants of free warren' specifically with the intention of enabling parks to be created; in many cases, as with chases, such deer parks were carved out of areas of former royal forest.

The great era of park creation was between 1200 and 1350, corresponding to the period of agricultural development and growing population, when sufficient surplus wealth was being produced to enable many noble and knightly families to indulge in hunting and, perhaps just as important, to demonstrate their status by creating parks on their estates. Their owners could call upon the services of their tenants to maintain and repair the park banks and pale and despite growing land hunger there was still some less fertile wooded land available in many manors which was well suited to emparkment. More generally, the

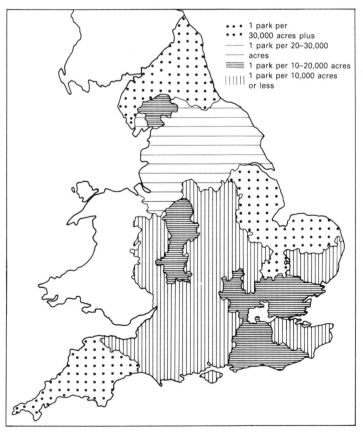

32 Density of medieval parks (after Cantor)

dismantling of the royal forests at this time resulted in
land becoming available, much of it wooded and ideally
suited for emparking. As in the case of moated homesteads, parks were thickest on the ground in the west
Midlands; in the Home Counties; and in Sussex. The counties with the least number of parks were in the remoter
western and northern parts of the country. It has been
estimated that by the beginning of the fourteenth century
there were as many as 3,200 parks in England. The
majority of these were relatively small, usually measuring
between 90–180 acres in size and normally owned by a
local lord, but others owned by the crown and magnates
were extensive – for example, the royal parks of Woodstock, and Clarendon in Wiltshire were both over 10 miles

33 The distribution of
medieval deer parks
in Staffordshire (after
Cantor)

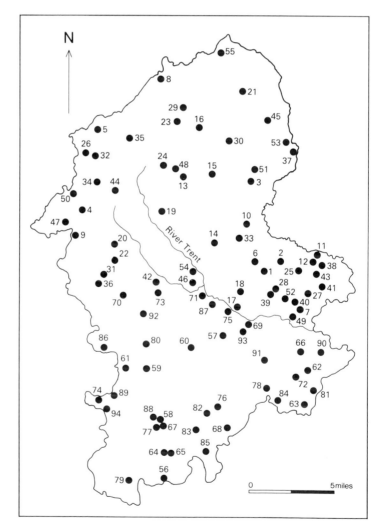

in circuit. The crown held about twenty parks, while the greater nobles could own up to a dozen each.

Woodland, forests and parks

Table 3 Staffordshire parks (after Cantor)

1	Abbot's Bromley	47	Tyrley
2	Agardsley	48	West Coyney
3	Alton	49	Wichnor
4	Ashley	50	Willoughbridge
5	Audley	51	Wootton
6	Bagot's Park	52	Yoxall
7	Barton	53	Blore and Swinscoe
8	Biddulph		
		54	Ingestre
9	Blore		
10	Bramshall	55	Quarnford
		56	Amblecote
11	Castle Park, Tutbury	57	Beaudesert
		58	Blakenhall
12	Castlehay	59	Brewood
		60	Carnnock
13	Caverswall	61	Chillington
14	Chartley	62	Comberford
15	Cheadle	63	Drayton New Park
16	Cheddleton	64	Dudley New Park
17	Colton	65	Dudley Old Park
18	Colton Old Park	66	Elford
19	Cublesdon	67	Ettingshall
20	Eccleshall	68	Great Barr
21	Elkstone	69	Handsacre
22	Ellenhall	70	Haughton
23	Endon	71	Haywood
24	Fenton Vyvyan	72	Hopwas
25	Hanbury	73	Hyde
26	Heleigh	74	Parshull
27	Highlands	75	Rugeley
28	Hoarcross	76	Rushall
		77	Sedgley
29	Horton	78	Shenstone
30	Ipstones	79	Stourton
31	Knightley	80	Stretton
32	Leycett	81	Tamworth
33	Loxley	82	Walsall
		83	Wednesbury
34	Madeley		
35	Newcastle	84	Weeford
36	Norbury	85	West Bromwich
37	Okeover	86	Weston-under-Lizard
38	Rolleston	87	Wolseley
39	Rowley	88	Wolverhampton
40	Shireholt	89	Wrottesley
41	Sinai	90	Harlaston
42	Stafford	91	Lichfield
43	Stockley	92	Bradley
44	Swynnerton	93	Longdon
45	Throwley	94	Pattingham
46	Tixall		

In the early Middle Ages the park normally consisted of an area of woodland and pasture (known as the laund) enclosed by an earthen bank, often with an inside ditch. The bank was normally topped by a wooden paling, but in some places the wooden fence was replaced by a stone wall, as in the case of Woodstock in Oxfordshire and Moulton Park, Northamptonshire. Occasionally a quickset hedge would serve in place of a fence and where the topography was suitable, for example, just below the crest of a steep slope, a paling fence alone might suffice. Water seems to have constituted an effective barrier to deer and some parks were partly circumscribed by rivers or marshy areas, as in the case of Sonning and Hamstead Marshall Parks in Berkshire where the northern boundaries were formed by the Thames and Kennet respectively.

The pale was sometimes set back from the boundary of the property and the space in between, known as the freeboard, was used to provide access to the pale for maintenance purposes. The upkeep of park pales posed a problem and the responsibilities of maintaining the royal park at Moulton fell upon the surrounding townships. Their obligations were recorded on stones carved with their village names which were inserted at intervals in the park pale, which in this case was a wall.

Linear earthworks which described the medieval park boundaries are also to be found in many places. Modern field boundaries will normally respect the cross-country course of a medieval park enclosure bank. The park perimeter usually followed a compact course to keep its length down to a minimum and a roughly elliptical or circular shape was common. The circuit was broken by gates for passage in and out of the park and occasionally by 'deer leaps'. These were devices which enabled deer to enter a park but not to leave it, for instance in a survey of 1251 we hear:

How the park of Brewham [in Somerset] belonging to Sir Robert de Mucegros was held enclosed with a hedge in the time of Richard and in the time of King John. In the time of King Richard the lord of the manor of Brewham was Richard, son of John, and he kept the park enclosed with a ditch and hedge and had deer in it all that reign. And when the said Richard, son of John, died . . . the wardship of his heirs . . . remained in the hands of the King until William de Montacute purchased it from King John and he kept the park enclosed with a ditch and hedge and had deer in it until King John, being angered against the said William de Montacute for a trespass done by him, took from him by way of ransom five hundred marks so that under the weight of this ransom the said William let the ditch and hedge of the park fall into decay and the deer go. Yet the park is still so enclosed that cattle cannot enter it . . . and the metes [boundaries] of the said park during the time of its enclosure were as under: from the ford of Wodessned towards Kingsettle along the old ditch to the house of Iweyn and thence southward around the croft of Iweyn to the house of Alexander Heyrun and thence along the old ditch to the house of Robert le Siviere, so that the house and croft of Robert are within the enclosure, and thence along the old ditch to the ford of Wodessned again; and all this enclosure and the beasts in it existed during the reigns of King Richard and King John.

As with the royal forests the principal beast of the park was the fallow deer, though red deer were also quite common and other animals such as semi-wild cattle appear in park records. Occasionally there are also references to hare parks and swine parks. Many favoured lords received gifts from the crown to help create new parks. In Buckinghamshire, for example, Richard Montfichet was given 100 live does and bucks from Windsor forest in 1202 for his park at Langley Marsh, and in 1222 Robert Manduit was granted five stags from Salcey forest to stock his park at Hanslope. At Middleton Stoney, Oxfordshire, there was a small deer park whose creation was authorised by King John in 1201 and in 1203 the king gave deer from Woodstock park to stock it (plate 40). This was later followed by the gifts of deer from Beckley park and Wychwood forest.

40 Middleton Stoney, Oxfordshire. The large house in the centre of the photograph was built in the 1930s by Lutyens. However, it occupies the southern end of what was once a medieval deer park, the boundary of which still survives as a boundary today

133

In 1295, 11s 8d was paid to the king's huntsmen for
catching wolves in Middleton park, which incidentally was
the last known reference to wolves in Oxfordshire. Just
a few years earlier, in 1281, Edward I had ordered the
extermination of wolves in the counties of Gloucestershire,
Worcestershire, Herefordshire and Shropshire. As early as
1311 Middleton park seems to have ceased to have been
important for its deer. A valuation of that year states that
the park was said to be worth 10s a year in pasture and
underwood if not stocked, but worth nothing if it held
deer. The last known medieval reference to the park was
in 1349, when a survey records 'a certain little park in
which there are wild beasts, whereof the pasture is worth
nothing.' However the boundary of the park is still
distinguishable as a bank and ditch surrounding the
present Middleton House and gardens.

A detailed survey of Madeley Great Park in north Staffordshire by Professor L. Cantor has provided us with
important evidence about the nature of the medieval park
economy, together with some insight of how the parks
were maintained. Madeley park was first recorded in 1275
when John de Whitmore surrendered to Nicholas de Stafford his rights in 63 acres of land and 3 acres of wood in
exchange for pasture for 16 oxen in Madeley park. Though
deer are not recorded before 1430, it seems almost certain
that they were present in the park from the beginning,
and were continuously present up to at least 1521 when
it is recorded that there were 300 deer there. In 1442–3,
some 80 cartloads of pales bound together with wattles
were used for the repair of the park pale and, in addition,
80 perches of ditch on the northern side of the park were
scoured. Two years later, the pales along the western edge
of the park were again repaired together with 60 perches
of new ditching 'in certain swampy places for the purpose
of setting and putting up pales there'. Repairs to the paling
and ditching around the park 'in various places where
most deficient' also occurs on another occasion between
1445 and 1512. The accounts also provide us with some
idea of the construction of the paling-fence, which in
1467–8 consisted of four pales between each two posts,
braced by two rails. 'Stipers' (possibly diagonal braces)
are also mentioned. The Great Park provided three main
sources of revenue other than from hunting. These were
pasturage, wood and turbary. Stone-mining, pannage,
rabbits and fishing were also mentioned occasionally.
After 1392, apart from the permanent disappearance of
sales of wood and fuel (charcoal), there are surprising

fluctuations in the amounts derived from pasturage and turbary which do not conform to the general trends of the national economy in the fifteenth century.

The fashion for creating and the enthusiasm for maintaining deer parks declined rapidly during the later Middle Ages, when many parks deteriorated, their boundaries being allowed to collapse, and hunting often ceased altogether. At this time some old parks were cleared of their

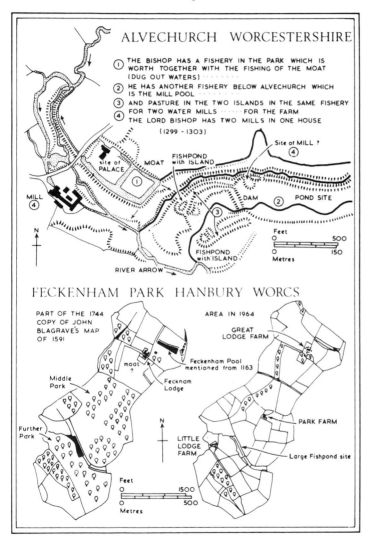

34 Internal features in the Bishop of Worcester's park at Alvechurch, Feckenham Park, Worcs before and after enclosure

woodland and enclosed; subsequently they were divided between freeholders or consolidated into single farms. Thus medieval hunting gave way to a more economic land use. Heath Park (Salop), for instance, was enclosed into a farm in the mid-sixteenth century and appropriately

135

assumed the name Heath Park Farm; its former limits can
still be traced from field boundaries. Similarly in Dorset,
for example, many of the medieval deer parks were
converted to other uses during the later Middle Ages.
Knighton Park in Canford was disparked in 1462 and
leased out for pasture, while that at Wynford Eagle had
been divided into pasture closes by the sixteenth century.
Apart from the boundaries other medieval parkland

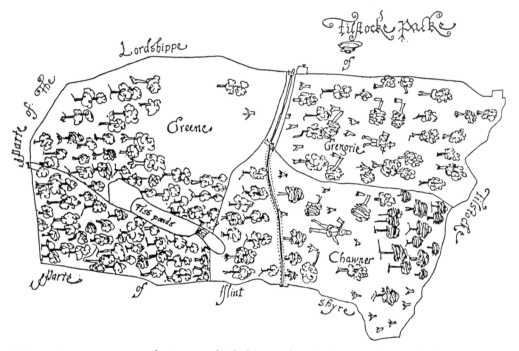

35 The enclosure of
Tilstock park, c. 1600.
Copy of original plan
(SRO 212/Box 466)
showing the division
and enclosure of
Tilstock park between
the farmers Greene
(missing), Gregorie
and Chawner, who
are busy clearing their
areas of woodland.
There is no scale or
north on the original
plan

features which have often left some legacy in the modern
landscape are the lodges, moated enclosures, fishponds
and rabbit warrens. Place-names incorporating 'park' and
'lodge' often indicate the former presence of such medieval
parkland.

Even in those parks where enclosure did not occur they
frequently just fell out of use, the herds dwindled and
there was insufficient labour to maintain them properly.
Many existed in name only, and increasingly, pasture
within them was leased out for long periods, a trend which
mirrored the contemporary decline of direct demesne
farming. On the other hand, in various parts of the country
tracts of arable and pasture land which could no longer
be properly farmed because of the labour shortage were
converted into parks, sometimes associated with sheep
farming. A case in point is Tusmore in northern Oxfordshire, where it is assumed a park was created on top of a

depopulated village and its fields in the wake of the Black Death. In 1279 Tusmore village comprised 25 households which were not particularly wealthy; in 1334 Tusmore paid about half the local average tax and in the collection of 1355 it paid nothing, for the village had been completely depopulated by the Black Death. The earthworks of the former village appear in pastureland near to the present Tusmore House. The total destruction of the village is confirmed by the wholesale tax reduction of 1355 and by the license granted in 1357 for Roger de Cotesford, lord of the manor, to 'enclose his hamlet of *Toresmere* and the highway from *Cotesford* to *Sulthorne* passing through it, the hamlet having been inhabited entirely by Roger's bondmen but now void of inhabitants since their death in the pestilence'. Roger was to make a new road on the north of the hamlet. This 'new road' is the road that now skirts the northern boundary of the park, between Souldern and Cottisford. However, these late parks were generally much

Woodland, forests and parks

41 Castle Bolton, Yorkshire, high up on the Pennines provides an excellent example of a decaying late medieval landscape. The castle itself had been built in the late fourteenth century to dominate a planned medieval village. On the left hand side are some early enclosures. The area at the top of the photograph was part of Bolton Park attached to the castle. The creation of the park involved a diversion of the road from Richmond to Bolton. The enclosure of arable land as can been seen from the traces of regular parallel field boundaries. Although the park survives as an open space it has been partly enclosed and no longer functions as a deer park!

137

larger than their predecessors of the early Middle Ages
and were neither managed as intensively nor as securely
enclosed. Indeed many of them may have been conceived
from the beginning for amenity rather than hunting parks
and several were attached to a new generation of fortified
manors and country houses.

Warrens

During the Middle Ages, the term *warren* was used in two
quite different ways. The first described a rabbit warren,
namely a place where rabbits were preserved and encouraged to breed. The second was used to define the exclusive
right to hunt in a specific place, the right of *free warren*.
This was the privilege granted by the crown to landowners
enabling them to create deer parks, but it also enabled
them to hunt smaller game – fox, rabbit, hare, wild
cat, badger, marten, otter and squirrel, pheasant and
partridges – over their estates. According to some authorities, the hare was the principal beast of the warren giving
the best sport when hunted fairly with hounds. The rabbit,
by contrast, was not much hunted for sport but was highly
regarded for its meat and skin. Unlike the hare, it was not
native to this country but appears to have been introduced
into England in the twelfth century. The first reference to
rabbits in England occurred in 1176 when they were found
in the Scilly Isles, but the first authenticated mention of
native mainland rabbits was not until 1235 when Henry
III made a gift of ten live rabbits from his park in Guildford.
Six years later, in 1241, the first reference occurs in the
same park to a coneygarth. During the next decade or so,
the number of warrens increased and in 1268, for example,
Richard Earl of Cornwall complained that his coneygarth at
Isleworth in Middlesex, was being plundered by poachers.
Other records indicate the scale of production: 2,000 rabbit
skins were delivered from Lundy Island in 1274, a further
200 skins were exported from Hull on one occasion in 1305,
and in 1270 the keeper of the estates of the Archbishop of
Canterbury supplied 200 rabbits to Westminster for the
royal feast on St Edward's day.

Rights of free warren were granted from the Conquest
onwards, and by the middle of the fourteenth century
such grants had become so common that the majority of
manorial lords seem to have enjoyed them. As with crown
licenses for other activities during the Middle Ages, the
granting of free warren was probably seen primarily as a
source of royal revenue. The actual *warren* was an
enclosure varying in size from a relatively small field to

a square mile or more, used for breeding rabbits. The enclosures were required to keep the rabbit in and vermin out. In the sixteenth century, for instance, Richard Fiennes enclosed his warren at Bloxham Grove in Oxfordshire with a wall, as a result of pressure from neighbouring farmers who objected to his rabbits escaping and eating their corn. A jury of commoners complained that in 1605 three warrens in Leicester forest had 'overspread and fed over a hundred acres of ground and more, to the oppression of the commoners and the utter exile of his Majesty's game.'

In addition to stone walls there are references to warrens being enclosed with wooden palings, wet moats and turf sods built up to a height of almost six feet. In the case of a larger warren, the lord of the manor might employ a warrener to look after it: for example, in 1300 the Earl of Cornwall paid his warrener at his manor of Oakham 6s 5d a year. Rabbits were also known as 'coneys' or 'conies' and warrens were also known as coneygarths or coneries, or in the case of one within Leicester Forest which was rather more than two acres in extent, a 'coninger'. The most common way of capturing them seems to have been with hawks, dogs and ferrets.

Medieval warrens have left their mark on the contemporary landscape. In Ashdown Forest in Sussex, for example, where they are known as 'berrys', they were enclosed with perimeter banks and ditches and contained earth banks in the form of long narrow banks known as 'pillow mounds' for the rabbit burrows. Such pillow mounds have often been mistaken for prehistoric burial mounds and are often found in places such as Dartmoor where they lie in close juxtaposition to prehistoric earthworks. Little is known of medieval techniques of warren management, and we have to rely on later accounts to provide more detail and confirm some facts of the early procedures. When writing of land improvements in the second half of the sixteenth century the surveyor John Norden suggested that fishponds should be dug in order to exploit a water-supply and 'As for Warrens of Conies, they are not unnecessarie, and they require no rich ground to feed in, but meane pasture and craggy grounds are fittest for them.' The profession of rabbit-keeper or warrener seems to have been well established, and later warrens provided an official dwelling for this functionary. Norden assumed that there would be a keeper if there was a warren and evidence of lodges is also to be found on a number of early maps and in place-names.

Chapter six

Industry, trade and communications

The difference between medieval craft and industry was not always obvious as the two activities often overlapped considerably. Most craft industry operated on a local basis producing consumer items such as leather, ceramics and metal goods. The exception to this was the textile industry which was concerned in part with the production of personal clothing, but also with a wide range of other products, and from the mid-fourteenth century it played a major role in the national economy. The majority of manufacturing industry was, however, linked to the constructional industry either in the form of building construction, or ship-building, or later on of weaponry. The raw materials for these industries were obviously restricted to the areas where the appropriate stone or minerals outcropped and to where there were sufficient timber reserves to provide building material and fuel. The individual nature of some industrial work, as well as its geographical location, tended to set those engaged in it apart from the routine of the villages of open-field England. Thus although the miners of north Yorkshire or the tinners of Cornwall would also have had small agricultural holdings, their homes for much of the year would have been in forest clearings, smelting iron, or within open-cast mines. Few areas of England were totally without such a basis for employment outside agriculture, and the role of the industrial smallholder in medieval England was an important one.

Nevertheless medieval industry was rarely totally disassociated from the broad agrarian base that dominated the national economy. In particular, craft industry tended to operate from within existing rural settlements. At Poteria (later Crockerton) in Longbridge Deverill in Wiltshire there were 25 smallholders with 4 acres of land or less. Of these two were millers; the others were entitled to make pots and paid 7d for their fuel if they worked for a full year, and 3½d if they worked for half the year. They also had to pay 4d if they took their clay from the lord's land, but only 2d if they took it from their own smallholdings. Similarly on the fringes of the deserted medieval village of Lyveden (Northamptonshire), which lay within the Rockingham forest, there was a twelfth-century iron-working site which was later used for pottery manufacture. Excavation here revealed a potter's workshop, various yards and pits, kilns, a pot-bank and a store-shed, but the potters were almost certainly still engaged in the village's agricultural cycle as well. At Brill (Bucks) the kilns for the famous medieval potteries were also worked in backyard areas. Barnack (Northants) was one of the best known sources of building stone anywhere in England during the Middle Ages, yet despite the surrounding pock-marked landscape, the medieval village of Barnack was no larger than its neighbours, and its present form gives little indication of the intensive quarrying that went on there. In such cases industry appears to have had little direct impact on the physical character of the villages, although the effect on the immediate landscape was in some instances very spectacular.

Many of the larger and the ancient shire towns contained a broad range of industrial activities. In the thirteenth century, for instance, listed among Gloucester's inhabitants were the following tradesmen: ironmongers, bell-foundry workers, cloth-makers, leather-workers, ship-smiths, parchment-makers, needle-makers, coopers, gold-smiths, glass-wrights, soap-makers, girdlers, mercers and drapers. Such a wide spectrum of activities would have been found in most major towns and only a very few towns had a specialised industrial economy; where such specialisation did exist was principally in the sphere of cloth manufacture, where to begin with at least the towns were more important that the countryside. The location of industrial activity was progressively broadened away from the towns by the development of new production centres based in industrial villages in the countryside. In the textile industry an increasing number of fulling mills were established in rural areas, sometimes, but not always, at the expense of adjacent urban centres.

The other major development during the early Middle Ages was the expansion of woodland-related industries. These included iron-smelting, charcoal-burning and glass-making. Although many woodland districts experienced this growth it was the Forest of Dean and the Weald area of Kent and Sussex which saw the largest developments. By the thirteenth century both these areas had major concentrations of charcoal-burners and iron-smiths and contained a strong representation of other woodland industries as well. Charcoal was an essential ingredient in

141

a wide range of industrial activities, and the charcoal-
burners formed peripatetic and isolated communities.
Charcoal, like faggots and other fuel, was exported from
forests both for the use of local landlords and for sale. But
probably the main market was provided by local fuel-
consuming industries. In the early Middle Ages charcoal
was made almost exclusively from oak, but recent analysis
of charcoal samples from various archaeological sites show

42 Nineteenth-century
photograph of a
charcoal burner raking
his newly fired
charcoal after it had
smouldered for
several days. From the
Morfe forest,
Worcestershire

that progressively charcoal was being made from a much
wider range of timbers. As timber reserves declined coal
gradually came to be used for some industrial processes.
At Alsted near Mersham in Surrey, for instance, fuel for
iron-working appears to have been supplied in the form
of coal, which came either from south Wales or Durham,
as well as from charcoal made from oak, ash, hazel and
wild cherry, sweet chestnut, guelder rose and willow.

Water– and windmills

Before discussing aspects of more specialised industrial
activity, reference should be made to the most widespread
industrial activity of all – milling. Mills, first powered by
water and later by wind as well, were found throughout
medieval England. Watermills were to be found in all areas
where there were streams capable of providing a sufficient
constant flow of water for at least a few weeks in the year.
It is not possible to obtain a realistic estimate of the number
of watermills operating at any one time: the Domesday
Survey records some 5,624 mills in those parts of England
which it covered, but although this figure almost certainly
incorporates a number of handmills, it is still probably
an underestimate. We should also remember that many

watermills were very small and may have enjoyed only a short life.

The creation of mills resulted in earth movement in the same way as that of fishponds or moated sites, with leats and dams for ponds. Although in some instances mills were rather ephemeral, in others they could represent a considerable capital investment. The example of the Earl of Arundel's mill at Acton Round (Salop) has already been quoted; another mill was erected on the Kingsland estate in Herefordshire in 1389 and cost £11 5s 7d to build which included expenditure on labour, the bed of the millstone, carriage of 38 loads of timber, the cost of hiring 24 oxen to carry one alder for the watercourse under the mill, bread and ale for the carters, 96 gross of nails, one hoop and spindle, tallow for the mill axle, moss, metal weights and two iron girdles for the mill axle. Abandoned water-mills have distinctive characteristics – a flat building plat-form by the side of the stream, together with empty ponds and channels. The mill leat or race is sometimes a useful pointer to the site of a former mill; it may be a straight channel cutting off stream meanders, which often have lines of willows growing along them. Straight stretches of stream in an otherwise meandering course often indicate the location of a long-lost mill site. Initially they were used exclusively for corn grinding but later on they were used to drive fulling mills, hammers in iron forges, and for a wide range of other industrial activities. In the first instance under-shot wheels were used, but eventually overshot wheels which required a greater head of water were introduced. An alternative form of water-driven mill was found in some coastal locations. At Tamar in Devon, for instance, there was a thirteenth-century tidal mill and such tidal mills seem to have been fairly common in other parts of western Britain.

In eastern and southeastern England, rivers frequently ran too slowly to turn a wheel and from the second half of the twelfth century an alternative form of power became available. This was the wind-driven mill which may well have been brought by crusaders from the Middle East, as windmills were well established in the Arab world by this time. In 1189 it is recorded that a constable of Henry II handed over a windmill in Buckinghamshire to Osney Abbey and during the next century windmills became common. Modification to the fixed windmill which had developed in Mediterranean lands became necessary in order to cater for the variable wind directions found in northwestern Europe. The result was the post-mill, consisting of a box-like wooden body carrying the sails and containing the gearing and the stones. This was mounted on a suitable braced-post on which it was turned so that the sails could face the wind. The tower mill, which consisted of a fixed tower in which the mill machinery was housed was capped by a rotating unit at the top. Such mills were particularly well suited for erecting on the walls of castles and towns. The earliest surviving post-mills date from the seventeenth century, but the sites of earlier wind-mills may be identified on the ground in the form of a circular mound, often with a cross-shaped depression in the centre. Further modifications were made to windmills during the later Middle Ages and in particular they were adopted for land drainage schemes, as well as for tanning, laundrying, sawing, and for crushing a variety of indus-trial commodities.

The textile industry

The processes involved in making woollen cloth, which was the most commonly produced textile of medieval England, began with the shearing and selection of wool fells (sheep skins), the standard of which was reflected in the quality of the finished product. In different parts of England there were different qualities of wool, which were used to make cloths such as the 'Stamfords', 'Lincoln Scar-lets' and 'Beverley Blues'. After shearing the wool was cleaned by beating and washing and then prepared for spinning by carding and combing. The combed wool was then spun into yarn, but although the spinning wheel was depicted on manuscripts from the fourteenth century onwards, there is little evidence that it was in common use in England before the sixteenth century. The spinning process appears to have been mainly undertaken on a domestic basis using a distaff and spindle. The wool was then woven on a loom, originally on an upright machine which was eventually replaced by the horizontal loom. After weaving the cloth was thickened or fulled. This was traditionally undertaken by trampling the cloth in vats filled with water and fuller's earth. The latter is a natural clay-like substance used because of its qualities of absorbing the grease and oils of the cloth. The cloth was then stretched and dyed on tenters using tenter-hooks and was finished off by being teazed and sheared. Only in exceptional circumstances, such as at Fountains Abbey, do medieval fulling mills survive, although place-names such as 'Walker', 'Tucker' and 'Fuller' all point to former locations of textile manufacture.

morá·

ꝑᵲſá·

ꝺuꞇá·

ꞇ ᴀuᴎá·

ᴀꞇᵲ

·ᵹᵹᴀᵲꞇ

43 A textile dyer at work, from a thirteenth-century manuscript

Table 4 (after Bowden)
The figures below show the movement of prices of wool and grain between 1209 and 1448, and the changes in the price of labour during the same period. The figures for *wool* are in shillings per stone; those for *wheat* are in shillings per quarter of grain; and those for *wages*, the product of a more complicated calculation, the rates in pence for threshing and winnowing three rased quarters of wheat, barley and oats on certain manors of the bishopric of Winchester.

Year	Wool	Wheat	Year	Wages
1209–18	1.93	3.22	1210–19	2.96
1219–28	2.04	4,71	1220–9	3.51
1229–38	2.92	3.81	1230–9	3.13
1239–48	3.04	4.64	1240–9	3.25
1249–58	2.65	4.66	1250–9	3.30
1259–68	3.61	3.95	1260–9	3.37
1269–78	4.16	6.26	1270–9	3.45
1279–88	4.56	5.28	1280–9	3.62
1289–98	4.05	6.15	1290–9	3.57
1299–1308	4.73	4.94	1300–9	3.85
1309–18	4.79	8.60	1310–19	4.05
1319–28	5.51	6.40	1320–9	4.62
1329–38	3.85	5.41	1330–9	4.92
1339–48	3.53	4.90	1340–9	5.03
1349–58	2.96	6.77	1349–59	5.18
1359–68	3.58	6.78	1360–9	6.10
1369–78	4.90	7.81	1370–9	7.00
1379–88	3.83	4.83	1380–9	7.22
1389–98	3.37	5.08	1390–9	7.23
1399–1408	3.92	5.70	1400–9	7.31
1409–18	3.99	6.27	1410–19	7.35
1419–28	3.21	4.98	1420–9	7.34
1429–38	3.72	6.17	1430–9	7.30
1439–48	3.36	5.89	1440–9	7.33

Industry, trade and
communications

44a Stamford sheep fair
at the beginning of
this century.
Stamford was one of
the first generation of
medieval wool
towns and grew
prosperous on the
wool industry.
Although it was later
surpassed by other
towns in its region, it
remained an
important woollen
centre into the
twentieth century

In the early Middle Ages England was a large importer of cloth and remained so until the middle years of the fourteenth century. At this stage the commercial manufacture of cloth, although undoubtedly widespread, was concentrated upon about a dozen towns mainly in eastern and southern England. In 1347–8 when cloth exports started to be taxed, around 12,000 cloths were being exported, while the home market took between 5,000 and 6,000 home-produced cloths and between 9,000 and 10,000 imported cloths. By the last decade of the fourteenth century more than 40,000 cloths a year were being exported, and around 10,000 a year retained for the home market, while imports of cloth had become insignificant.

The 1330s marked the midway point between the 'urban' cloth industry of the thirteenth century and the 'country' cloth industry of the fifteenth century. Although the respective roles of town and country in the making and marketing of cloth in the early to mid-fourteenth century is still a matter of debate, new growth in the textile industry seems to have been principally in the rural areas, with the towns, which had been the backbone of the thirteenth-century industry, fluctuating in their fortunes. In

44b St Mary's church, Stamford, from the south. Stamford boasts a considerable number of medieval churches built from the proceeds of the early wool industry

the 1330s the difficulties of the town weavers had intensified. By 1334 the weavers of Northampton, of whom there had formerly been about 300, had apparently disappeared completely, and numbers were also dwindling in London, Winchester, Oxford and Lincoln. Yet despite this decline these towns and other former centres of cloth-making such as London, York, Newcastle, Lincoln, Norwich and Oxford remained among the wealthiest in England. The shift in textile production from the town to the countryside has conventionally been attributed to two causes. First the growth of the powerful guilds during the twelfth century, whose restrictive practices are blamed for the search for new production centres, and second the arrival of the water-driven fulling-mill, first recorded in this country in 1185. This mill, which worked with an

147

overshot waterwheel, required a good head of water to propel it. Such a head was not readily obtained in most urban centres, although some places such as Ludlow, a town largely free of manufacturing guilds, could boast as many as five in the fourteenth century.

The vast majority of the new mills appear therefore to have been sited in the countryside; the sustained demand for English woollen textiles led to the expansion of the

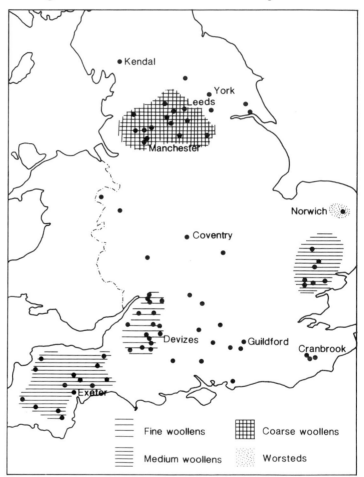

36 The cloth industry in the later Middle Ages (after A. R. H. Baker)

rural cloth manufacturing industry in the West Riding, the Lake District, Wiltshire and the West Country, in the Mendips, the Cotswolds, the Kennet Valley and East Anglia. As the market for home-produced cloth grew, so the demand for 'Ludlow's' and 'Cotswolds', 'Stroudwaters', 'westerns' and 'worsteds' began to replace that for the traditional cloths. By the fifteenth century up to half of the working population in some parts of the country were involved in cloth production. This rural-based industry involved the expansion of old centres and the creation of new ones. Paradoxically, these new centres were expanding at the same time that many other local rural settlements, based purely on agriculture, were declining. In Wiltshire, for instance, dyers, fullers and weavers were drawn out of the towns to the sites of the new mills in the valleys around Salisbury. Eventually, however, the Wiltshire clothiers shifted their attention to the northwest of the county between Malmesbury and Westbury, and to the southeast around Mere. These were traditional areas of pastoral dairying, where the owners of smallholdings had time to combine dairying with another occupation, and where the prosperous Wiltshire cloth industry eventually made its home.

The early woollen industry did not necessarily influence the form or outward appearance of the villages from which it operated. Early industry was largely part time, but in the later Middle Ages the cloth-working villages of the Cotswolds and Suffolk housed large numbers of independent weavers and accordingly contained a considerable proportion of smallholdings and cottages. This often resulted in a less regular settlement than was to be found in wholly agrarian communities. Frequently the only obvious sign of textile manufacture would have been in the form of buildings adapted for industrial use – the spinning gallery or insertion of large attic windows to provide light. In contrast during the fifteenth century public buildings, which frequently provide the most obvious manifestation of local industrial activity, were being built in the form of ornate parish churches. As the scale of industrial activity increased, through better technology and large-scale financing, so too did its impact on the pattern of rural settlement. During the later Middle Ages it was the cloth industry which above all generated wealth and in many cases the houses and public buildings reflect this prosperity as well as the churches. Lavenham in Suffolk is the classic example, but there are numerous others in the Cotswolds, in the southwest and in the Pennines, although here much of the evidence has been swept away or consumed by the overwhelming impact of later industries.

Lavenham has a composite village plan, dominated by the parish church, which started around a square and grew outwards as a result of medieval prosperity. This wealth of the late fifteenth and early sixteenth centuries came to East Anglia where church-building still satisfied both private piety and public ostentation. It also led to

149

45 Kersey in Suffolk was an important medieval textile town which retains many half-timbered weavers' cottages. A valuation of the manorial arable at Kersey in 1396 lists arable, meadow, pasture and woodland, but finishes with the income from the fulling mill which shows that textile manufacture was integrated into the every day village agrarian life. The Kersey cloths were narrower and lighter than the traditional broadcloths, but were soon taken over and manufactured in other parts of the country

a virtual rebuilding of the medieval village in a single architectural style, with the result that the tradesmen's shops, the cloth halls, the inns, the houses of the merchant clothiers and even the weavers' cottages still reflect a distant prosperity. Lavenham's fame was short-lived as the locally made blue broadcloth was replaced by the New Draperies which were manufactured elsewhere. After the textile boom the village largely reverted to agriculture and was therefore spared the rebuilding and reconstruction that came to other longer-lived clothing towns such as Sudbury and Hadleigh.

The late medieval cloth industry was capable of transforming rural villages into major towns. Lavenham raised itself from an obscure country village in the early Middle Ages to the rank of the 20th most wealthy town by 1525. In Gloucestershire, Stroud, originally an outlying hamlet dependent chapelry of the manor of Bisley, rose to a position of industrial prominence in the Cotswolds. Dr Carus-Wilson in her research on the Stroud valley pointed out the intensification of industrial activity both in the main valley and its tributaries, principally that of Nailsworth. So great was the demand for water power that there was considerable competition for even short stretches of water. Between 1447 and 1459, the fragmentary account rolls of Bisley record the granting of sixteen water leases for portions of the water-courses; each was carefully defined by reference to particular mills, bridges, houses, meadows, or mill-leets. Thus William Bigge was granted a new lease for life at 4s 6d beyond the old rent of 6d for the part of the water-course from his own house to 'Walkbridge' and from Walkbridge to 'Ladysmore's mill'; Thomas Mody, with his wife and son, part of the water-course from the upper part of the meadow called Stubbing to the mill of William Whittington; and William Banknok part of the water-course from Brimscombe Bridge to the lower end of the meadow called Freremede. One stretch of the water is defined as 'extending to Rekheyend', indicating that there was a meadow set aside for the racks or tenters on which the cloth was dried.

The expansion of the rural cloth industry is exemplified at Castle Combe in Wiltshire, where during the first half of the fifteenth century there was an impressive industrial development along the local stream. Among the new buildings at Castle Combe was a fifteenth-century church

37 Marshfield, a planned Somerset town which grew prosperous on the wool trade (after R. Leech)

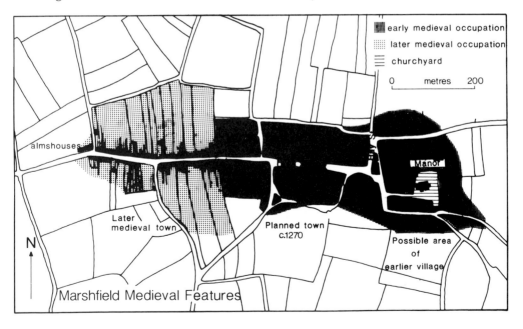

early medieval occupation

later medieval occupation

churchyard

0   metres   200

almshouses

Manor

Later medieval town

Planned town c.1270

Possible area of earlier village

N

Marshfield Medieval Features

tower with stone carvings based on cloth-working
implements. Here a growing class of craftsmen with no
agricultural holdings lived in the valleys of Nethercombe,
while yeoman cultivators lived on the heights above the
wooded valley at Overcombe. Even in the old part of the
town this pressure was felt and in 1454 William of Worcester made a comprehensive survey of the manor, which
revealed how the character of Castle Combe had been

46 Today Castle Combe is an idealised tranquil Cotswold village. However, it was an important textile centre from the fourteenth century onwards. In the fifteenth century the church tower was rebuilt with decorations based on cloth-working implements and a row of cloth workers' houses just below the church was also rebuilt. As late as the seventeenth century it was renowned for having the most celebrated sheep fair in north Wiltshire and John Aubrey the diarist, recorded 'that sheep masters do come (to Castle Combe) from Northamptonshire'

transformed by the cloth industry. 'In the said manor', he
wrote, 'are 2 vills, one called Overcombe, in which reside
the yeomen who are occupied in the cultivation and
working of the land which lies upon the hill, the other
Nethercombe in which dwell the men who used to make
cloth, like weavers, fullers, dyers and other artificers.' He
tells also of the fifty new houses that had been built largely
by the clothier tenants since 1409.

In 1409 the Castle Combe estate had passed to medieval

entrepreneur Sir John Fastolf who lost no opportunity to extoll the virtues of the Castle Combe textiles, placing considerable military orders for local red and white cloth 'for the great livery of the lord [the Duke of Clarence] beyond the sea'. From the invasion of France in 1415 down to 1440, when he retired from the wars, Fastolf was constantly equipping troops to serve under him. 'For the space of 22 years or more', wrote William of Worcester, 'Sir John bought every year to the value of more than £100 of red and white cloth of his tenants in Castle Combe.' 'In this manner,' continued William 'he divided the rents and profits of his manors of Castle Combe, Oxenden and Bathampton Wyly among his tenants and clothiers of Castle Combe, and his doing so was one of the principal causes of the augmentation of the common wealth and store of the said town and of the new buildings raised in it.'

The important role played by textiles in the late medieval export trade meant that they provided the crown with considerable revenue. The very fact that cloth exports were

47 Chipping Campden, Gloucestershire, was a product of the late medieval Cotswold wool industry. The fine perpendicular church at the top of the photograph was built on the proceeds of wool and the prosperity of the town below with its stone houses and public buildings developed on a similar basis. Note the regular parallel property boundaries demarcating the strips of the burgage plots

153

taxed has meant that a considerable body of documentation has survived, perhaps distorting the role they played
in the overall economic picture. None the less, quite apart
from the documentary record, the scale of enclosure for
sheep farming, the great East Anglian wool churches, the
market and guild halls and the wool merchants' houses,
both town and country, all stand as a silent testament to
the dominance of wool in late medieval England.

Iron and coal

Iron has been produced in Britain since well before the
Roman conquest and during the Middle Ages it became
an increasingly important commodity. One medieval attitude to iron is reflected in an *Encyclopedia* written about
1240 by a Franciscan monk, Bartholomew, who called the
use of iron 'more needful to men than the use of gold.
Without iron', he went on, 'the commonalty be not sure
against enemies; without dread of iron the common right
is not governed; with iron innocent men are defended;

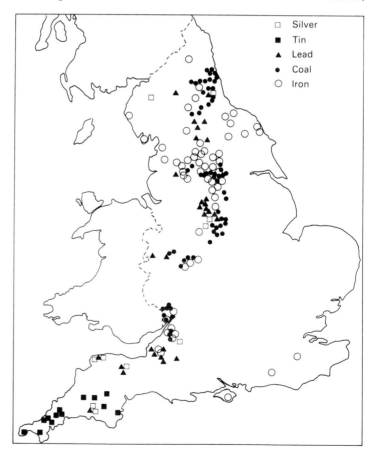

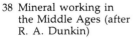

38 Mineral working in
the Middle Ages (after
R. A. Dunkin)

and foolhardiness of wicked men is chastised with dread of iron. And well-nigh no handiwork is wrought without iron; no field is eared without iron, neither tilling craft used, nor builded without iron.' There was an increasing demand for iron for arms and for constructional purposes during the twelfth and thirteenth centuries, which led to the expansion of industrial iron-working in the southwest, particularly in the Forest of Dean. Giraldus Cambrensis in his itinerary through Gloucestershire and Wales of 1188 had described the Forest of Dean as 'abounding with iron and deer', and the city of Gloucester as 'celebrated for its iron manufacturers'. In all of the main areas of production it seems that working was limited more by the local exhaustion of supplies of wood for charcoal-making than by a scarcity of supplies of iron ore. There is evidence of increased coppicing during the fifteenth century and of a growing use of young and small trees. Such was the demand that coppices were planted even in remote places even where iron production was on a small scale, as for example at Barnard Castle (Co. Durham) in the mid-fourteenth century.

The iron works in the Forest of Dean benefited from having a broader catchment area for their charcoal. Of the 27 forges operating in 1255, 23 appear to have obtained their charcoal partly, or entirely, from outside the forest. Nevertheless by the late thirteenth century, forest records reflect the real concern being felt about the inroads being made into the timber resources by the charcoal workers, for although coal was readily available and could be used in the forging process, it could not be employed in the major task of iron smelting.

Within the Forest of Dean by the thirteenth century

39 A Forest of Dean miner depicted on a medieval brass from Newland, Gloucestershire

there were forges of very different sizes, one forge
belonging to the king was estimated to be worth about £50
a year, but there were also numerous small, often itinerant
forges (the *plures forgie errantes*) of which some 58 were
recorded in a Dean document of 1282. Such forges often
consisted of temporary structures which were worked on
a seasonal basis and could be easily abandoned, with the
iron-workers moving on to sites with access to new fuel
resources. Small forges and peasant smithies were found
in many other woodland areas – for instance dozens of
such sites have been identified in the Weald – at places
where ore was available close to a water supply and timber
for fuel. Excavation at Minepit Wood near Rotherfield in
Sussex, has produced evidence of a medieval iron-working

40 Medieval bloomeries
in the Weald (after D.
Crossley)

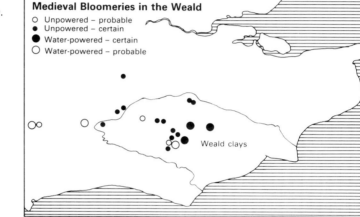

site of the fourteenth and fifteenth centuries on the site of
an iron-works that had been in use in the Iron Age and
then in the Romano-British period. The medieval site
incorporated a roasting furnace in which the ore was
broken up and the water removed from it. A smelting
furnace, the mines from which the ore was produced, slag-
heaps both with ore and refuse, and the whole complex
was enclosed in a small paddock which was surrounded
by wattle and daub fencing. In Knaresborough forest, in
the early fourteenth century, six small forges (alternatively
called 'nailsmiths') paid a total rent of 22s and in 1297 a
lorimer paid 4d for his forge. Men with surnames derived
from specialisation in the iron industry are found in nearly
all forest documents. The surnames Smith and Marshall
are common in Wealden villages and Smiths, Marshalls
and Lorimers frequently appear in forest records. Arrow-
smith and Cutler are also found occasionally, often in
contexts which show their owners to be peasants. For

example, two smallholders on Cannock Manor in 1297 were surnamed Smith, whilst a Marshall at Rugeley held 4 acres. Three men surnamed Smith, by far the most common surname of this sort, pannaged pigs in Rockingham Forest in 1295.

Increased iron production was made possible by technological advances, and was stimulated by the demands of war. The application of water power to bellows, providing an artificial draught for smelting, was more widely adopted after about 1350, and may, in some instances, have been encouraged by labour shortages after the Black Death. The use of water power to work bellows was not new in the later Middle Ages, but the first unequivocal reference to water-powered hammers comes from the

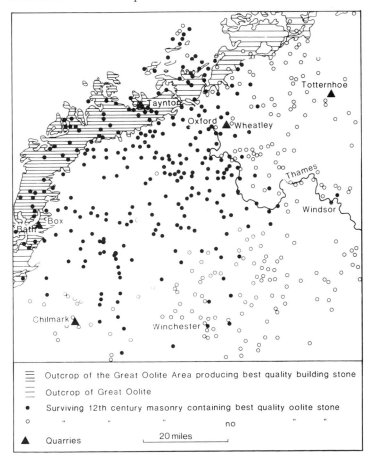

41 Distribution of fine building stone from the Oolitic limestone outcrop in the Cotswolds (after E. M. Jope)

≡ Outcrop of the Great Oolite Area producing best quality building stone

= Outcrop of Great Oolite

● Surviving 12th century masonry containing best quality oolite stone

○   "   "   "   no   "   "

▲ Quarries   20 miles

Weald in the 1490s, where the works at Newbridge, in the parish of Hartfield in Ashdown Forest, included a 'great water hammer'. The most important change in the iron industry during the later Middle Ages, however, was the

157

introduction of the blast furnace. The first definite reference to a blast furnace comes from Newbridge in the Weald in 1496, an iron-works commissioned by the crown to manufacture iron for armaments to be used in the Scottish war. An account for 1496–7 tells of axles, wheel-rims, cast-iron bullets and shot being carried to the Tower of London.

Although a number of medieval iron furnaces have been excavated at places such as High Bishoply, Co. Durham, and Basedale, N. Yorkshire, surviving physical remains of manufacturing industry are comparatively rare. More evidence survives from the mining of iron ores, although even here medieval mines and quarries are difficult to distinguish from later workings, with which they are often frequently closely associated. Ironstone could be worked by open-cast mining or by sinking bell-pit mines which were used during the Middle Ages to obtain iron ore from seams lying some way below the surface (plate 48). A bell

48 Bell-pit coal mines on Catherton Clee Hill in south Shropshire. Miners seeking for iron and coal during the Middle Ages and later have created a landscape of low pitted mounds over this hillside. Some of the bell-pits have subsequently been enclosed in a pattern of irregular fields by squatters from the late Middle Ages onwards

pit was a relatively shallow pit ranging from 9 to 12 feet deep, about 6 feet in diameter at the top and gradually widening to about 12 feet at the bottom, thus resembling a bell or beehive in profile. The amount of ironstone which could be quarried using this technique was limited, as there came a point at which the mine would collapse in on itself. Although this must have happened on many occasions, references such as that to a miner being crushed to death in 1357, working a pit at Hansworth in Yorkshire, are relatively rare. The ore was brought to the surface manually by ladder or later by a simple winch. Around the mouth of the mine quantities of waste were dumped and once the mine was abandoned and a new shaft sunk, all that remained was a low circular mound with a depression at the centre. Such traces of bell-pit mines have been identified in Sussex, Lancashire, Shropshire and Yorkshire. At Bentley Grange, West Yorkshire, the earthworks of bell-pit iron mines created by the monks of Byland Abbey and dated to the early thirteenth century, clearly sit on top of ridge and furrow, providing a rare stratigraphical relationship which enables us to deduce an early medieval date for the ridge and furrow.

The timber shortage of the later Middle Ages, which was brought about by increased domestic as well as industrial demand, encouraged the substitution of coal for wood wherever it was technically possible. Coal was widely worked on a small scale throughout the later Middle Ages, but, except for the Tyne valley, there was no district from which coal was regularly carried in large quantities for more than a few miles. Coal was nevertheless used for a range of activities including lime-burning, for agricultural and building purposes, for smith's work (although charcoal was preferred if available) and for baking, brewing and salt-making. The bell-pit technique was also used for extracting coal right up to the Industrial Revolution, but during the fifteenth century, pits were sunk deeper than previously and precautions taken against flooding. A 'colepytte' at Kilmersdon (Somerset) was deep enough in 1437 to have an adit or drainage channel and a pit at the same place was said in 1489 to be deep and dangerous: the 'wark' or spoil from these pits in the outcrop areas remains today in mounds of considerable size. There is also evidence to suggest that in many places coal was not greatly valued. In Durham, for instance, bell pits were excavated through a 5–foot thick coal seam without working it, in order to reach ironstone deposits, but the coal excavated in the process was discarded. A number of references to coal are disdainful. In 1260, for instance, Walter de Clifford granted out land for assarting on Brown Clee Hill in Shropshire together with a license 'to dig coals within the forest of Clee or to sell or to give it away'. By the early fourteenth century, however, the traffic in 'sea-coal' from the Tyne to London was sufficiently well established for a tax to be levied on it. Coal, however, was not very popular with Londoners either, who in 1307 complained about the smell, claiming that 'the air is infected and corrupted to the peril of those frequenting and dwelling in those parts'.

Documentary references to miners of ironstone or coal are rare; when it was found close to the surface ironstone seems to have been broken with short iron pick hammers. An order given to the sheriff of Hereford in 1245 required him 'to send to Chester 12 miners of the Forest of Dean well skilled in their art with 4 iron hammers for breaking rock and 6 crows for raising it.' Miners' picks and shovels are carved on the font of Abenhall church, Gloucestershire, dated about 1450.

By the later Middle Ages the Shropshire coalfield was beginning to develop as an important centre of industrial activity partly as a result of the role of monastic institutions. The origin of monastic involvement in the iron industry has now been traced back to 1397 when crown permission was obtained by James 'Mynor' of Derbyshire to work a mine of copper and silver within the lordship of Wenlock Priory. At the time of the dissolution, Wenlock Priory was working two iron foundries as well as ironstone quarries in Shirlett forest. One of the first references to iron-working here was in 1559 when a man was killed digging in the Shirlett mines. The Priory also had coal mines in Little Wenlock at this period. At Wombridge Priory, situated in the middle of the Shropshire coalfield, coal from two pits brought in £5 a year at the time of the dissolution and there was also a small ironworks at Oakengates. The rather pitiful monastic remains of Wombridge are now engulfed by nineteenth-century coal and iron workings. Most significant of all, the Cistercian abbey at Buildwas, just upstream from Coalbrookdale and Ironbridge, had a small iron forge on their demesne in the sixteenth century, possibly representing the beginnings of the Coalbrookdale iron industry. At the dissolution these ironworks were taken over and developed by families such as the Reynolds, the Baldwins and later the Darbys, whose names are closely associated with the later Industrial Revolution.

Other extractive industries

Silver and lead were precious commodities, the one needed for coinage and ornament, the other for roofing and piping. The two minerals were mined together in the Mendips, and in a number of other localities. Lead was worked continuously from the Roman period onwards in North Wales and during the Middle Ages in the Mendips. Lead was also worked on the Isle of Man. The first reference to this activity was in 1246 when the monks of Furness Abbey were granted the right to work the mines there. Derbyshire was the most productive lead-mining area in the Middle Ages, although the available evidence suggests that output was highly variable. The ground between the rivers Dove and Derwent in central Derbyshire is still scarred with old lead workings wherever the veins of ore approach the surface. In the Middle Ages there was a general right of prospecting on the moors, the crown's interest being served by a royalty of 1 dish in 13 of molten metal. As some of the best established mining areas were on manors of the royal demesne, such as Wirksworth, Bakewell, Ashford-in-the-Water and Hope, the industry is relatively well documented. The lead from these remote centres played an important part in the economy of northern Europe. In the 1180s 100 carretates of lead were sent from Derbyshire to the Cistercian house at Clairvaux in Burgundy: £33 6s 8d was allowed to the sheriff for the lead, a further £9 13s 11d was needed to move it to the Humber estuary, and a further £6 13s 4d for its transport in two ships to Rouen. The important retail market centres were at Derby, Chesterfield and Wirksworth, although the bulk of the export trade was conducted via London. At the end of the thirteenth century two groups of rich silver mines were found in Devon at Combe Martin and the Bere Mines, where production continued throughout the Middle Ages, and by 1485 over a thousand miners were employed at the two centres. Technological improvements were brought about by an influx of experienced European engineers who appear to have introduced considerably improved extraction techniques.

Throughout the Middle Ages the production of tin was limited to the southwest of England. Tin working was an extractive industry very similar to lead mining, both in the processes involved and in the degree of independence from seigneurial authority which the tinners enjoyed. The tinners of Devon and Cornwall were licensed to dig as and where they chose. In the first surviving stannary charter of

1201, they were given the right of:

> digging tin and turves for smelting it at all times, freely and
> peaceably and without hindrance from any man,
> everywhere in moors and in the fees of Bishops, abbots and
> earls . . . and of diverting streams for their works . . . just
> as by ancient usage they had been accustomed to do.

During the thirteenth century Devon outpaced Cornwall in
the level of tin production but after 1300 Cornwall overtook
Devon and remained ahead for the rest of the Middle
Ages. The early fourteenth century was a period of exceptional activity in tinning, and the charters of Edward I in
1305 had the effect of encouraging the industry by
confirming the ancient privileges of the stannary men,
which included exemption from ordinary taxation.
Production was severely curtailed by the Black Death, but
it recovered again by the late fourteenth century. For most
of the Middle Ages, workers washed their debris down
the valleys into the rivers, damaging arable land, and
silting up harbours in the process. At one stage it was
claimed that up to 250 acres a year of good farm land
was being destroyed by the tinners' activities. During the
fifteenth century various statutes were introduced to limit

49 Evidence of tin mining on Dartmoor. The tin was extracted from the ground by a process known as 'streaming' by which water was directed over tin-containing deposits. It has left an irregular corrugated landscape of former artificial water courses

this damage, but with little effect. In the later Middle Ages the crown appears to have introduced German iron-workers in order to improve techniques and increase production.

The major extractive industry during the Middle Ages was of course stone quarrying. Most stone was used locally although some acquired a wider reputation and was moved about more. In most cases stone buildings were constructed or repaired with stone brought from quarries close to the site. In 1232, for example, the Friars of Exeter were allowed to take stone for their church from the quarry located near the castle ditch. Similarly in 1357 stone for the repair of Nottingham castle was obtained from 'the quarry below the castle'. One quarry for Adderbury church (Oxon) was actually sited in the rectory garden and was filled up when the chancel was completed in 1418. Quarries were not always so conveniently sited and carriage from sources only a few miles from the building work could be costly. Repairs to Tutbury castle (Staffs) in 1314 involved moving freestone from Winshill quarry about 6 miles away at a cost of 7s 6d 'the hundred', but the actual cost of the stone was only 4s 'the hundred'.

Some of the finest stone came from the Jurassic lime-stone escarpment which runs from Lincolnshire in the northeast to Dorset in the southwest. Stone from Barnack in Northamptonshire, which had been quarried exten-sively during the later Saxon and Norman period, was carried as far as East Anglia and the Fens in the Middle Ages. Peterborough Abbey and many of the fine fenland churches were built of Barnack stone. In 1176 Sawtry Abbey's right to use 'the ditch which they had made at their own cost to carry stone [from Barnack] for the building of their church' was confirmed by Pope Alexander III. However, the stone for Wells cathedral came from the quarry at Doulting, just 7 miles away. The much valued Cotswold stone from Taynton found its way down the Thames to Windsor and London, but the quarries producing Bath stone were essentially land-locked and despite its qualities its main use was local. Marble from the Isle of Purbeck was a much prized stone for pillars in buildings such as Salisbury cathedral and the Great Hall at Winchester. A large proportion of ornamental stone was supplied ready worked and cut to measure from quarries which were given patterns and instructions on how to cut it. At Corfe there was a flourishing school of monumental masons working the marble. In 1385 £30 6s 8d was paid to 'Thomas Conon, marber [marbler] of Corfe for making 13

163

stone images in the likeness of kings, to stand in the great hall' at Westminster.

Despite these important domestic sources the famous white stone from the Caen region of Normandy continued to be imported into southern and eastern England throughout the Middle Ages. Caen stone was used for the rebuilding of Canterbury cathedral at the end of the twelfth century, and it was also used in Westminster Abbey and the Tower of London. In 1429 Caen stone for London Bridge was brought at 2s 6d a ton, but its carriage was 5s a ton. The quality of Caen stone made it particularly suitable for mouldings and carving and it was used for the Eleanor crosses. The great perpendicular nave of Winchester cathedral, which was inspired by William of Wykeham (1367–1404) and executed by his master mason, William Wynford, was also built of stone from Normandy. Similarly in the second half of the fourteenth century the magnificent Neville screen, which stands behind the high altar of Durham cathedral, was made of Caen stone. The screen was actually carved in London, possibly by Henry Yevele, the master architect of Westminster Hall, and then brought in pieces by sea to Newcastle.

The actual processes of stone quarrying are well documeted in some of the building accounts. For example, when Magdalen College, Oxford, was being built in 1474, the accountant records:

> First, I paid to Henry Baily and John Chamberlayn his partner, of Hedington, for the digging and removal of the earth lying over the quarry, which earth was 60 ft. square in area (*superficie*) and 8 ft. in depth down to the stones called le freebedde, and also for the digging and removal of stones in the said earth which are called grete pendant and small pendant – £3 6s 8d. Also I paid to Walter Bladon of Hedington for digging and removal of earth, being in length 72 ft. and in depth 7 ft. down to the stones called le cropperagge, and in breadth 22ft. – 40s.

In addition to stone for building, stone slates for roofing were used extensively for important buildings. An early reference to slates occurs in 1238, in the order to roof with slate (*sclata*) a mill at Woodstock, in which neighbourhood laminated limestone suitable for splitting into slates is found. For work at Cambridge castle in 1286 'sclatestone' of Peterborough was employed. But the most famous quarries were those of Collyweston in Northants. These were used extensively at Rockingham castle, and for instance in 1375, 9,500 stone slates were brought at 8s the thousand, and in 1390, 4,500 'sclastones' were brought at

6s 8d the thousand, carriage to the castle being at the rate of 3s the thousand, and for Oakham castle 5,000 'sklat' were bought at 6s 8d the thousand at Collyweston in 1383. As the manor of Collyweston belonged to the Lady Margaret, mother of Henry VII, her building accounts naturally contain a good many references to slates – in 1504, 'sclatt to the hillyng [i.e. heling, or roofing], of the new house'.

As in earlier times, salt was an essential commodity in medieval England. By the 1330s the main coastal producing area was in Lincolnshire, but substantial amounts of salt were also produced elsewhere along the south and east coasts, notably in Norfolk, Kent and Sussex. Inland, salt was produced from the brine springs of Worcestershire and Cheshire whence it was exported throughout Midland England and through Chester to Ireland. The salt industry of Worcestershire and Cheshire consumed great quantities of turf and wood in the boiling of brine from salt springs. Along the east coast, the last recorded evidence of salt-making at Fleet in Lincolnshire comes from 1455; here and elsewhere along the east coast decayed salterns survive today as relict features – clustered masses of irregularly shaped mounds, some of them 18 to 20 feet high. In the northeast, along the coasts of Durham and Northumberland, coal began to be used for boiling brine in the sixteenth century, and this resulted in considerable development especially at South Shields at the mouth of the Tyne.

The late medieval fuel shortage resulted in the search for sources other than timber and coal. These included peat. One unexpected result of the use of peat as an industrial fuel was the creation of the Norfolk Broads, now known to be a product of cutting turfs or turbaries (*turbaria*). An analysis of Barton Broad, which lies in the parishes of Instead and Barton, serves as an example of how the medieval turbaries flooded to become shallow lakes. The documentation for Barton shows that the cutting of turves gave way to the extraction of *mora*, a form of wet peat, which was dug or dredged from beneath standing water. In many places the peat floor lies little more than 6 feet below the present level of the broad, so that in an early stage of flooding the floor would not have been difficult to reach from the uncut balks, or from a boat. The *mora* was shaped into 'bricks' and left to dry out before it could be used as fuel. Evidence for such flooding is provided by the rising costs of extraction, and by the eventual cessation of turbary income in the accounts of

165

manors such as South Walsham which had been able to
produce over 200,000 turves a year in the 1260s. It is
known that the kitchens of Norwich Cathedral Priory were
consuming about twice this amount each year in the early
fourteenth century. Places that had once yielded rents for
turbaries were now having their fisheries valued instead:
fishery income begins in Barton records in 1422, at the
very time when *mora* are recorded being dredged from the
'private pond-water of the lord of the manor'. It has been
estimated that in all more than 30 million cubic yards of
peat were taken from the Norfolk Broads.

Manufacturing industry

The medieval industry for which we have the most
surviving archaeological evidence, in the form of tens of
thousands of sherds, is the pottery industry. Pottery
production increased rapidly during the early Middle
Ages. Along with iron artefacts, which show a similar
distribution and increase in quality, it was important not
just in extending the range of manufactured goods, but in
satisfying a consumer demand both for luxury goods for
the aristocracy and for basic equipment for every hearth
in the country. During the early Middle Ages production
moved out from towns such as Stamford and Thetford
and became widely dispersed in rural areas. There was a
proliferation of regional styles giving rise to a wide range
of pottery types. By the fourteenth century there were few
areas in England which did not have their local pottery
industry. At the same time techniques of potting improved
rapidly: the increasingly common use of sand rather than
shell or limestone as a tempering agent made the use of a
faster wheel possible, while improved throwing techniques enabled development of taller and narrower
shapes. These developments were accompanied by the
use of more advanced kilns firing to higher temperatures.
The basic cooking pot continued to be made throughout
this period, though in decreasing quantities in many areas,
owing to the wider use of bronze or iron cooking vessels.
Jugs or pitchers formed a large proportion of output, and
it is these which best show the distinct regional variations.
Throughout the thirteenth and the first half of the fourteenth centuries these vessels were elaborately decorated
with designs in painted and trailed slips of different
colours. Frequently they had applied ornamentation of
human figures, animals, faces and abstract designs, and
sometimes with combinations of different types of glazes
– a trend which paralleled and was in many cases

influenced by similar developments in western Europe and Scandinavia. Along with other aspects of the economy during the fourteenth century the pottery industry over much of England seems to have suffered an almost complete collapse and in many areas decorated and other good-quality pottery ceased being produced.

Much fifteenth-century pottery was plainly utilitarian and of relatively low quality. By the middle of the century,

50 Medieval pottery manufactured in Nottinghamshire. There is a plain storage jar on the left and a regular half glazed jug on the right. In the centre is a more elaborate glazed jug with applied decoration.

however, several areas, particularly in the Midlands and around London, had once again begun to produce household wares on an industrial scale. New and distinctive types of vessels such as large 'bung-hole' pitchers, skillets, bowls, plates and cups, as well as the more usual small jugs, many of these in graded sizes, began to be manfactured. The development of some types, such as the Tudor green wares in Surrey, has even been attributed to an influx of potters from the Continent, introducing superior techniques. Despite the wealth of archaeological evidence, documentary references to pottery manufacture are rare. Kingston-on-Thames may have been an early centre of the trade, as in 1260 the bailiffs of that town were ordered to send a thousand pitchers to the king's butler at Westminster. At Graffham, Sussex, in 1341 one of the sources of the vicar's income was a 'composition from the men who made clay pots, which is worth 12d', but the most common form of entry is a record of sums paid by potters for leave to dig clay. Thus at Coningsborough (Yorks) in 1348 a sum of 3s yearly was paid for the digging of clay to make pots, and at Hanley in Worcestershire in 1350, after the visitation of the Black Death, it is noted that the potters who used to pay 13s yearly for clay are dead.

167

At Cowick in Yorkshire in 1374 as much as £4 14s was 'received from potters making earthen vessels, for clay and sand taken in the moor at Cowick'. Similar entries occur here every year for about a century, while at Ringmer, in Sussex, small dues of 9d a head were paid yearly by some half a dozen potters for a period of well over 200 years. Still earlier, in 1283, a rent of 36s 8d called 'Potteresgravel', was paid to the lord of the manor of Midhurst.

In dealing with the documentary history of pottery we are met by one or two complications. For instance, the term 'potter' was constantly applied to the makers of metal pots; and it has also to be borne in mind that the commoner table utensils were often made of wood. At the election feast of the Drapers' Company in 1522 'green pots of ale and wine with ashen cups were set before them at every mess', the green pots were presumably pottery but the cups were wooden.

At the beginning of the thirteenth century, developing from pottery manufacture, the making of floor and roof tiles was well established. London building regulations dated 1212 record that tiles could be used instead of thatch, and the evidence points to their becoming increasingly popular during that, and still more during the following, century. Nevertheless in all the mass of detailed instructions for the construction and repair of buildings issued by Henry III there appear to be only a few references to tiled roofs. In 1236 William de Burgh was ordered to cause the roof of the king's chamber at Kennington to be stripped and re-covered with good tile. The Wye tileries, belonging to Battle Abbey, had an output of about 100,000 tiles. The price was 2s 6d the thousand in 1355, but the usual cost in building accounts of the second half of the fourteenth century is from 4s to 5s 6d. At Langley in 1366 some were bought from Simon Molder of Ruislip at 3s, and others from Richard Tielere of Botley at 4s 6d. For work at Wallingford 36,000 tiles were obtained in 1365 from Nettlebed at 4s the thousand and in 1390 the price at that tilery had dropped to 3s 4d the thousand with carriage extra.

During the fifteenth century complaints were made of the lack of uniformity in the size and quality of the tiles. It was said that many of the tiles then being produced would last only 4 or 5 years instead of 40 or 50, and this is borne out by the many series of manorial accounts, which show that a surprising amount of tileing repairs had to be carried out every year on the farm buildings. To remedy these defects, an Act was passed in 1477 regulating the process of manufacture and the size of the products.

Until the middle of the fourteenth century, most bricks used in Britain were imported from the Low Countries. The earliest definite reference to the making of wall tiles (the word brick was not used until the fifteenth century) was in 1335 at Ely and during the early fifteenth century places such at Tattershall castle were built of brick, often under the direction or influence of European craftsmen.

Although window glass was known in Anglo-Saxon England, it was only rarely used in domestic houses during the Middle Ages. By the second quarter of the twelfth century the glazing of church windows was common and the use of pictorial glass was so common-place that the austere statutes of the Cistercians expressly forbade such use in their own churches. Surprisingly enough there is no documentary evidence for the manu-facture of coloured glass in England, and as late as 1449 Henry VI brought John Utyman from Flanders to make coloured glass at Eton and to instruct English craftsmen in the techniques. In ordinary domestic houses glass windows remained a luxury throughout the Middle Ages. One early sixteenth century commentator records that 'Paper, or lyn clothe, straked a crosse with losyngs, make fenestrals instede of glasen wyndowes'. But in 1441, when Peterhouse built a great dovecote on their estate at Thri-plow they spent 22d on the glazing of one of its windows. Although glass-making was found in many woodland areas the chief centre of medieval glass production was Chittingfold in Surrey. Production here was first recorded in a grant of land to Lawrence Vitrearius about 1226; frag-ments of glass and broken crucibles have been found on a site here. Conclusive evidence for a major glass industry in the Surrey/Sussex Weald using local sand from Hambledon and fuel from local woodland is provided by the exchequer rolls of 1351. The medieval English glass industry appears to have been stimulated by glass-makers from France, although there were long established Wealden families in the industry. It was backward in comparison with its French counterpart and there was relatively little expansion until the sixteenth century. The quality of the products was never as good as those of Normandy and glass continued to be imported from various regions of France on a large scale.

Communications
Most manufactured goods were distributed locally, finding their outlets through the hundreds of small village and

town markets that were operating throughout the Middle Ages. The markets ranged from small weekly gatherings in villages to the specialised commodity markets of the larger towns. Sometimes markets developed at the junction of the principal trading routes and in some cases they simply acted as market centre for areas which had no town nearby – often carrying the place-name prefix 'Chipping' or 'Market'. Long distance transport on a regular basis was required only for items such as best stone which moved principally by water.

Many places also had annual fairs, but the great international fairs found in eastern England in the thirteenth century had declined in importance by the end of the Middle Ages; their functions had been assumed by the permanent and increasingly complex trading arrangements of the towns. Most journeys were relatively short, but there were long-distance communications, which became increasingly important. The network of overland communications that operated during the Middle Ages was a complex one. The Roman road system had largely disintegrated but surviving stretches of road between Roman centres which were still occupied in the Middle Ages continued to be used. The abandonment of Roman towns such as Wroxeter in Shropshire, Silchester in Hampshire and Alchester in Oxfordshire led to the abandonment of the road systems that had served them. Under the Romans the road system had worked as a national network used to convey goods from throughout Britain and the Empire. No such integrated economy or road system existed in the Middle Ages. Medieval roads, unlike their Roman counterparts, with few exceptions were not metalled. The medieval concept of a road was more of a right of way than an actual physical trackway, none the less there was an intricate pattern of roadways performing different functions operating in Medieval England.

Any consideration of roads in the Middle Ages has to be based upon the Gough map, c.1360. The essence of the modern road pattern existed in the early fourteenth century, except that very few roads crossed the country from southwest to northeast. London was at the hub as it had long been, and Coventry was the great crossing point in the Midlands. On the roads there were a wide range of travellers, on foot and on horseback, merchants with packhorses, carts, and occasionally with great four-wheeled wagons. Carts were used to transport goods such as fish, grain, flour, wine, salt, cloth, hay, faggots and brushwood, peat and stone, and less frequent loads of iron, tin and military weapons. The carriage of Exchequer goods from Westminster to York in the early fourteenth century took between 10 to 14 days; the journey from Malmesbury to Carlisle in 1318 took 12 days; London to Gloucester was an 8–day return journey. Travel and methods of transport by road formed one of the few aspects of life in England in the early fourteenth century that the Black Death and the next century scarcely altered.

One of the most useful sources about medieval transport is provided by the many and complicated royal itineraries. Such itineraries, for which complete records often survive, present the best data from which the road network can be reconstructed. The royal court had an arduous circuit, visiting palaces, castles and ecclesiastical sites in southern and central England on a regular basis. Such movement was in part to maintain a royal presence, but as we have seen it also had an underlying practical purpose, which was to feed the retinue that accompanied the king and his peripatetic government. It was no accident that many of the stopping-off places were sited near to royal forests where there was a readily available source of food for such large numbers. King John, for instance, is recorded as having made 360 moves in 1245, visiting some 145 royal manors, 129 castles, 46 religious houses and 40 other places. Altogether John made 1,378 recorded moves compared with 1,458 by Edward II, but remarkably Edward I made almost 3,000 moves during his reign.

It addition to this royal traffic there appears to have been a regular cart link between towns such as London, Bristol, Coventry, Leicester and Chesterfield. Such cartways were known as *viae*. The *via regia* was common to all while the *communis strata* belonged to cities or even individuals. Lesser tracks for packhorses were known by the name of *vicus* while footways were called *iter*. Villages surrounded by their open fields had numerous lanes and trackways leading out onto the fields, while others joined up hamlets and single farms. Where such routes were reasonably direct they were often of considerable antiquity, but where the course contains frequent changes of direction, they normally post-date the enclosure of the open fields as they were obliged to pursue an indirect course to avoid pre-existing arable furlongs.

In places, particularly where the trackways ran over heavy clay, their courses were moved from one site to another in preference to maintaining a single line. The resulting hollow or sunken ways which are characteristic of the modern communication network of rural Devon and

171

Cornwall, are to be found in various other parts of the
country, often overgrown but marking the lines of former
communication. The freedom of medieval roads to move
or spread out in part explains why they have otherwise
often left relatively little trace in the modern landscape.
Their general tendency not to follow straight lines has also
meant that, while they may well show up in territorial or
administrative boundaries, they are not directly as easily
identifiable, because their course is not as obvious as that
of their Roman predecessors.

Separate routeways were established for the distribution
of salt from the Cheshire and Worcestershire production
areas and the name 'saltway' often marks the lines of these
former trading routes, which generally avoided towns in
order to minimise the amount of tax payable. Similarly
drove-roads, which ran across central England from the
uplands of Wales and Scotland, normally ran independently from the general communication network.

One of the few areas where we have any indication of
actual road construction during the Middle Ages, apart
from in towns, was in the Fenland, where the need for
access to the low-lying islands brought about the construction of causeways for the passage of foot and wheeled
traffic. The Isle of Ely with its fine cathedral and market
town was served by two landward causeways. On the
southeast Stuntney causeway led across the Ouse to
Soham and the high ground near Newmarket, while to
the southwest a road led out to Haddenham and Aldreth
where a long neck of firm ground protrudes into the Fen.
This causeway, built in the early Middle Ages, still carries
a modern routeway.

As well as transport by road there was movement along
the navigable rivers and also coastal traffic. Thus, boats
sailed to Southampton with herrings and stockfish from
the east coast, with coal from the northeast, with wheat,
malt and iron from nearby Kent and Sussex, with ropes,
sails and cordage from Bridport and with Purbeck stone
and marble from Poole.

Medieval towns

Throughout the Middle Ages the majority of people dwelt in the countryside in villages, hamlets and isolated farmsteads. Even at the height of urban expansion and prosperity in the early fourteenth century it is doubtful if more than one in ten would have thought of themselves as townspeople, while in 1200 none of the towns, with the exception of London, was very large. Bristol, York and Newcastle might have numbered 10,000 inhabitants, but most of the others would have had fewer than 5,000, including a considerable percentage with less than 1,000. Yet towns have probably received more scholarly attention than any other aspect of medieval life. One of the reasons for this is that, in general, urban records tend to survive better than those relating to the countryside, and therefore provide the historian with a readily accessible source of information. Borough records cover not only town government and administration, but also a wide range of social, demographic, economic and commercial aspects of urban life, and have enabled the compilation of detailed topographical studies of medieval towns such as Oxford, Canterbury and Winchester, as well as a number of other towns covered by the *Atlas of Historic Towns* volumes.

As we shall see, the dividing line between town and village was a fine, not to say frequently blurred, one. Many villages displayed urban characteristics during the period up to about 1350. Some took the form of fleeting and forlorn aspirations, but others displayed more tenacity and some of the proto-towns managed to succeed. Still others were hybrids with characteristics of both town and village. For example, by the mid-thirteenth century, although burgage rents and market tolls represented the principal source of revenue at Clare, Suffolk, nevertheless the community never became a fully fledged borough. Two examples from Norfolk are worth quoting here. The first is Castle Rising, where a decayed town and port lie to the north of the impressive castle remains. A large church containing architecture contemporary with the castle tells us something of the size of the former settlement here. An impressive market cross lies to the east of the church

173

in the old market square, which is now a village green. Not far away at Castle Acre another decayed medieval town lies in the western lee of the great earthwork castle. The massive town defences, thought by earlier historians to be Roman, formed part of a defensive complex contemporary with the medieval castle. It can be seen that the southeastern corner of the medieval borough has been abandoned and given over to allotments, while the modern village lies in the form of a little planted unit outside the northern defences, with the wide Market Street lying partially over the northern town ditch.

On the other hand a number of towns which started out life confidently armed with borough charters, gradually, or in a few cases abruptly, faded into a state of rural tranquillity. License and privilege could help, given favourable conditions. but geography and commercial viability were usually the ultimate arbitrators. The acquisition of market and borough charters have conventionally been seen by historians as essential requirements for successful medieval towns. However, in reality such legal license confirmed status and potential upon the recipient, at the same time as providing revenue for the grantor. Obtaining a borough charter no more guaranteed commercial success than did the erection of town walls, although as it happens the majority of successful towns did ultimately achieve full borough status.

Medieval towns had three main functions. These were commercial, administrative and strategic, although a number of towns did develop other specialist functions based, for instance, upon industrial production or on scholarship. In the century following the Norman Conquest strategic and administrative functions tended to be most important, particularly in the larger urban centres, but by the later Middle Ages trade and commerce were far more important to the majority of English towns. The Normans had used the town and the castle as the means of at first dominating and then administering their newly won kingdom. Initially the ancient shire capitals were used as political and ecclesiastical bases, but as relatively stable trading conditions were restored new generations of strategic towns were created in the west and the north. These were followed by new or greatly expanded towns whose main function was marketing; during the early Middle Ages population pressure prompted existing towns to grow and led to the creation of a considerable number of new towns throughout England and parts of Wales.

After about 1350 the fortunes of some towns declined

along with those of the surrounding countryside, and as late as 1500 several of the old corporate towns do not seem to have recovered fully. There is little evidence for the continuing expansion of suburbs during the fifteenth century and some towns, which relied upon cloth manufacture, were seriously affected by the growing competition from rural-based industries. Added to which the plagues that had been inflicted upon the whole country

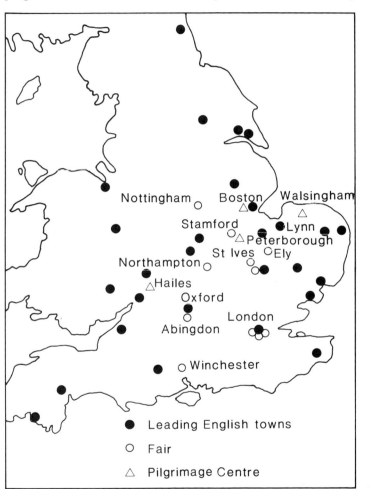

42 Sites of important towns, fairs and pilgrimage centres in the Middle Ages (after J. F. D. Shrewsbury)

Nottingham   Boston Walsingham
Stamford   Lynn
          Peterborough
     St Ives   Ely
Northampton
  Hailes
  Oxford
       London
Abingdon

  Winchester

● Leading English towns

○ Fair

△ Pilgrimage Centre

in the fourteenth century became a particular phenomenon of the towns in the fifteenth, sapping them of their energy and their population. In a number of towns there were repeated complaints about buildings being neglected, streets being left unpaved and townspeople attempting to evade heavy taxations. In part these were levied to cover the effects of disastrous fires which became an increasing threat to the late medieval urban population, which was housed largely in timber-framed buildings.

There was a significant decline in the number of markets by 1500. For instance, of 45 markets found in early medieval Staffordshire, only 20 had survived into the late Middle Ages, and the picture in other counties was very similar. Not until the Great Rebuilding of the late sixteenth and early seventeenth centuries did many towns revive, although some were never to regain their medieval glory and were to sink back into rural backwaters. Only a few reverted to mere village status, but where the woollen industry had boosted communities into small towns and then abandoned them as quickly as it had arrived, the pattern of change was very dramatic. In the Cotswolds, Chipping Campden, Stow-on-the-Wold, Northleach and even Cirencester all display ornate parish churches, guild-halls and market-places reflecting their former status. Such centres were typical of a new generation of small industrial towns grown wealthy largely on the proceeds of the flourishing textile industry in the later Middle Ages. There were many small towns which for a short period enjoyed considerable prosperity. All are towns where wealth disappeared as rapidly as it had arrived. Today we find such places 'delightful' and 'charming', but perhaps we should remember that they owe their charm to the fact that they stopped succeeding in the sixteenth and seventeenth centuries. Had they continued to prosper then Broadway and Bourton-on-the-Water would have more in common with Reading or Swindon than they would with other rustic Cotswold retreats.

The picture of urban decline during the later Middle Ages, which emerges from the analysis of certain towns, is no doubt an accurate one, but the historical record does contain some serious contradictions. For despite setbacks, a comparison of the taxation records of 1334 and 1524 shows that some towns continued to prosper throughout the later Middle Ages and most important of all there is a marked increase in the total proportion of urban wealth during the period. Naturally the fortunes of individual towns differed quite markedly, but collectively they had strengthened their grip on the national economy. Even the decline in the number of market towns hides the fact that there was a polarisation of trade and commerce in a smaller number of successful towns. There was increasing centralisation epitomised by London which was increasingly important as the largest and most prosperous urban centre in the land. There were 85 parishes within the city wall and Westminster, Southwark and other outlying 'villages', which were closely associated with its daily life, would have ranked as major provincial towns elsewhere in the kingdom. London contained between 14 and 18,000 households, giving it a total population of about 60 or 70,000. The crowded character of the city is vividly illustrated by a late thirteenth-century enactment, where we hear that the houses

> are so close together that in many places there is no vacant land and some occupy a neighbour's walls where they have no right at all; and occupy them maliciously, as by putting into the said walls beams and corbels or chests or cupboards; and . . . such purprestures are made in cellars and rooms where no-one can enter and know the same, except the occupier's household, and . . . are concealed during many years and not perceived.

Table 5 Wealth of medieval towns *c.* 1300

	Assessed wealth £		Assessed wealth £
London	11,000	Beverley	500
Bristol	2,200	Cambridge	466
York	1,620	Newbury	412
Newcastle upon Tyne	1,333	Plymouth	400
Boston	1,100	Newark on Trent	390
Great Yarmouth	1,000	Peterborough *cum membris*	383
Lincoln	1,000	Nottingham	371
Norwich	946	Exeter	366
Oxford	914	Bury St Edmunds	360
Shrewsbury	800	Stamford	359
Lynn (King's and South)	770	Ely *cum membris*	358
Salisbury	750	Luton	349
Coventry	750	Barking	341
Ipswich	645	Hull	333
Hereford	605	Scarborough	333
Canterbury	599	Cottingham, Yorks. E.R.	330
Gloucester	541		
Winchester	515	Derby	300
Southampton	511	Swaffham	300

By the 1520s the City of London alone was almost 10 times as wealthy as Norwich, then the leading provincial city, and more than 15 times as wealthy as Bristol. In the subsidy of 1543–4, London paid 30 times as much tax as

Norwich, and well over 40 times as much as Bristol. At that date even the suburb of Southwark, across the river, paid more tax than Bristol. London contributed as much in 1543–4 as all the other English towns put together. By 1600 its population was probably about four to five times as great as it had been in 1334. London's prosperity was based upon an increasing share of England's trade, particularly the cloth trade, as well as an increasingly centralised government, which brought with it the fortunes associated with a capital city.

Gradually London usurped the trading functions of many provincial towns. During the fifteenth century the distribution of cloth in York, for example, was taken out of the hands of the city's traders first by West Riding merchants and later by London merchants able to supply, in return for textiles, a large variety of imported goods which previously had not been obtainable from local traders. By the early sixteenth century much cloth manufactured in Devon was being sent to London and thence exported to the Low Countries, rather than being exported to France from West Country ports as had been the custom previously. The ever increasing influence of London's merchant class was clearly demonstrated in Southampton. From the mid-fifteenth century Londoners had taken a leading part in Southampton's commerce, using the town as an outport for trade between England and the Mediterranean. Eventually London merchants penetrated into every branch of commerce in Southampton, gradually swamping local merchants by their larger capital resources. Increasingly London dominated overseas trade as it came to dominate the English economy in general.

An anonymous writer of 1497 said that apart from London there were only two towns of importance in the country, Bristol and York, but in this he was misinformed, for there was another town which experienced a remarkable and spectacular growth during the later Middle Ages – Norwich. In 1334 Norwich was the sixth richest town in England, with an estimated population of about 6,000, but by the end of the Middle Ages it had risen to second position. It was the chief market town of one of the most thickly populated and prosperous districts of medieval England. The main market-place came under so much pressure that subsidiary ones developed, for example horses were sold outside the churchyard on St Stephen's, an area now appropriately known as Rampant Horse Street. A wide range of commodities came into Norwich including wool, bread corn, barley, pigs, sheep, cattle, fish, shell-fish, poultry and dairy produce, vegetables, herbs and salt. Even in the thirteenth century there were over 130 trades and occupations recorded. These included the principal trades of leather-working, textile-working, and metal-working. There were also many imports – fish from Sweden, Caen stone, timber, steel, olive oil, dye stuffs, ash, alum, mill stones – and luxuries such as wine, furs, fine woollen cloth, silk, beeswax, and sugar. After

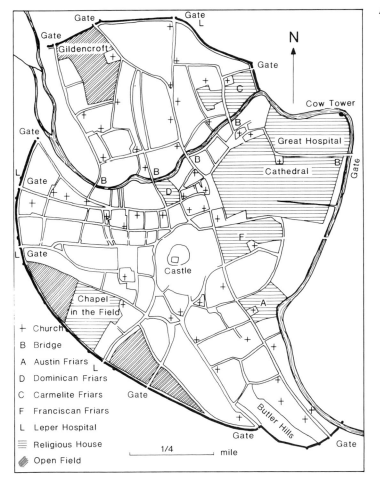

43 Norwich in 1348

1194 when Richard I granted a charter giving the citizens the right to elect their own city governor there was considerable migration from the surrounding countryside. In the thirteenth century the defences were strengthened and the enclosed area greatly extended. A new bank and ditch were made in 1253 enclosing an area of almost one square mile, which was far larger than most medieval boroughs. This extension was partly made in order to provide larger marketing areas within the town. Similar walled extensions occurred at other successful towns, such as Hereford.

Along with other large towns Norwich appears to have suffered badly during the middle years of the fourteenth century. In 1357 it is recorded that shops and market stalls were left empty so long that they were falling down, and that after the plague and famine of 1369 the overcrowded churchyard of St Peter Mancroft was extended southwards

44 Norwich in the early seventeenth century (Speed)

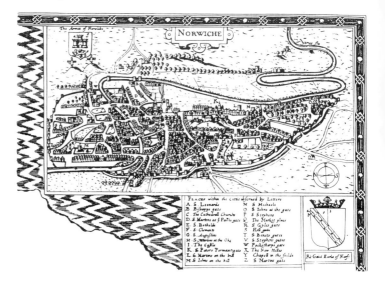

by taking in part of what had been the cloth market. By the end of the fourteenth century, however, there was a recovery, led by the expanding textile industry which attracted agricultural workers from the marginal lands close to Norwich, as well as traders from throughout Europe. By the later fourteenth century Norwich was the chief seat of worsted manufacture and this was reflected in the rebuilding of a number of municipal and ecclesiastical buildings. In the century after the Black Death all four orders of friars built new churches and conventual buildings of considerable grandeur. St Peter Mancroft was rebuilt and reconsecrated as was St Mary in the Fields and many of the parish churches. Municipal buildings such as the Market Cross and the Guildhall were also rebuilt. Perhaps even more impressive than the churches and the public buildings were the houses. Cunningham's perspective view of 1558 which is probably the earliest such view of any English town, shows a picture of substantial two-storeyed late medieval buildings, many of which seem to have been constructed between 1440 and 1525. Recent excavations in the city have confirmed that the 'great rebuilding' which was later to transform rural England, was accomplished in Norwich at the end of the Middle Ages, when it 'changed from being predominantly one-storeyed to being predominantly two-storeyed'. All this would seem seriously to call into question Leland's description of Norwich in 1530s as 'a city of decay'.

Although no medieval towns were able to survive on specialist activities alone, the fortunes of some were certainly enhanced by performing specialist roles and important trends began to emerge in the fourteenth and fifteenth centuries. London, as already noted, was the prime example, as it developed the administrative and fiscal characteristics of a capital city, and those centres in East Anglia and the west where textiles began to dominate have already been discussed. During the Middle Ages Oxford and Cambridge began to develop as important centres of learning, and in the case of Oxford at least, the coming of the university seems to have in part offset a

51 Oxford. The centre of the city is dominated by the University, several of whose constituent colleges were founded in the later Middle Ages. In the foreground is Christ Church, which was created by Cardinal Wolsey in the early sixteenth century out of St Frideswide's monastery

severe economic decline during the later Middle Ages. Oxford began to acquire a reputation of a place of learning early in the twelfth century. Theobold of Etampes called himself Master of Oxford and was lecturing to over 60 students as early as 1117. Towards the end of the same century some of the English scholars who were ordered by Henry II to leave the University of Paris arrived to take up studies in Oxford. Masters and students alike seem to have been attracted to Oxford by its central position in southern England and by its remoteness from ecclesiastical control. At this stage the University was no more than a guild of teachers and scholars, who combined together for mutual protection and convenience. The early years of the University were not without their problems. For instance, after two clerics had been hanged by townsmen in 1209, the students left. Some moved to Cambridge and did not return until 1214. In 1264 some students moved to Northampton to avoid involvement in a dispute between the crown and Simon de Montfort, while in 1334 half the scholars of Oxford went to Stamford after serious rioting between rival student groups, but they were ordered by the king to return to Oxford immediately. Despite these upheavals the University grew rapidly during the thirteenth century, partly under the influence of the friars who began arriving in 1221. The first chancellor of the University was appointed in 1214 to act as a representative of the Bishop of Lincoln, under whose aegis the University nominally operated. One of the first men to be appointed as chancellor was Robert Grosseteste who later became Bishop of Lincoln himself. To begin with there were few specific university buildings, and ceremonies and meetings took place in the church of St Mary Virgin, but in about 1320 Thomas Cobham, Bishop of Worcester, built a congregation house with a small library on the north side of the church. The first building specifically planned and built by the University was the Divinity School (completed in 1490), one of the finest examples of fifteenth century vaulted architecture. Over it was built a library named after Humphrey Duke of Gloucester its principal benefactor. Both buildings now form part of the Bodleian Library complex. The first colleges began to appear during the second half of the thirteenth century. The earliest was Merton College endowed by Walter de Merton about 1263–4, which was established in order to enable 11 graduates to study for their MAs. It was not until William of Wykeham, Bishop of Winchester, founded New College in 1379 that the characteristic layout of all subsequent colleges was adopted. Wykeham had been a surveyor of the king's works and he took a great interest in the buildings. This close association between the University and the church, explains his use of the monastic plan of quadrangles, cloisters and chapel. New College was intended for 70 scholars from Winchester School, another of his foundations, and as the largest educational institution in Oxford, was the first to cater for undergraduates. Later other colleges such as Magdalen College, founded in 1458 by William of Waynfleet, Bishop of Winchester, were to copy this design.

Despite the establishment of a number of colleges during the fifteenth century, including Lincoln founded in 1427, and elaborate building schemes for other foundations, the fifteenth century appears to have been a period of regression in Oxford. By 1450 the number of students had fallen to about 600 compared with 3,000 in the fourteenth century and many of the halls were closed down. Early in the sixteenth century the university complained that numbers were falling again because abbots were no longer sending their monks to be educated and parents were unwilling to expose their sons to heretical ideas. Oxford and Cambridge survived the dissolution and unlike the monasteries were able to build on their medieval reputations, eventually coming to dominate their mother cities.

Another town which had a specialisation of a rather different nature was Bath. Bath clearly shared in the prosperity of Somerset, which was the premier wool-producing county in the late fourteenth and fifteenth centuries. Chaucer in the Tale of the Wife of Bath went so far as to claim that its cloth was superior to that of Ypres and Ghent. In addition to the wool trade, there were the priory and the church which had doubled up as the cathedral for the diocese of Bath and Wells. During the Roman period Bath had been the main spa centre in Britain and it would appear that interest in the baths was revived perodically during the Middle Ages, possibly linked with attempts to promote Bath as a major pilgrimage centre. One of the earliest references to the baths comes in the *Gesta Stephani* (1138) when they were recorded as 'most delightful to see and beneficial for health'. King John visited the town on a number of occasions, and Henry III spent money on repairing the wall around the King's Bath in addition to his house in the city. The crown's interest in the baths then seems to have lapsed until the sixteenth century. During the Middle Ages there are, however, various references not only to the King's Bath, which was said by

Leland to be used by 'gentlemen', but also to the Cross Bath which lay immediately to the east of St John's Hospital on the site of one of two hot springs in the southwestern part of the town. It was recorded that this bath was much used by 'people diseased with lepre, pokkes, scabbes, and great aches'. There was also the hot bath – alternatively known as Alesy's Bath during the Middle Ages – which, according to Leland, 'for at

52 Bath. The first known pictorial representation of the city, dating from the mid-fifteenth century from an illuminated initial to the 69th Psalm of David in a Book of Hours of Henry Beauchamp, Duke of Warwick. The walled city with the Abbey church is on the right. The figures outside represent Henry III immersed in the river and the Bishop of Bath and Wells and the Prior of Bath. Note the sheep grazing outside the city walls

cumming into it Men think it wold scald the Flesch at the first, but after that the Flesch ys warmid and it is more tolerable and pleasaunt'. Other medieval baths referred to were the Lepers' Bath, the Mild Bath and the Priory Bath. Leland completes his account by noting that:

> The Colour of the Water of the Baynes is as it were a depe blew Se Water, and rikith like a sething Potte continually, having somewhat a sulpherous and sumwhat a pleasaunt flavour. The Water that rennith from the 2 smaul Bahthes goit by a Dike into avon by West bynethe the Bridge. The Water that goith from the *Kinges Bath* turnith a Mylle, and after goith into Avon about Bath Bridge. In all the 3 Bathes a Man may evidently se how the Water burbelith up from the Springes.

Improved overland communications were later to enable Bath to prosper through her hot springs. but the seeds of this success had been sown during the Middle Ages.

Markets
The creation of markets and fairs, either by means of royal grants or by the action of more locally based interested

parties, reached a climax in the thirteenth century. A network of chartered and prescriptive markets and fairs was established throughout England by 1300. The charter simply represented the legal recognition of the right of a community to hold a market. Many markets were, however, held without such charters while the granting of a charter did not necessarily lead to the creation or expansion of a market area. It is clear, however, that the

45 Markets and fairs in medieval Derbyshire (after B. E. Coates)

need for adequate market facilities, with or without market or borough charter, was of primary importance in the shaping of many medieval towns (and villages). Between 1227 and 1350 the crown granted market rights to more than 1,200 places in England and Wales, underlining an intense interest in trade and in the profits accruing from it. Some developed quite intricate functions, while others remained obscure villages and hamlets. As already noted in many of the newly expanded centres the dividing line between town and village was far from obvious. Clare in

185

Suffolk, for example, was said in 1086 'always to have had a market', but apparently its 43 burgesses were then a new group appended to what was essentially a rural manor. By the mid-thirteenth century, however, burgage rents and tolls from the market and fair were the principal revenues drawn from Clare by its lord. It never became a fully fledged borough, but it clearly developed some essentially urban characteristics even if it remained of modest size.

The abbots of Ramsey played an important role in creating St Ives as an urban appendage to the Huntingdonshire manor of Slepe. This settlement was conveniently situated to provide a meeting place for merchants from the East Midlands and foreign merchants coming down the Ouse; the abbey exploited the advantages of the site by building a bridge over the river, obtaining the grant of a fair in 1110 and encouraging the building and repair of houses and shops. Even so, agriculture was never pushed entirely into the background at St Ives, for its commercial life was centred on its fair, which lasted for just one week each year. It was in practice a temporary or periodic town which never achieved municipal standing. Similarly Chipping Campden (Gloucs), was created a borough by Hugh de Gonneville in 1173 and became one of the main marketing centres for Cotswold wool, but it, too, never entirely outgrew its agricultural characteristics (see plate 47).

Market grants could lead to the physical expansion of an existing village, and in some cases could dramatically change village morphology. In the prosperous Essex countryside, market charters were obtained from places such as Castle Hedingham, Burnham-on-Crouch, Hatfield Broad Oak and Newport, but none of their names survive in a list of markets in 1575. Yet in each of those villages it is possible to recognise the effect that the market made by causing the main street to be widened in order to accommodate it. At Linton (Cambs) there was a deliberate attempt to create a market-place in the village, which led to the development of the small town and subsequently to the moving of the market-place. While at Caxton (Cambs) which obtained a market grant in 1248, the village was moved from its original site to a much more commercially attractive position (c. 1250–80), probably in an attempt to benefit from the commercial potential of the main road. An open triangular space in the centre of the village is known as the market-place and was used as such into the eighteenth century. Another Cambridgeshire example, at

53 Chelmsford in the late sixteenth century, from a contemporary map. The large triangular market-place is typical of many market towns of the Middle Ages and the number of encroachments within the market demonstrate that it was successful.

Whittlesford, appears to have had a market-place or green laid out deliberately on the outskirts of the village in the early thirteenth century. The village then grew around it and later beyond, rather than along the main street down to the ford as might have been expected. Such examples of fundamental changes to medieval settlement geography were far more frequent than is appreciated; often a casual reference to a market or to burgesses in manorial records will be the only hint concerning what were often significant changes to the village layout.

In Saxon *burhs*, in which defence was a major consideration, no permanent market areas appear to have been provided within the town plan. Trade was largely carried out in churchyards and open areas within the town defences. In the early Middle Ages there remained a close relationship between the church and market-place, and in many cases, as at Newport (Salop), and numerous other examples the church occupies a central island in the market. There was often a connection between the

187

parochial saints' day and the dates on which local fairs and weekly markets were held; markets were also often held on Sundays until the late thirteenth century. The Statute of Winchester (1285), however, ordered that 'Henceforth neither Fairs nor Markets be kept in Church Yards for the Honour of the Church', and the creation of a considerable number of new town market-places appears to date from about this time. In the older established towns extra-mural market areas were developed, or in some cases an area may have been cleared within the town to create room for a market. At Oxford there is evidence to suggest that Cornmarket Street was widened in the Norman period to accommodate a market within the walls, though the large market areas of Broad Street and St Giles were sited outside the town defences. At Warwick and Wallingford too properties also appear to have been cleared in order to create town-centre markets.

54 Aerial view of Brackley, Northamptonshire, showing the broad open market-place characteristic of so many planned boroughs of the Middle Ages. The location of a church on the top right hand side of the photograph, well away from the main town centre, indicates that this was a site of an earlier settlement and that the new town of Brackley was laid out some way away from the original centre. The area around St Peter's church became known as the 'old town' during the later Middle Ages. In the fourteenth century Brackley was a staple town for wool and just a mile to the south-east was a great tournament ground at Evenley, both of which brought prosperity to the town during the later Middle Ages

The market was a trading place where town and country people congregated, but it was also a place of supervision and regulation. A number of well defined market shapes evolved or were designed to meet these needs. It was necessary to provide sufficient space for free movement within the market areas, while at the same time creating access and exit points which were capable of being controlled and suitable for the collection of tolls. This requirement often led to very narrow market entrances, which can still be found in many small towns today. Their presence is frequently the cause of modern traffic congestion. The long rectangular open space was a common form of market area, as at Clare (Suffolk) and Chipping Norton (Oxon), while funnel and triangular-shaped market areas were frequently created in southern and central England as at Hereford, Ely (Cambs), Woodstock and Bicester (Oxon). A less common but more striking form was the bow-shaped market area to be found at Thame (Oxon), and Marlborough (Wilts). In larger towns there were sometimes several markets, often with quite different shapes.

Sometimes it is difficult to identify medieval market areas because of encroachment or infilling which has altered their original shapes. In many cases it was a logical process for canvas stalls to be replaced by tiled *shoppa,* as the lord of the market, whether king, seigneur or burgess, saw that it was in his interest to have permanent rather than temporary market stalls. Encroachments consist of blocks of buildings occupying part or even all of the old market area. Today these buildings or their successors can be identified as they rarely possess attached gardens or closes, and are usually separated from the old market frontage by a narrow lane. Naturally enough it was in the most successful market centres that encroachment was most frequent. In the case of Ludlow (Salop) encroachments virtually blocked off the eastern end of a large broad rectangular market, completely hiding the substantial parish church of St Lawrence, with its fine late medieval porch. The market authorities generally displayed an ambivalent attitude to encroachments, for while they did contribute to congestion they also brought in a secure revenue. Ironically at Thame, the Bishops of Lincoln were persistently fined for encroachments which had been made in the market area, which they themselves had created.

Hereford provides an interesting example of a Saxon town that was adapting throughout the Middle Ages to meet increasing commercial pressures. The Saxon town was based on St Ethelbert's cathedral and the crossing of the river Wye. The grid of streets in the vicinity of the cathedral dates from the ninth century and the modern inner ring road precisely follows the line of the Saxon and later medieval defences. The shape of the *burh*, which has been revealed by excavation in recent years, was distorted by the insertion of a great Norman castle on the eastern side and by the growth of the cathedral precinct. The

46 Hereford town plan

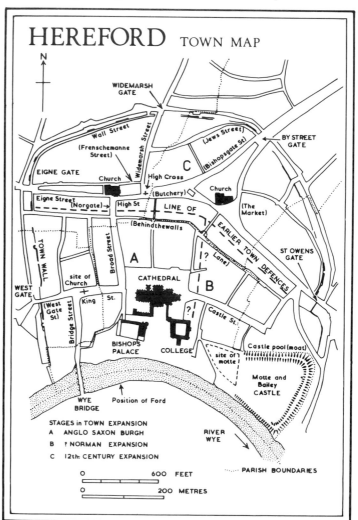

gradual westwards expansion of the cathedral and its associated buildings effectively filled up the interior of the early Saxon town. Accordingly when a new area to the north of the early town was enclosed within the defended area in the early Middle Ages a broad new market area was laid out running east to west at total variance with the traditional north-south axis of the town. Subsequently this and another market area were almost completely infilled. All Saints' Church originally occupied an island in a rectangular market running from the Eigne Gate to the High Cross, but encroachment has reduced this to two narrow, roughly parallel streets. A triangular market nearby occupied the northeastern area of the town but the whole of the centre of this area was infilled. The markets

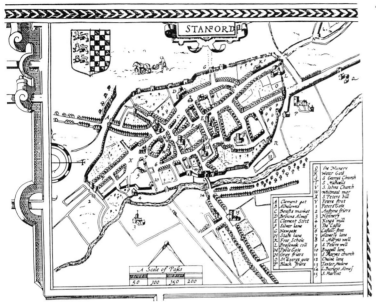

47 Speed's plan of Stamford, in the early seventeenth century

thus extinguished were then replaced by streets of specialist traders, such as the butchers in Butchers Row, while later on the livestock markets moved right outside the town centre. John Speed's town plans of the early seventeenth century, included as insets to his county maps, reveal just how many other county towns had infilled their centres in this way. In his *Theatre of Great Britain*, London 1614, Speed included plans of some 50 towns (Table 6).

Table 6 Speed's town plans

Chichester, Winchester, Newport (IOW), Southampton, Dorchester, Exeter, Launceston, Bath, Salisbury, Westminster, London, Colchester, Ipswich, Norwich, Cambridge, Hertford, Bedford, Buckingham, Reading, Oxford, Gloucester, Bristol, Hereford, Worcester, Warwick, Coventry, Northampton, Peterborough, Huntingdon, Ely, Oakham, Stamford, Leicester, Lincoln, Nottingham, Derby, Stafford, Lichfield, Shrewsbury, Chester, Lancaster, York, Richmond, Hull, Durham, Kendal, Carlisle, Berwick, Newcastle.

Lesser medieval place-names are often able to provide a useful source of information about the economy and development of the town – many of these place-names are more permanent than buildings. Specialised market names, such as Bull Ring, are often retained and are of value in reconstructing the function of such areas within the town plan. The common name 'Shambles' or the earlier 'Fleshshambles', is usually indicative of a meat market, and is derived from the Old English *Scamel*, Latin *scammelum*, meaning a little bench. Some names such as 'Newland' at Eynsham (Oxon), Pershore (Worcs), Whitchurch (Salop), Banbury (Oxon) and Cogges-by-Witney (Oxon) indicate newly settled land, often in the form of a planned extension. The names Old Town at Stratford-upon-Avon and Brackley (Northants) indicate the earlier village from which the town has developed. Street names can also indicate phases of a town's development: for instance, Old Street, Ludlow (Salop), and the many New Streets, as at Deddington (Oxon), were often contemporary with the town's medieval expansion. Street names often indicate former occupations and hence the status of particular areas of a town. 'Rother', 'Chipping' and 'Shambles', as well as simple 'Market' names, indicate places or streets where general markets were held. Specific types of market are indicated by such names as Cornhill and Cornsteading (London and Ottery St Mary, Cornwall) And Butcher's Row (Shrewsbury); and Butchery Lane, Draper, Mercer's Row, Woolmonger Street, Wood Hill, Horse Market, Sheep Street and Mare Hold (now Mayor Hold) in Northampton. In Pontefract, for instance, a remarkable collection of commercial trading names round the church of St Giles represents the infilled market-place west of the medieval town.

Town defences and suburbs

In 1086 about 48 towns appear to have had some form of communal defences. These were largely the Saxon *burhs*, many of which had reused Roman fortifications for their town walls. By about 1200 the defences in most of these towns had been neglected, to the point where they were of little use and it is quite clear that in the century and a half after the Norman Conquest, communal or town defences were not considered to be important, the emphasis being on private castle-building. From about 1200, however, the situation changed, and work on stone-built town defences began again. Obviously town walls were designed with defence in mind, but they did have other functions. Not least was the restriction of access and exit to the town, which was essential in order to control trade and levy tolls. Town walls were also seen as symbols of municipal status, and in those places such as Coventry where the construction of walls went on well into the fifteenth century status rather than defence seems to have been the primary motive for building them.

There is some evidence of work on urban defences in the later years of the twelfth century, but the greatest stimulus seems to have been in the early decades of the thirteenth when the threat of invasion and growing civic pride led many towns seriously to consider the erection of town walls. During the remainder of the thirteenth century, and to a lesser degree during the following two centuries, there was a steady increase in the number of towns which built defences. By 1500 there were few major regional centres in England and Wales which were not surrounded by defensive walls of some sort. Much of the documentary evidence comes from the record of what are known as 'murage grants'. These were the permissions

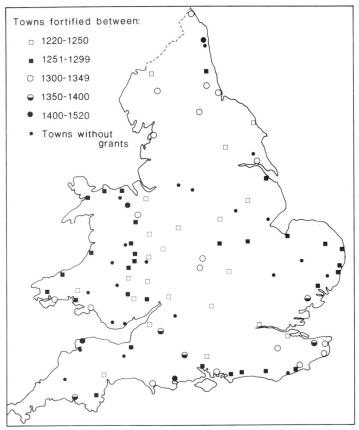

Towns fortified between:

□ 1220-1250

■ 1251-1299

○ 1300-1349

◑ 1350-1400

● 1400-1520

• Towns without grants

48 Distribution of towns in receipt of murage grants (after Turner)

granted by the king to levy a toll on goods coming into the town, the proceeds of which, in theory at least, were to be used for the provision of town defences. However, murage grants were only recorded for about half (51) of the 108 walled towns in the thirteenth century.

There were also the walled towns of North Wales established by Edward I which were financed directly by the crown rather than by a levy on goods. The most notable

49 The planted walled towns of North Wales (after M. Beresford

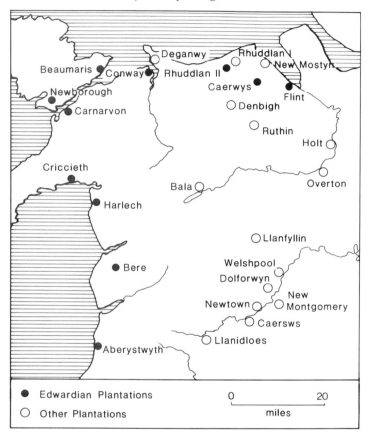

examples of these are the virtually complete circuits of Conway and Caernarvon. The walls of Conway, built between 1284 and 1287, form part of a larger defence scheme, the main element of which was the great castle. The walls are roughly triangular in plan with a circuit of about a mile. There was an outer ditch on the southern and northwestern sides, but on the northeast the river Conway formed the outer defence. There were 21 towers and 3 double-towered gates. The walls of Caernarvon which were built c. 1283–6 were also linked to the castle. There are also substantial remains at Denbigh including the Burgess Gate and the Goblin Tower, but only slight remains at Rhuddlan, where the defences were of earth and timber, and virtually nothing at Beaumaris. In mid-Wales there are no remains of the Edwardian defences at Aberystwyth and only earthwork remains at Montgomery. In South Wales there are good visible, but by no means complete, remains at Tenby and Pembroke.

In England the outstanding surviving town walls are at York and Chester, with less complete but still substantial

5 Castle and planned town at Caernarvon in north Wales. The town was built alongside the castle as part of Edward I's policy of conquering Wales at the end of the fourteenth century. By 1312 there were 124 burgage plots in the town

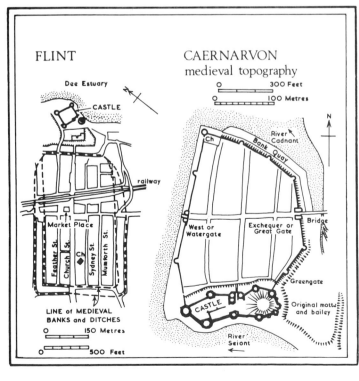

50 The medieval topography of Flint and Caernarvon

remains at Canterbury, Southampton, Oxford, Norwich, Yarmouth and Newcastle. In addition to these there are sites where the principal remains are in the form of a gateway as at Rye, Winchelsea, King's Lynn, Hartlepool, Warkworth, Alnwick and Beverley. At its greatest extent the town wall of York was over 3 miles long, while at Chester the circuit is about 2 miles long and is virtually complete, although it has been considerably altered, and none of the original gates survive. On the north and east the medieval walls follow the line of the legionary fortress, making use of original Roman work. King Charles's Tower stands at the northeastern angle of both the medieval walls and the original Roman fortress. Although originally built in the late thirteenth or early fourteenth century the tower was almost entirely rebuilt in the seventeenth century after considerable damage suffered in the Civil War. The Water Tower stands at the end of a short spur wall at the northwest corner of the medieval defences, and was part of the defences of the harbour, which is now Chester racecourse. The remains of outer town walls tend to be less extensive. The existing walls at Canterbury belong to the late fourteenth and early fifteenth century, although they represent rebuilding of an earlier system. At Southampton about half of the original circuit of about a mile has survived including 13 towers and 4 gates. Other sites with visible remains of walls include Newcastle-on-Tyne, Norwich, Oxford and Yarmouth. At a number of other places the principal remnant of the town defences is a gatehouse. These tend to have survived because the accommodation above the gateway was useful for domestic or business purposes.

The survival of town defences is variable and it is often difficult to track down long stretches of wall. Turrets and gates have a better survival record, often because of their sheer size or their suitability as town gaols down to the nineteenth century, but many have been destroyed within the past century as increasing traffic demands brought about their removal. At Canterbury, Lincoln and Southampton massive gateways survive, either isolated on traffic islands or still vulnerable to passing traffic; an extreme example is at Canterbury where the buses had to be specially designed to negotiate the narrow gateways of West Gate. There remain only short pieces of the long defence line of Norwich which together with the river Wensum stretched for 2½ miles. London's city wall has also suffered badly over recent centuries, buried in the dense concentration of buildings that have used it as a convenient back wall, but the clearing of Second World War bombed sites and more recently development within the City has exposed some impressive stretches, of which the Barbican site is now the best example. In a considerable number of other towns, although the walls have gone, their alignments can still be clearly traced through the road pattern, the alignment of property boundaries and breaks of slope. Two particularly good examples, where the urban topography reveals the line of the medieval defences are at Shrewsbury and Bath. Very few towns have lost all trace of their walls, although those of Barnstaple, for instance, have left nothing obvious on the ground. Field-work may often help in the identification of lost ditches and some defences are still remembered in street names as in Walfurlong in Tamworth (Staffs) and Walditch (now Joyce Pool) in Warwick. Gate names can be useful in the south of England but in the north the name often means a 'road' or 'way', and hence some care is necessary in their interpretation. It is important to remember, however, that long after their defensive function had ceased the town's defences continued to be used as parish and other forms of administrative boundaries.

The cramped nature of the medieval town within the walls was accentuated by the large amounts of space devoted to non-residential purposes. At Exeter, for example, the cathedral close occupied almost a third of the town, with the castle taking another small area, while at Lincoln, excluding the large walled suburb of Newport, the castle and cathedral together controlled over a third of the old Roman town area even though much of the cathedral close lay outside. With the expansion of many towns in the early medieval period it is not surprising that extensive surburbs later developed beyond the walls. At Bristol, Lincoln and York the new suburbs were provided with defences through an extension of the walls, while other towns stretched their jurisdiction over their suburbs but did not have the protection of a wall. Many continental towns have a series of walls that mark successive phases of growth, some of them covering the post-medieval period, but similar examples from England are rare. Groups of foreigners who often established separate quarters are revealed in place-names such as Petty France (Westminster), French Street (Southampton), Danes Gate (Lincoln), Fleming Gate (Beverley), and also in the forms Jewry or Jury, indicating the location of the medieval Jewish quarter.

Town churches and religious houses

At the time of the dissolution of the monasteries urban houses suffered particularly badly. Only two of the great urban monastic churches, Gloucester and Chester, became cathedral churches, whilst a handful of others such as Tewkesbury and Evesham survived as parish churches. The dissolution was often followed by widespread pillaging of monastic sites to provide building stone for other parts of the town; sections of the magnificent abbey church of Bury St Edmunds can be recognised in fragments of carved stonework scattered throughout the town's buildings. In some places the monastic precinct and some of the associated lesser buildings have survived. For instance, Wells cathedral precinct is clearly demarcated by two rows of houses built for the Vicars Choral about 1348, and on either side are the houses of cathedral officers such as the Master of the Fabric, Archdeacon and Chancellor. Anti-clerical feeling that developed in the towns in the later Middle Ages was of such dimensions that monasteries and cathedral closes began to protect themselves more effectively from the populace. Thus the Bishop of Bath and Wells built a substantial moat around his palace in the early fourteenth century, crossed through a

56 The cathedral at Wells with the virtually fortified bishop's palace on the right. On the left is a row of medieval houses, which houses the cathedral clergy and is known as the Vicar's Close.

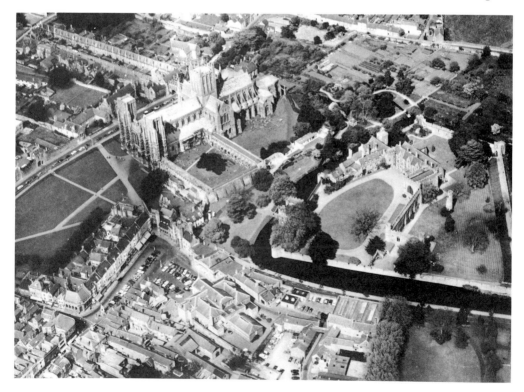

defended gateway that was added in the following century. The massive gateways that survive at Bury St Edmunds and St Albans are to some extent a reflection of the anxiety that beset fourteenth-century abbots. In some towns the dissolution of religious houses within the town provided space for urban expansion, but despite this the form of the precinct was frequently preserved, as for example the precinct of the Greyfriars, Worcester, which can be traced partly from surviving remains and property boundaries.

Although many ecclesiastical buildings such as urban monasteries, chantry chapels and hospitals have fared badly, the medieval church has survived as the most visible remnant of the medieval town. Almshouses or hospitals stood a better chance of being undisturbed, although those which were of a secular nature from the start are now the most conspicuous. Lord Leycester's Hospital in Warwick was one of the few late medieval timber-framed buildings to survive a fire that destroyed much of the town centre in 1694. It was formerly a guild house, which had been transformed into almshouses in the late sixteenth century. Browne's Hospital in Stamford founded by William Browne in the reign of Henry VII as an almshouse is a well-known example of a late medieval building which still continues to perform its original function.

The high density of medieval churches in the major towns of London, York, Bristol and Norwich was a note-worthy feature of the townscape, although many of the original structures have not survived to the present day. Norwich now boasts the highest number of medieval chur-ches of any English town, although many no longer perform an ecclesiastical function. Shire towns throughout the country tend to have a large number of parishes, but in eastern England even relatively small towns contained up to a dozen medieval churches. In the older established towns parish churches and other ecclesiastical buildings were to be found every few streets, and although some of these churches can be explained in terms of guild associ-ations, the majority of them reflected the very high densi-ties of population which were to be found in most quarters of the medieval town. In contrast, the newly planted towns are often characterised by a solitary medieval church sometimes serving a large parish.

The church-market-place relationship in many of the new towns was also of considerable importance. Boston's famous 'Stump' dominates its massive market-place,

57 Aerial view of Boston, Lincolnshire, with the famous tower or 'Stump' which dominates the adjacent market-place.

acting not only as a beacon for vessels across the dangerous sands of the Wash, but also as a reassurance to the town's burgesses of the success of their new venture. For those towns where population pressure brought about the creation of a second parish (or, as at Heden in Yorkshire East Riding, and New Salisbury, three) within the medieval period the new churches were primarily functional and did not carry as much civic status as the market church.

Table 7 The founders of towns (after Beresford)

England	No.	%
Kings alone	21	(12)
Seigneurs alone	77	(45)
Bishops alone	25	(15)
Abbots alone	31	(18)
Unknown	18	(10)
Total	172	

Wales	No.	%
Kings alone	29	(35)
Seigneurs alone	39	(46)
Bishops alone	6	(7)
Native princes alone	5	(6)
Unknown	5	(6)
Total	84	

Table 8 Areas of planted towns contrasted with mother parishes, census of 1801 (after Beresford)

	Acres	Area of Mother parish
West Looe	4	2,661
East Looe	1	3,193
Oakehampton	10	9,542
Bishops Castle	11	5,638
Mitchell	15	7,022
North Shields	36	2,285
Newport, I.O.W	59	9,579
Tregoney	69	2,300
Stony Stratford	70	4,240
Weymouth	77	1,702
Harwich	87	1,392
South Shields	90	4,225
Boroughbridge	95	2,241
Uxbridge	99	4,845
New Lymington	100	1,415
Losthwithiel	110	6,790
Hartlepool	137	2,465

New towns of the Middle Ages

Considerable emphasis has been placed upon the legal and commercial elements in medieval towns, but until fairly recently relatively little attention has been paid to the story to be gleaned from town topography. The publication of Maurice Beresford's *New Towns of the Middle Ages* (1967) was responsible for demonstrating the importance of ground plans in understanding a town's history and in particular just how many English and Welsh towns had deliberately planned origins. However, in the mid-nineteenth century the phenomenon of the medieval new town had already been identified, although this discovery was not followed up subsequently by urban historians. Mr Hudson Turner in his book *Some Account of Domestic Architecture in England from Edward I to Richard II* (1853), wrote an account which could have been based entirely on observations of Ludlow or Salisbury:

> There is, however, still another class of towns which were entirely founded in the Middle Ages, built from their foundations on a new site for some specific object, which have not been specifically noticed. These towns are more regular and symmetrical than most modern towns, and are built on an excellent scientific plan, combining very close packing with great convenience for individuals, while the principal streets are wide, open and straight, crossing each other at right angles only. There are always two parallel streets at a short distance one from the other and connected by short streets at frequent intervals; between these principal streets and also in parallel lines are narrow streets or lanes. Corresponding to the modern mews and employed for the same purpose: by this means each plot of ground for building on is of a uniform size and shape, a parallelogram with one end facing a principal street and another a lane. In some towns each building plot, or, when built upon, each house, was also divided by a narrow passage or court leading from the principal street to the lane, serving as a water course and surface drain. Sometimes when a large house was required two plots were thrown together and the passage omitted; and in some towns these narrow passages were not used at all.

The earliest of new towns came into being immediately after the Norman Conquest, often outside monastic establishments at places such as Abingdon, Battle and Bury St Edmunds, or outside a castle in the case of Ludlow. The presence of water, either as a river or along the coast, acted as a natural break-point in many travellers' journeys and hence proved particularly attractive for new-town foundations, and accordingly those established on coastal positions such as the new towns at King's Lynn, Boston and Kingston-upon-Hull were often the most successful. In the case of Newcastle-upon-Tyne the Norman castle acted as the pre-urban nucleus, overlooking the new river bridge as well as the Great North Road and thus combining a strategic situation with one of considerable economic advantage. Subsequently an open settlement (*suburbium*) developed round the hill, with a market by the river and a church on the plateau. The combined bridging point and estuarine seaport soon grew as an important borough trading in wool, leather, and other merchandise and became the outstanding coal export centre of medieval England. The town spread along the river bank and over three adjoining plateaux; so that the fourteenth-century town wall encompassed the pre-urban nucleus, the *suburbium*, the medieval harbour quarter, the recently incorporated village of Pandon, and three roadside extensions on the plateau with new markets, three additional churches, six urban friaries and other religious houses in peripheral positions.

Towns sited at river crossings were also assured, at least in prosperous well-populated areas, of a good start. Stratford-upon-Avon, Hungerford, Ludlow, and Chelmsford had little problem in filling up their burgage plots. In 1086 Stratford-upon-Avon had no burgesses, and appears to have been just a small rural settlement, but it had grown considerably in the twenty years after the Conquest and continued to do so during the twelfth century. By 1182 the number of peasant landholders had practically doubled, although the settlement was still primarily rural in character. At the end of the twelfth century John de Coutances, Bishop of Worcester (1196–8) decided to found a borough and market town here. On 25 January 1196 he obtained a charter from Richard I for a weekly Thursday market following which he formally created a borough, laying it out in the uniform thin rectangular building plots referred to by Hudson and which are known as 'burgages'. These were to be held by 'burgage tenure' at a money rent of 1s a year in lieu of all feudal services. Burgesses were also exempt from tolls. In 1214 Bishop Walter Grey also obtained the grant of a fair to continue for two days on the eve of the Trinity. Like so many medieval new towns Stratford was grafted on to an existing settlement or township, with three streets running parallel and three at right angles to the river. A sinuous curve in the alignment of some of the burgage plots suggests that they could well have been laid out on top of open-field strips. A similar usage of former arable strips is known from other medieval new towns, most notably Thame (Oxon). The burgage plots had frontages of almost 60 feet and stretched back some 200 feet, which would have provided the burgage with sufficient space to erect a substantial town house. The typical fourteenth-century burgess's house would have consisted of an entrance passage and several rooms on the ground floor facing the street with other buildings around the garden or courtyard behind. Frontages were often subdivided between several dwellings, each with a door leading on to the main street.

In Stratford the wealthiest man paid a rent of 18s, that is the equivalent to 18 burgages, but the majority held single burgage plots or even less. In 1251–2 over two thirds of the original burgages were still undivided, and most of the rest were split only into two. Although there are references to plot subdivision as early as the thirteenth century, when half – and even quarter-burgages were recorded, the excavation of some town sites has suggested that many original urban property boundaries are of considerable antiquity. In Westwick Street, Norwich, basic

51 The regular layouts of Stratford-upon-Avon and Thame

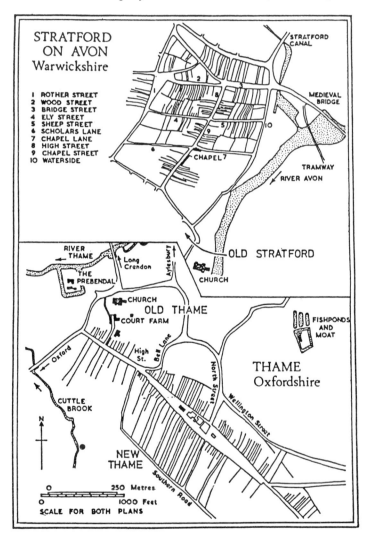

property boundaries remained unchanged from the twelfth to the eighteenth centuries, while excavations in nearby Oak Street have revealed a similar pattern over a shorter time period. Even when the town experienced considerable population expansion in the sixteenth and seventeenth centuries, this was carried out within the medieval boundaries, by infilling and adding further storeys. When subdivision did occur it tended to force changes in the building alignment, the long-axis turning at right angles to the street. Stamford and Stratford-upon-Avon both clearly exhibit this phenomenon.

In a detailed survey of 1251–2 there were two very distinct parts to Stratford: first the manor of Old Stratford,

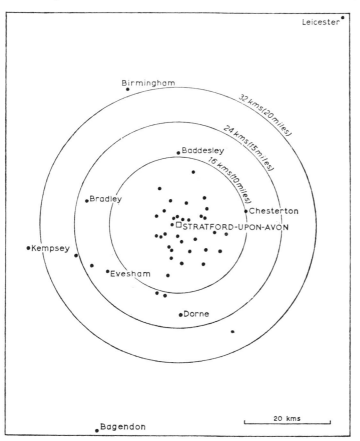

52 Immigration into Stratford-upon-Avon to 1252 (after E. M. Carus-Wilson)

and second the new Borough of Stratford. In the manor there were some 70 tenants, which represented a considerable increase over 1182; about 50 were customary tenants holding land in villeinage. In the borough there were 234 tenants holding 250 burgages, 54 pieces of ground, 14 shops, 10 stalls, 2 ovens, and 2 dyepans. Only two tenants' names survive which are coincidental in both surveys, so altogether there were over 300 tenants. This represented a six-fold increase within half a century. The two communities were administered quite separately with distinct manor and borough courts, and this separate jurisdiction of rural parish and urban borough provided a constant source of friction. A draft charter drawn up as late as 1600 sought to bring all the parish into the borough, but it was never completed and consequently the townspeople were obliged to use the church at Old Stratford until eventually a chapel of ease was built within the town in 1855. At their foundation many such chapels were initially only endowed with a chapel of ease, the rights to the important offices of baptism, marriage and burial being reserved by the existing church out of whose parish the town was carved. It was not uncommon for the ancient parochial centre jealously to guard its rights and refuse to hand them over to the new usurper. At New Woodstock, Oxfordshire, for instance, although the mother church at Bladon founded St Mary's as a dependent chapelry the little parish church did not relinquish its ecclesiastical domination of the busy town until the nineteenth century, while at Henley-in-Arden the shape of the administrative boundaries shows clearly how a new borough had been cut from the parish of Wootton Wawen. There was no church at Henley until 1367 when the Bishop of Worcester permitted a chapel of ease to be built at the townsmen's charge in view of the inconvenience of reaching Wootton Wawen church two miles away in bad weather. At Market Harborough (Leicestershire), built within the parish of Great Bowden, the new town was not granted its own church until a century after its foundation and even then Great Bowden retained the rights to burial. Hence the tall spired church of St Dionysius still has no churchyard or burial ground.

The surnames of the inhabitants of Stratford suggested that 90 percent came from villages or hamlets within a 12–mile radius, and most of these were from the rural area within 6 miles of the town, an area which corresponded to the Stratford market area. As there was already a well established town at Warwick only 8 miles away Stratford's success may on the surface appear surprising. Additionally Alcester and Henley-in-Arden came into existence as new commercial centres at about the same time as Stratford. These too were no more than 8 miles distant. However, Alcester and Henley served the Forest of Arden, an area which was being rapidly colonised at that time, while Stratford, like Warwick, was ideally sited to serve both Arden and the Felden. Furthermore, down the street, the Roman road from which the town took its name, merchants could reach the wool-producing Cotswolds. Stratford's prime advantage, however, was its location at

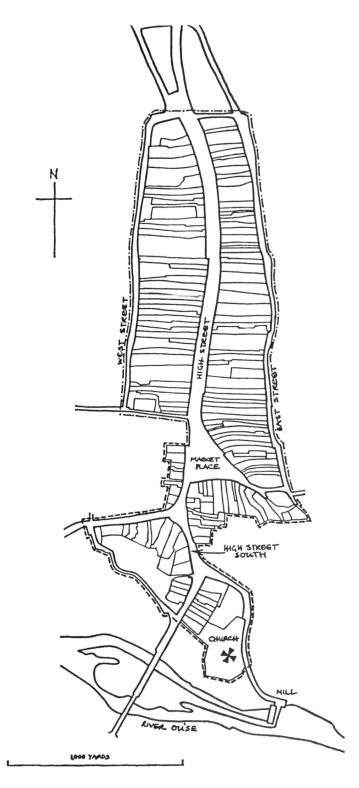

N

WEST STREET

HIGH STREET

EAST STREET

MARKET PLACE

HIGH STREET SOUTH

CHURCH

MILL

RIVER OUSE

1000 YARDS

53 Olney, Bucks. A
borough added to a
village but with no
physical separation
(after M. Beresford)

the junction of these lines of communication with the navigable Avon, then part of the great waterway system of the Severn valley, looking to Gloucester and Bristol as major markets and as ports from which Midland products could be shipped.

By no means all the new planted towns were successful and relatively few were founded after 1300. One of the few medieval foundations after 1348 was Queenborough in north Kent, which was intended as a naval base for

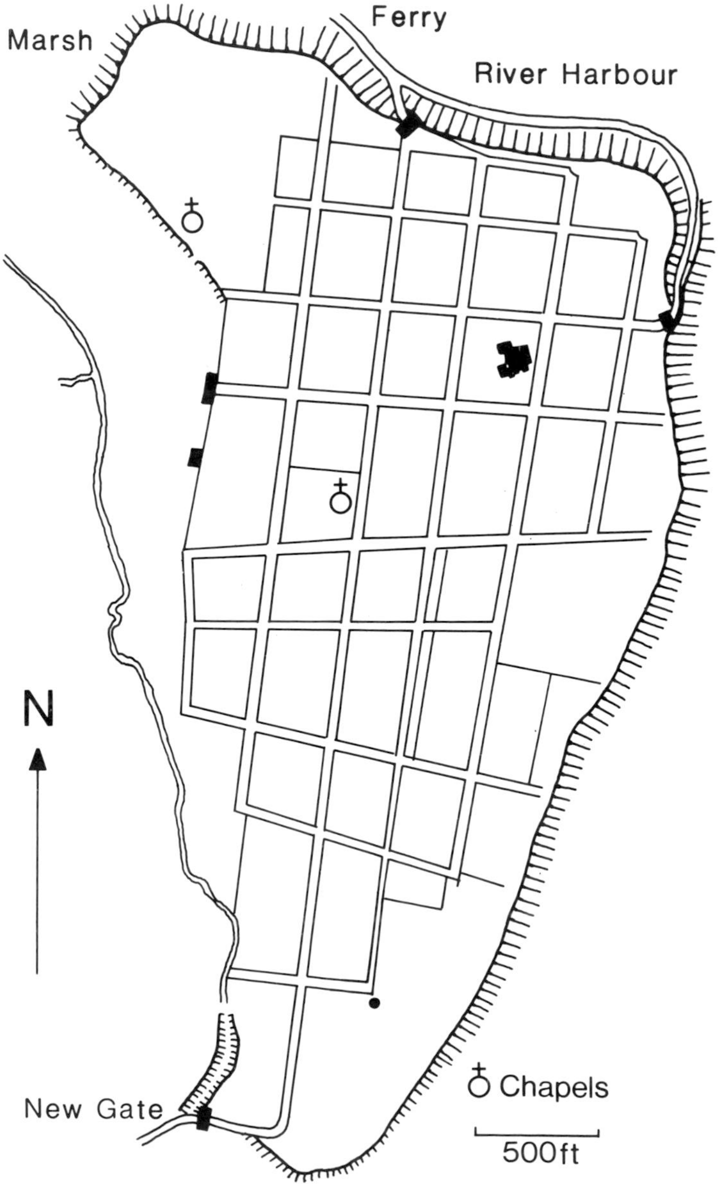

54 The regular laid-out grid pattern of the unsuccessful port of New Winchelsea, Sussex. Edward I planned the town at the end of the thirteenth century. Late foundations such as New Winchelsea were particularly vulnerable and it failed for a variety of reasons, but mostly because of coastal silting which made the port inoperable

Marsh

Ferry

River Harbour

N

New Gate

Ő Chapels

500 ft

use during the French wars. The town was founded to
accompany the new castle on the western edge of the Isle
of Sheppey, and named after Edward's queen, Philippa,
in the last year of her life. The castle can now only be
identified as a circular area of open ground near to the
railway station. The broad High Street runs in an almost
straight line from the station to the river bank where there
is a small quay. The town appears never to have consisted
of much more than the burgage plots on either side of the

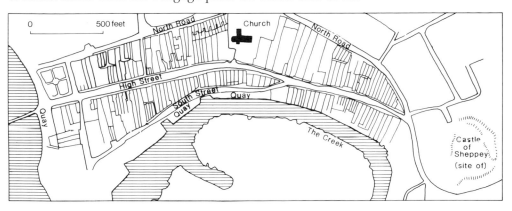

High Street. The parish church stands near the Town Hall
on the north side of the High Street; despite the town's
royal foundation in 1607 there were disputes concerning
the tithes which had to be paid to the mother church of
Minster. The town's foundation charter sets out the events
and crown's motives: the king,

55 Queenborough. One
of the last medieval
planned towns, it was
created by Edward III

> out of care for his subjects and realm and their protection has
> lately founded and fortified in a suitable place in the island
> of Sheppey where there is a broad and deep arm of the sea
> convenient for ships to put in at, a town and castle which
> he has named the Queen's Borough. In order that many
> might more readily come and live there he granted borough
> status, two markets a week, two fairs a year, the right to elect
> a Mayor and two bailiffs, together with independence from
> the jurisdiction of the Cinque Ports.

In July 1368 Queenborough replaced Sandwich as the
Staple Port along the coast of Kent and Sussex from
Gravesend to Winchelsea and from the same date the
customs duty on cloth was also collected at Queenborough
instead of Sandwich. This privilege lapsed as early as
January 1378 and Sandwich resumed its traditional role of
Head Port for this section of coast. Thereafter Queenborough declined. Its single main street is a vivid reminder
that late foundations stood much less chance of success,
even if they did have exalted patronage.

Any town coming late into the race, when agricultural

activity was already in recession and a century of decline lay ahead, needed exceptionally good fortune. In 1286 Edward I established Newton on the shores of Poole Harbour as a port from which Purbeck marble could be exported, but despite generous privileges offered to new settlers, the town never seems to have operated successfully and by 1558 only one cottage remained. On the Isle of Wight the similarly named Newtown, founded in 1256

58 Aerial view of Newtown (Francheville), Isle of Wight, which was founded by bishops of Winchester and went into a gradual decline during the later Middle Ages. It now survives in the form of field boundaries which mark the former burgage tenements

by the Bishops of Winchester, experienced a slower decay, but by the eighteenth century it too had gone. Even if a new town thrived during the early medieval period it did not necessarily maintain the same prosperity subsequently. New Buckenham in Norfolk which was founded in the mid-twelfth century is now no more than a small village, yet was initially successful and by 1305 over 170 tenants were recorded here and when the medieval church was constructed to replace the chapel that had formerly served the town, it was placed outside the arranged town plan.

Many of the newcomers failed because they were sited within areas already well served by market centres. Eastern England was both highly populated and highly urbanised in the early Middle Ages and therefore there had to be exceptional circumstances operating for late plantations to survive. Another principal reason for shrinkage or failure was the loss of a strategic function and the inability to develop a commercial base instead. Along the Welsh Marches there are a group of such towns, created initially by the Normans to subdue the Welsh, which withered away during the later Middle Ages. Today

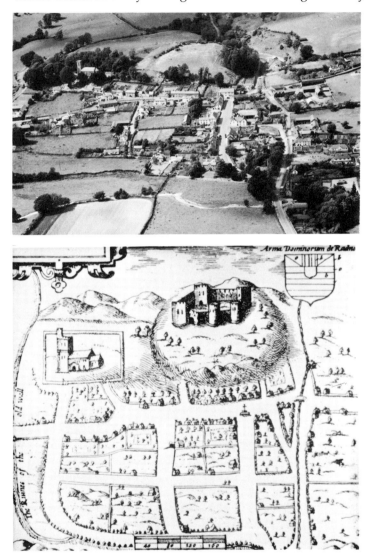

59a Aerial view of New Radnor which lies two and a half miles to the west of Old Radnor in the Welsh borderland. This town was built in the mid-thirteenth century as a fortified town but it never really succeeded, as can be seen from plate 59b.

59b A plan of the decayed town of New Radnor from Speed's *Theatre of the Empire of Great Britain*, 1611

the landscape of the Marches is littered with places that were once granted market charters and the rights of boroughs, towns which have since failed completely. A rectangular-shaped field where cattle graze, as at Huntingdon, may be the sole visual evidence of a former market-place. Narrow high-hedged fields as at Richard's Castle mark the plots that attracted the burgesses to a newly founded borough eight centuries ago. Deep lanes and foot paths indicate the lines of former streets, and the once formidable castle of a forgotten founding Marcher lord is now no more than overgrown mounds.

At Caus in the parish of Westbury in the foothills of the Long Mountain a few miles from Shrewsbury there are the earthworks of a massive fortified town and castle created by the Corbet family. Sited on a high ridge, it commanded the valley road from Shrewsbury to Montgomery. The ruins of a massive earthwork and stone castle with outer fortifications now have to be disentangled from the undergrowth; nothing except earthworks remains of the borough. The town appears to have been created by Roger Corbet in 1198 and it is recorded that by 1349 there were 58 burgesses living here. In the mid-fifteenth century much of the town appears to have been burnt down during the rebellion of Sir Griffith Vaughan. By the time a survey was made of the site in 1521 the castle was being recorded as being in 'grete ruyne and decay'; thus the borough of Caus faded away in the later Middle Ages and is remembered now by its earthworks, and its place-name.

In the words of Maurice Beresford, Caus was like 'a prehistoric monster crushed beneath the weight of its own armour' which was incapable of adjusting to the new economic conditions of the later Middle Ages. Today apart from a single farm the site is completely deserted. The great tree-covered motte and bailey and the line of the town ramparts can be clearly identified, but here and there are more subtle remnants of this once important town in the form of stone buttresses, wells and hidden sections of the town wall.

Another town with a rather similar history lies further west into Wales beyond New Radnor; this is Cefnllys. The site of Cefnllys stands on a rocky spur 300 feet above the wooded gorge of the river Ithon. The Mortimer family built a castle here between 1240 and 1246, at the same time as other outposts at New Montgomery and Paincastle. It is recorded that in 1332 Cefnllys had 20 burgesses and a survey of 1360 records it as a borough. But it would appear that this highly exposed settlement had little chance of long-term success and was already in decline by the time that Edward I led his attack on Wales. A document of 1383 mentions only 10 burgesses here. Like other border boroughs of its type the earthworks of the actual town are difficult to disentangle. Only a short stretch of street with possible burgage plots can be identified as earthworks within the rampart of the Iron Age fort, and like so many of its colleagues it has been extensively robbed by stone quarrying. Like Caus it is dominated by a massive motte and castle defence. At the close of the sixteenth century the antiquary Camden described Cefnllys as a 'lonely

ruin', but surprisingly it survived as a 'rotten borough' into the nineteenth century.

At Huntingdon on the Welsh/English border in Hereford a borough was created in the late twelfth century as part of a policy of political reprisal. In 1173 after a rebellion against the king, the honour of Kington, a planted borough close by, was suppressed and absorbed into the new Marcher kingdom of Huntingdon. This was granted to William de Braos and, as a result, Kington castle was abandoned sometime before 1230 and the government of the lordship was settled at Huntingdon. The outlines of the new borough were sketched out between the castle mound and the church. Ironically Huntingdon failed to make any real progress and the successful town in the area was Kington-in-the-Fields which had been laid out in a valley bottom some distance away from the old borough of Kington with its church and castle. Huntingdon is today perhaps one of the most spectacular of the failed border boroughs, occupying as it still does a little territorial enclave which projects into Wales. The borough boundary

60 Aerial view of the failed Marcher town of Cefnllys. The medieval borough occupied an Iron Age hillfort, but its isolated upland location meant that it could not prosper by trading during the late Middle Ages and it therefore went into a decline. By the time the antiquarian Camden came here he was able to describe it as a 'lonely ruin'. Nevertheless it survived as a rotten borough into the nineteenth century

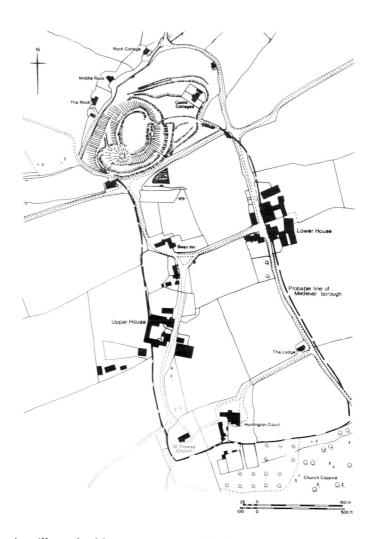

56 Huntingdon,
Herefordshire, a
failed medieval
borough planted on
the Welsh border

is still marked by a pronounced indentation in the border. The earthworks here take the form of an extended outer bailey marking the town precinct and the lumps and bumps of the medieval settlement indicate former town houses. Its situation, however, is so rural that it is difficult to imagine that the settlement ever harboured any urban ambitions.

Another site where today it is difficult to imagine that there was ever a town is Richard's Castle near Ludlow. In 1304 there were some 103 burgesses here. However like Huntingdon and Caus and Cefnllys, Richard's Castle went into a decline in the later Middle Ages. Now only the church of St Bartholomew survives, noted because of its detached bell tower, along with the earthwork outlines of the borough. The reasons for its failure appear to be largely commercial. Sitting on a high bluff looking eastwards it was to some extent rather uncomfortably situated and as Ludlow thrived in the later Middle Ages so the commercial fortunes of Richard's Castle must have declined. A little to the south, Wigmore occupies a very similar situation and although a village with a market area survives here, only the enormous earthworks of the castle and former borough give some indication that this was the capital of the great medieval Mortimer kingdom.

Chapter eight

The church in the later Middle Ages

The fortunes of the medieval church accurately reflected the fortunes of the nation as a whole. By the late twelfth century the austere Romanesque was giving way to the more flamboyant and architecturally adventurous Gothic, which developed in the Ile de France and rapidly spread to Britain. The thirteenth century provided the optimum economic and social conditions for large-scale enterprises of church building and rebuilding. These conditions persisted into the early decades of the fourteenth century by which time the cost of foreign wars followed by the agricultural crises and the Black Death saw an end to the era of architectural development. The fortunes of the monasteries also reflected the general economic climate of the period. They enjoyed considerable prosperity during the thirteenth and early fourteenth centuries, followed by a period of stagnation and decline which lasted well into the fifteenth century and finally enjoyed a brief Indian Summer in the later decades of the fifteenth and early sixteenth centuries, before they were extinguished during the fourth decade of the sixteenth century.

Although many parish churches were rebuilt or modified between 1350 and 1500, using the late medieval perpendicular style, there were no perpendicular cathedrals and few perpendicular monastic churches. Only Great Malvern and Sherborne were essentially perpendicular, and both of these involved the adaptation of an existing fabric rather than a completely fresh start. Even when Bath Abbey was rebuilt by Bishop King in the early sixteenth century the entire church was less than half the length of its Norman predecessor. The 150 years between the accession of Edward III and the Battle of Bosworth Field is an age of contradictions, during which fine new parish churches were built while others were left to decay. Dr Bridbury has argued that the later Middle Ages provide 'an astonishing record of resurgent vitality and enterprise', while others have seen it as a period of universal decay. The testimony of church building during the later Middle Ages shows that the conspicuous wealth of both the monasteries and cathedrals had largely slipped away. The grand buildings of the fifteenth century were largely on a local scale and church building and rebuilding was undertaken on a much more selective basis. Thus we find the great perpendicular enterprises at Boston, Yarmouth, Hull, Lavenham and Collumpton being undertaken at the same time that some of the greatest Romanesque and Gothic cathedrals and monastic parish churches in the land

were allowed to deteriorate and a considerable number of humbler parish churches contracted or were closed down. In the words of Richard Morris, 'far from being a period of architectural decline the later Middle Ages saw redoubled building activity, but at a neighbourhood level.'

One of the reasons for the relative paucity of new church building in the fifteenth century was that quite apart from

there being less money available from the traditional
benefactors – the crown, the nobility and monastic estates
– such funds that there were often found their way into
different building enterprises. It is no accident that in the
fifteenth century those patrons who were putting their
money into churches often showed a preoccupation with
towers. It has been pointed out that of all the elements
which went to make up a great church, a tower was the

57 Graph representing
the number of
building projects
started and those
actually in progress
during the Middle
Ages (after R. Morris)

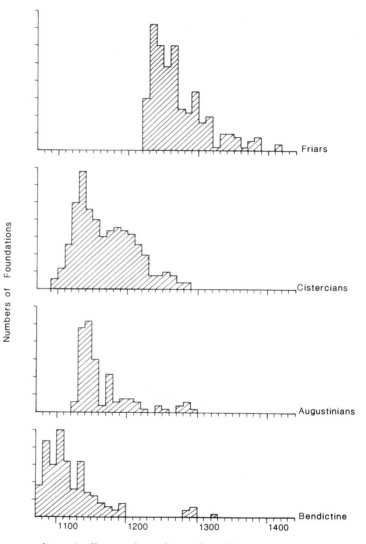

most liturgically useless but also the most impressive.
Howden, York, Gloucester, Great Malvern, Norwich,
Durham and Chester all had fifteenth-century towers or
spires, while at Canterbury in 1493 Cardinal Morten
commissioned John Wastel to double the height of the

central tower. In prosperous East Anglia and the Cots-wolds it was the ostentatious spire and porch that received attention during the fifteenth century. At Swaffham in Norfolk, however, the church was rebuilt from ground level in the fifteenth and early sixteenth centuries, with funds provided by wealthy parishioners. The *Black Book of Swaffham* records that John Chapman and Catherine, his wife, contributed the north aisle, with the glazing, seating

and paving of the same, and with the further gift of £120 'to the makyng of the New Stepyll'. More than at any other time money was going directly into those projects that would make the most immediate impact. Typical of this movement was the rebuilding of Dunster church (Somerset), where in 1442 the parishioners contracted a mason to build a tower, 'with three angle buttresses . . . battlements and pinnacles, 100 feet in height. The parish shall bring all materials to the churchyard . . . and pay

62 The spire of the parish church of Weobley, Herefordshire, dominates the small medieval 'borough' and the surrounding countryside. It was a product of the late Middle Ages and of the prosperity brought to the region by the wool industry

him 13s 4d for every foot built, and 20s for the pinnacles.
He shall complete the work within three years.'

Elsewhere from the crown downwards money was
going into buildings and monuments which reflected a
different economic, and to some extent social order.
Market crosses and market halls, almshouses and places
of learning – schools and colleges. The most ambitious
of the fifteenth-century foundations was King's College,
Cambridge, which began on Easter Sunday 1441 when the
young King Henry VI laid the foundation stone of the
gateway, which was to be one of the principal architectural
features of the new college. On 12 March 1448 Henry
issued the document known as his 'Will' which laid down
his architectural scheme with considerable precision. The
king wanted the college as a whole to be built 'in a large
fourme, clene and substancial, settyng a parte superfluit
of too gret curious werkes of entaille and besy moldyng':
in other words it was to conform to the simpler style
of perpendicular architecture which was then becoming
fashionable. The work was to be financed by an annual
payment of £1,000 from the revenues of the Duchy of
Lancaster beginning at Michaelmas 1447 and continuing
for at least twenty years.

The most remarkable feature of the church was the great
height and length of the aisleless body which despite its
size was designed as a chapel to be used solely for
collegiate purposes. The chapel was the only portion of
Henry VI's design that was completed and even this was
not ready for use until half a century after his death, for
the project fell victim to the Wars of the Roses. Some of the
difficulties which faced the builders after the Lancastrian
defeat at the battle of St Albans (23 May 1455) are described

63 The chapel of King's
College, Cambridge,
built in the second half
of the fifteenth
century. The later
Middle Ages saw a
significant move away
from ecclesiastical to
secular sponsored
building, but the
chapels at Cambridge
and Eton formed parts
of larger schemes and
provide us with some
of the grandest of all
medieval church
buildings

in a memorandum by Provost Wodelarke:

> When Henry the Sixth, founder of the college, was taken prisoner by the Earls of Salisbury and Warwick, they pledged their word to him, in order to gain his goodwill, that they would hasten the completion of his church and royal building operations in Cambridge; and they ordered me to use all possible despatch in getting together, by the help of royal letters, as many stonemasons and other workmen as I could, with the view of carrying on his buildings at Cambridge, and especially his collegiate church, so that all the workmen might reach Cambridge at the same time.

The twin foundations of Henry VI's Eton College and King's College Cambridge have a special place in the history of medieval architecture. More than any other surviving buildings, with the exception of Westminster Abbey, they represent the personal patronage of architecture by an English king in the Middle Ages. Eton and King's College were Henry's own conception, and according to Colvin they can be seen as 'the one permanent achievement of a reign which saw neither political nor constitutional progress'. It has been suggested that if Henry had been a more effective ruler, both colleges could perhaps have been completed in his lifetime. Nevertheless the two chapels, Eton still without its nave, and Cambridge without its quadrangle, are amongst the greatest architectural achievements of medieval England.

58 Eton College as planned by Henry V (*right*) and as actually built (*left*) (after Willis and Clark and the Royal Commission on Historical Monuments)

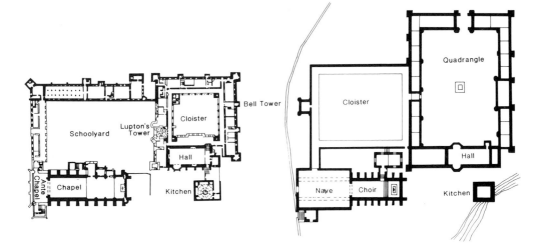

The cathedrals

Without doubt the crowning glory of the English church in the Middle Ages was the cathedral. Even today they represent England's greatest public buildings, and until the Industrial Revolution they were the largest buildings in the land. After the Norman Conquest the diocesan map of England had been largely redrawn, with the transfer of bishoprics from rural to urban settings. By 1200 this process was almost complete and England was divided into seventeen large dioceses which survived right up until the Reformation. It was partly because they were so few and so large that their mother churches – the cathedrals – unlike many of the multitude of provincial cathedrals in continental Europe, became so grand.

Another major difference between England and the Continent was that during the Middle Ages almost half the English cathedrals (seven) were also the abbey churches of great Benedictine monasteries, of which the bishop was also abbot. These were Canterbury, Rochester, Winchester, Worcester, Durham, Norwich, Ely and Bath. The latter, which served intermittently or jointly with Wells as the cathedral for Somerset, was also a Benedictine house. Carlisle, which was created a bishopric in 1133, was also an Augustinian monastery. The other medieval cathedrals were served by secular canons. These were clergy who did not follow a prescribed rule of life and derived their income from the endowments which were called prebends. The chapter, which was responsible for administering the cathedral's affairs, was made up of those who held the prebends, known as the prebendaries. At the time of the dissolution of the monasteries, those cathedrals which had always been run by secular clergy – London, York, Lichfield, Hereford, Exeter, Lincoln, Chichester, Wells and Salisbury – became known as the Old Foundation, while the monastic cathedrals were refounded and, together with Henry VIII's new cathedrals, are known as the New Foundation.

After the Conquest the Normans set about rebuilding the cathedrals in their newly won land in the Romanesque style, and thus by 1200 little of their Saxon predecessors survived. Although some cathedral churches such as that at Durham stand as magnificent, virtually complete monuments to the Norman achievement, the work of building and rebuilding continued throughout the Middle Ages. Only Durham and later the cathedral at Salisbury were completed within a generation. The others took much longer to finish and were continually being added to or amended. Rebuilding or restoration was a constant feature of the medieval cathedrals because of damage caused either by fire or subsidence, which were both permanent threats. In some cases increased revenue allowed an extension or even a complete rebuild in a new architectural style more suited to the tastes of contemporary sponsors.

Salisbury cathedral was exceptional in a number of ways, not least because it had no immediate Norman or Saxon predecessor as the bishopric was not transfered to its present site until the thirteenth century. In the first instance in 1075 the dioceses of Sherborne and Ramsbury had been amalgamated and incorporated into the new

64 Salisbury cathedral, one of the few cathedrals built in one continuous process during the thirteenth century. In the background lies the town of New Salisbury which replaced Old Sarum, a little to the north

diocese of Sarum. Old Sarum, however, eventually proved to be an uncomfortable and unsuitable site for a castle, city and cathedral and there was constant friction between the garrison and the clergy. About 1200 Peter de Blois, a canon of Sarum, wrote a letter expressing his delight on the decision to transfer the cathedral from a place which he regarded as 'ventis, expositus, sterilis, aridus, desertus' and in 1217 Bishop Richard Poore petitioned the pope to build a new cathedral in the Avon valley below the ancient fortification of Old Sarum. The papal bull of Honorius III, dated 1219, finally authorising the move confirms all the disadvantages of Old Sarum. 'Let us descend joyfully to the plains, where the valley abounds in corn, where the fields are beautiful and where there is freedom from oppression.' Old Sarum became a quarry for building materials, and was finally deserted in the fifteenth century. However, it remained a 'rotten borough' up until the 1832 Reform Act.

Before Salisbury cathedral moved its location the bishop already had a house, presumably on the site of his later palace, called New Place at the 'Old Salisburys' by the river. In 1219 a graveyard was consecrated and a wooden chapel built. The foundation stones of the cathedral were

59 Plan of New Salisbury, Wiltshire, showing the dominant location of the cathedral (after M. Beresford)

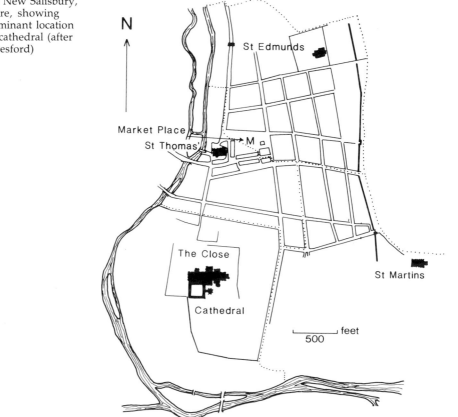

laid the following year and by 1225 the east end was sufficiently advanced for three altars to be consecrated. As land was plentiful a spacious layout was adopted, another of the Old Sarum canons, Elias of Durham, supervising the work. In 1258 the cathedral was consecrated. Salisbury was the first English cathedral to be built on an unoccupied site, without the constraints of having to accommodate previous buildings or adapt or adopt older ground plans. However, even at Salisbury not everything was complete by the time of the cathedral's consecration. The west front of the cathedral was not finished until 1265, while the cloisters date from between 1263 and 1270 and the chapter house was finally completed in 1284. The cathedral's crowning glory, its spire, resulted from a last-minute change of design – originally it was to have had a much squatter steeple. The spire, which was built between 1285 and 1310, is 404 feet high and the highest in England; it was constructed around an interior wooden scaffolding which still survives, as does the windlass which was used to haul up the stone from below.

An important source of money for major church-building enterprises such as Salisbury cathedral was derived from the practice of 'appropriating' the revenues of parish churches. From the twelfth century onwards lords who possessed the right to appoint clergymen to livings and to enjoy the revenues accruing to parish chur-ches (because their ancestors had founded the churches) frequently made these rights over to monasteries. The result is that the monks became responsible for main-taining the chancels of churches. Many parish churches show evidence of their chancels being rebuilt anew in a more stately style at this time, often using designs copied from the mother church. A less desirable effect was that they put in a poorly paid *vicar* (from the Latin meaning 'in place of') and took the rest of the revenues, which were then used to pay for building programmes. An example of a great church in financial difficulties, recouping its revenues by this system was in 1363 when the revenues of the parish church of St Thomas were given over for six years, to pay for repairs at Salisbury cathedral. The cathedral stood roughly in the centre of an area of some 90 acres bounded on the north and east and partly on the south by a wall with a ditch outside it. The ditch may have been dug to mark out the precinct at its foundation, but royal license to build the wall was not obtained until 1327. Four years later permission was granted to remove stone from Old Sarum for the purpose, but the shortage of stone was still causing difficulty in the middle of the fourteenth century and as a result the southern section of the wall was never completed. The southeast quarter of the close was set aside for the bishop's palace, and as the chapter was a secular one the clergy required houses, the building of which began in 1219. Elias of Durham built Leadenhall as a pattern for the houses of his fellow canons. On the western and northern sides of the close they were laid out along two walks set well back from the cathedral. Those on the west had particularly spacious gardens leading down to the Avon.

The bishops of Salisbury provided more than the physical framework for the town's development: they saw to its spiritual, intellectual, and social needs. Bishop Richard Poore himself appears to have invited the Franciscan friars to the city. They were settled on episcopal land on the outskirts between 1225 and 1228; the Dominicans followed later and obtained a building site at Fisherton, just outside the city boundary. The friaries quickly expanded and by 1285 each contained 40 friars, and just a few years later the friars minor were rebuilding or extending their house in stone, granted to them by the king from the decaying cathedral of Old Sarum. Bishop Richard Poore was also an active patron of the Hospital of St Nicholas, which was charged with the duty of caring for the poor, the sick and travellers and was also refounded and rebuilt on a new site in the 1230s.

In 1262 the buildings of the College of de Vaux were erected close to the Hospital. The college was designed for twenty scholars and has often been claimed as the first university college in England, being founded two years before Merton College, Oxford. After the suspension of Oxford University in 1238, a number of university masters and students from Oxford, attracted to the facilities offered by the new city as a centre of learning, had settled in Salisbury. It seems likely that for a period after this migration, the city had an incipient university organised under the chancellor of the cathedral. Although it failed to survive as a university, the college continued to prepare students for other universities, while functioning as a college for university graduates. A later foundation of 1269, the College of St Edmund, was also intended to promote learning. Its thirteen priests, under a provost, were to attend lectures in the neighbouring theological schools, as well as attending to the parochial duties of the new parish of St Edmund.

The cathedral church at Ely evolved from an abbey when

the huge diocese of Lincoln was subdivided in 1109. The Norman church was completed around 1189, but although the framework is still basically twelfth-century, Ely's most striking features are Gothic. These amendments to the original design were in part a result of the growing prosperity of eastern England during the High Middle Ages and partly as a result of accident. The Galilee porch at the west end was added in the thirteenth century, and later in the same century Bishop Hugh created a magnificent presbytery, which was consecrated in the presence of Henry III in 1252. However, Ely's two greatest glories were still to come and were the work of a group of medieval clerics who created some of the most remarkable buildings

65 The lantern of Ely cathedral, one of the most daring architectural schemes incorporated into any cathedral in the country

in the kingdom. Alan of Walsingham, sacrist in the abbey, was in charge of the building programme of the Lady Chapel when, in 1322, the Norman central tower collapsed. The chronicle of building records that he was bewildered and did not know 'where to turn or what to do'. He then conceived a unique plan to construct a huge octagonal lantern to replace the tower. The lantern rises up on corner posts, each cut from a single oak tree obtained from Chikissand in Bedfordshire. Alan of Walsingham's head is appropriately carved on his masterpiece. The Lady Chapel was set between the presbytery and the transept, with the widest stone vaulted roof in England, and is, in common with other great East Anglian

66 Fan vaulting in the retrochoir at Peterborough cathedral. This dates from the later fourteenth century and marks the beginning of some of the most delicate and inspiring of all medieval architecture. During the Middle Ages the cathedral formed the centre of one of the most important Benedictine monasteries in the land, but at the time of the dissolution the church was saved and became the seat of a new bishopric

churches, light, spacious, and beautiful.

The fourteenth century saw Ely virtually complete. An octagonal belfry tower was built at the west end, at the same time as the collapse of the northwest transept and that is why the cathedral has its distinctive and curious off-centre appearance. Early in the sixteenth century the two fine chantry chapels of Bishop West and Bishop Allcock were added, built of clunch, a peculiarly hard form of local chalk. However within a few decades the monastery was dissolved, statues in the Lady Chapel and elswhere were smashed and defaced, and the latest and finest shrine to St Etheldreda was destroyed. Nonetheless Henry VIII refounded the see and Ely remained a cathedral.

The rise and fall of the monasteries

By 1200 the majority of English monasteries had been established. The English and Welsh countryside had houses of Augustinians, Benedictines, Cluniacs and Cistercians. At the beginning of Henry VIII's reign in 1517 there were about 180 larger monasteries with as many as 700 smaller communities. It has been estimated that in 1217 there was a monastic population of about 12,500 which increased to about 17,500 by the mid-fourteenth century. The religious communities owned up to a fifth of the nation's wealth, which was largely derived from their extensive estates. A considerable proportion of this wealth was used for the construction and repair of monastic churches and conventual buildings.

Buildings and re-building went on well into the fourteenth century, and sometimes as with the castles, original wooden buildings were replaced by stronger and finer stone equivalents. New foundations by the major orders were, however, relatively rare after 1200, although King John founded Beaulieu in 1204 and there were some new foundations in Wales following Edward I's campaigns. Royal patronage was often involved, indeed required, during this final phase of monastic creations. Even so such foundations were not necessarily immune from difficulties, for instance problems could arise if the founder died before any proper provision was made for the continuance of the work. Edward I began the construction of his great monastery at Vale Royal in Cheshire in 1277. He intended it to be more magnificent than his grandfather John's foundation at Beaulieu and larger than his uncle's church at Hailes. The foundation of Vale Royal Abbey was the fulfilment of a vow made by the future Edward I

229

during a perilous sea-crossing in the winter of 1263–4, but because of the Barons' Wars nothing was done until 1270, when the first foundation-charter was issued at Winchester. The original intention was to establish an abbey at Darnhall in Delamere forest, and a colony of Cistercian monks from Abbey Dore in Herefordshire lived there for several years. Meanwhile a better site had been found four miles away, to the north, at a place to which Edward gave the name of Vale Royal, and here, on 13 August 1277, he laid the foundation-stone of the new abbey. Temporary buildings were erected to accommodate the monks while their new monastery was being built. Edward wanted his new abbey to be the largest Cistercian foundation in England, but its construction was to be a long and expensive task.

Edward's original intention was that the building of Vale Royal should be financed out of Cheshire's revenues. On 10 January 1278 one of Edward's clerks, Leonius, was made chamberlain of Chester, and with this office was combined the custody of the works at Vale Royal. For the next three years Leonius acted as chamberlain and keeper of the works, and his account of 'the expenses incurred in the works of the lord king at Vale Royal' has been preserved. The master of the works was Walter of Hereford, one of the foremost masons of his day, and one who in later years was to be heavily involved in the king's military works in Wales and Scotland. He received a salary of 2s a day, which was nearly five times as much as the wages of the highest-paid working masons. His principal assistant in 1278 was John of Battle, then at a comparatively early stage in his career, but later to be master mason of five of the crosses set up by Edward I in the memory of Queen Eleanor. Masons from throughout England worked on the Vale Royal project, some of them bearing names indicating a connection with other Cistercian houses such as Furness, Roche and Dore. In 1285 considerable trouble was caused by the imprisonment of a mason named John of Dore who, with other Vale Royal workmen, was accused of killing deer in Delamere forest.

The stone used in the building of the abbey was taken from the quarries at Eddisbury about five miles to the west of Vale Royal. The stone was trimmed in the quarry and then taken to the site of the abbey to be shaped by the masons. The carriage was provided largely by one-horse carts, some of which completed two journeys a day. Many thousands of journeys were made each year, and the roads appear to have been sufficiently good to enable stone to be moved even during the winter. Some stone came from further afield and in 1287 the abbot contracted with Master John Doget and Ralph of Chichester for a supply of polished Purbeck marble columns, capitals and bases for the cloister. As the abbey was situated in the midst of a well-wooded royal forest ample supplies of timber were available, and the builders were licensed to take all the timber that was required from the forests of Delamere and Mondrem. Large quantities were already being used to build lodges, workshops and houses for the masons and other workmen. In March 1278 Leonius paid ten diggers and other 'common workmen' for levelling the site of the abbey in order to set out the foundations. During the first few years work on the project was pursued with great energy, but as time went on payments fell into arrears as war broke out in Wales, and the money for the abbey was used for the construction of castles and the maintenance of troops. Finally the king lost interest, and refused to make any further contributions to the works, which dragged on throughout the fourteenth and fifteenth centuries. Although the monastery was occupied the church was never finished, and its walls and vaults remained exposed to the wind and weather. In the great

67 The Cistercian abbey of Roche which takes its name from an outcrop of rock in the valley nearby. It was founded in 1147 indirectly from Fountains, with which its plan has some similarities, with the church on the left hand side, the main claustrial buildings around the cloister to the right, and outer buildings centred on a stream. There is a dramatic account of the selling up of Roche: 'Every person had everything good cheap. . . . It would have pitied any heart to see what tearing up of lead there was and plucking up of boards, and throwing down of the sparres. . . . The lead was torn off [the roof] and cast down into the church, and the tombs in the church all broken . . . and all things of price either spoilt, carted away or disfaced to the uttermost'

231

gale of 19 October 1360 the nave collapsed, its columns falling 'like trees uprooted by the wind'.

Thus although royal patronage could provide a source of strength in the first stages of a building enterprise, financial prosperity could only be guaranteed if the foundation was backed by large landed estates. The oldest and wealthiest Benedictine abbeys like Peterborough, Ely and Glastonbury had been founded before the Norman Conquest and had accumulated enormous endowments. Peterborough, for example, possessed practically the whole of the Soke of Peterborough, much of the middle and lower Nene valley and had expanded into the neighbouring counties of Leicestershire, Rutland and Lincolnshire to such an extent that it was named 'the golden burgh'. It is therefore not surprising that it was able to finance ambitious rebuilding programmes during the Middle Ages.

68 The Benedictine abbey of Bardney lay in the Fens eight miles to the east of Lincoln. It escaped dissolution in 1536 but was involved in the monastic rising of 1536 and six of its monks were executed, the remainder surrendering the abbey two years later. The aerial photograph shows the abbey has been systematically robbed leaving no above ground masonry. The layout of the monstery has to be identified from the earthworks and spoil heaps left by the robbers. It is particularly interesting because the earthworks of the surrounding area present farm buildings storage areas, barns, animal compounds and fishponds. Such a photograph gives a better impression of the area covered by a monastic complex than is normally provided by an examination of the surviving central ruins alone

The surviving ruins tend to emphasise the ecclesiastical
and communal nature of most monastic life. The church
and the associated conventual buildings were the finest
and most substantial structures of the abbeys and priories.
Even with their roofs removed and after centuries of
robbing they still provide an impression of their former
splendour. However, it should be remembered that they
would have been surrounded by lesser, but none the less
essential, buildings and structures which were used for a
wide range of agrarian and industrial purposes. In recent
years scholars have begun to recognise and investigate
some of those elements, which were so essential to a
successful monastic operation. These included watermills,
fishponds and in some cases, as at Bordesley Abbey,
Worcestershire, an impressive industrial complex.
Frequently these have survived in the form of earthworks
which cover an area far in excess of what is normally
thought of as forming the monastic ruin.

The lands lying next to the foundation would have been
worked from the abbey farm, which often lay adjacent to
the conventual buildings. However, in the case of outlying
estates, their economic potential was exploited through
granges of which abbeys such as Strata Florida had 13 and
Tintern 11. Such granges were largely independently
controlled estates, supposedly not more than a day's
journey from the mother church (*Grangia juxta abbatiam*).
In layout the farmstead was arranged round one or two
courts. Accounts for Merthyrgeryn grange in the parish of
Magor (Gwent) towards the end of the fourteenth century
give some idea of the buildings normally found. These
included a mill, a garden, pigsty, an old and new byre,
cow-house, sheep-cote, hen-house, stable and granary.
Very occasionally complete buildings from such monastic
granges have survived in the form of tithe barns such as
that belonging to Beaulieu at its grange of Great Coxwell
in Oxfordshire. In parts of the country granges were at the
forefront of colonisation and deliberately sited on marginal
land. For example Meaux Abbey founded a group of
granges on the north Humber shore in Yorkshire. From
granges at Ottringham, Tharlesthorpe and Keyingham a
systematic programme of drainage and reclamation was
carried out despite a series of major reverses in the fourteenth century. At Salthaugh flooding was so bad in the
mid-thirteenth century that the monks were compelled to
demolish the grange and rebuild it on higher ground close
by.

The Cistercians were often at the forefront of such

ventures. Their technology reached a high level of achievement and the energy they demonstrated throughout the Middle Ages was formidable. The Cistercians, however, fell victim to their own prosperity and just as they had started as a reforming order, so they too were followed by reformed orders of canons, notably the Premonstratensians, the Gilbertines and the Victerines. The Gilbertines had double houses consisting of monks and nuns living in the same precinct, but separated both in their domestic and liturgical arrangements. One of the last orders to appear on the English scene was the Carthusian, which although based on a community, required strict isolation and silence from the monks who spent most of their time in their separate cells, meeting together only infrequently for communal worship or meals. The dominance of the church and refectory characteristic of the other main orders did not apply therefore in Carthusian houses, where the great cloisters took their place as the main architectural feature. The first English house was founded at Witham, Somerset, in 1180, but altogether no more than ten houses were founded in England and Wales. A number of other minor orders also appeared at about this time, including the Tironenisians and the Trinitarians as well as the Premonstratensians and Gilbertines.

The final groups of religious houses were those of the mendicant friars who arrived in England in the first half of the thirteenth century and rapidly overtook the enclosed orders in popularity. They tended to establish their houses in or on the edges of towns, often physically linked to the town walls, which meant that at the time of the dissolution the buildings were readily robbed or converted to other uses. Accordingly many of their sites are known only through documentary references or place-names. One of the features of the friaries in the later Middle Ages was their appeal to mainly urban labourers through their preaching. This lead to the development of so called 'preaching churches' with large naves capable of holding the considerable congregations which the friars attracted.

Two other orders whose organisation was somewhat different from mainstream monasticism also made an impact. They were the two military orders of the Knights Templars and Knights Hospitallers. The former had originated along crusade and pilgrimage routes to provide shelter and sustenance for Christian travellers. During the twelfth century they spread to England where they established a number of houses whose main functions were to train new members and provide a home for retired soldiers. Once the crusades were at an end the Templars became something of a problem and the order was finally abolished in 1312, at which time they possessed approximately twenty houses in England. Most of these were then made over to the Hospitallers who had about fifty commanderies in Great Britain at the dissolution.

Like a number of other orders one of the chief sources of income for the Hospitallers was derived from the

69 A Franciscan friar from *Piers Plowman* (1427)

keeping of sheep. In some cases the flocks were considerable, for example in 1338 the Hospitallers' manor of Hampden in Middlesex owned 2,000 sheep. We can compare this figure with that of some of the major Welsh

Cistercian houses, such as Margam, which in 1291 had
5,285 sheep, and Tintern which had 3,264 sheep. By the
fourteenth century some monasteries had become
wealthy, partly as a result of their own economic efforts
through sheep farming and extensive land reclamation.
The Cistercians were amongst the major wool producers
in the kingdom. Tintern particularly stands out because of
its quality wool, though it produced less in quantity than
Fountains Abbey. Tintern wool fetched the highest price
of English monastic wool at 28 marks per sack.

At the same time many other monasteries were subject
to severe financial problems because of declining benefactions and taxation. Moreover there was a decline in the
number of men and women coming forward to be monks
and nuns as the opportunities for literate men and women

60 Medieval wool-
producing houses in
Lincolnshire (after D.
M. Owen)

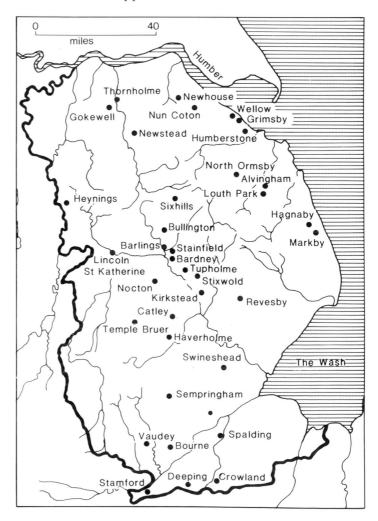

outside the monasteries increased. This decline appears to have become a major problem after the Black Death. It halved the number of monks and regular canons and in particular it affected the principal monastic centres of the Benedictines and Cistercians with extreme severity. Although there was a revival in monasticism in the late fourteenth century the number of monks in 1400 was still only about two-thirds of what it had been a century earlier. As a result of labour shortage the Cistercian abbots, for example, like other great landowners, were obliged to divide up their large farms into smaller units which could then be leased out for shorter periods. Moreover the growth of nationalism and anti-papal feeling had manifested itself in the crown's confiscation of a number of alien priories who owed their allegiance to continental mother houses, most notably Cluny in Burgundy. These 'alien' monasteries, as they were known, were obliged to pay heavily for royal letters patent of denization in order to be treated as native. Much Wenlock Priory (Salop) paid £400 for this privilege in 1395, and Thetford Priory paid £100 two years later. Smaller houses were unable to afford such sums, and Minster Lovell (Oxfordshire), a priory dependent on the abbey of Ivry in Normandy in the thirteenth and fourteenth centuries, was suppressed by Henry V. The lands and the inhabitants of these suppressed priories usually went to other, larger houses – Henry V was particularly keen to use their revenues to enrich the Carthusian house he founded at Sheen, London. The process was finally completed in 1414 when all remaining alien institutions were taken over.

Monastic plans did not remain unchanged throughout the Middle Ages. The greater monasteries of the twelfth and thirteenth centuries had been in the forefront of European architecture, and their buildings provided the monks with living conditions that were as good as, and in the case of sanitation usually better than, those of their lay contemporaries. By later medieval standards these conditions were regarded as poor, and the monks were to some extent prevented from refurbishing their living conditions by the great legacy of buildings they had inherited from earlier centuries, and by the fact that practically no convent could shoulder the financial burden of complete replanning when the tide of benefactions had begun to ebb.

When Pope Benedict XII issued new constitutions to the Benedictines, Cistercians and Augustinians, between 1335 and 1339, a widespread change had already begun to leave

237

its mark on monastic buildings in general, and this is recognisable not only in the design of new buildings but also in the conversion of old ones to new uses. Many factors contributed to these changes including an increased emphasis on the value of a university education in monastic life; the growing importance of the abbot's quarters in relation to the rest of the establishment; the reduced number of brethren in many houses and above all, a general desire for better standards of material comfort and privacy. This reached its most extreme form in a few houses where the most characteristic feature of a medieval monastery – the cloister – was abandoned. The early sixteenth-century reconstruction of the cloister at Forde was undertaken in a manner which shows that it no longer served its old purpose, and the conversion of the frater at Lindisfarne involved the abandonment of the cloister alleys. At Valley Crucis, the eastern alley of the cloisters was blocked by the external stairs to a hall and chamber which the abbot had made for himself by appropriating the northern end of the dorter.

By the early sixteenth century the medieval monastic plan had therefore outlived some of its usefulness, and only the accident of the dissolution prevented this from becoming as clear in England and Wales as it did on the Continent. By the time of the dissolution a large number of smaller monasteries and nunneries had already fallen into decay, and many others had greatly reduced numbers of inmates. In 1497 John Alcock, Bishop of Ely, secured papal permission to close down St Radegund's nunnery in Cambridge and converted its buildings and endowments to the use of his newly founded Jesus College. A few years later John Fisher, Bishop of Rochester had, in similar fashion, applied the property and revenues of two small nunneries to the support of his new college of St John's. In the 1520s Cardinal Wolsey started a similar, but much more ambitious, project which involved the suppression of no fewer than twenty-nine assorted religious houses in order to acquire endowments for a grammar school at his birthplace, Ipswich, and another new college at Oxford. Even so at the time of the dissolution there were still almost 900 religious houses of the various orders operating in England and Wales.

Houses with a net annual income of £200 or less were suppressed from 1536; the larger establishments were dealt with in 1539 and 1540. Dissolution led to the destruction of some buildings which, if they had survived today, would have ranked amongst the masterpieces of European architecture. Among the most serious casualties were Abingdon, Hyde, Barde, Reading and Winchcombe which were all completely destroyed. Several major royal foundations were also destroyed including Vale Royal and Henry II's church at Waltham. Often an aisle or nave was saved from destruction because it was already in use for parochial worship. This accounts for the relatively large residue of Benedictine and Augustinian buildings and the

high fatality rate of churches which belonged to the reformed orders. These latter generally excluded laymen and hence had inspired little local loyalty. None of the nine major Cluniac priory churches survives as anything more than a ruin.

In certain instances, as at Selby and Tewkesbury, the parishioners managed to acquire almost all of the monastic church for their use, and a handful of the great monastic churches survived without parochial intervention, for in step with the suppression of the monasteries went a programme of diocesan reorganisation. The Benedictine order supplied new cathedrals at Chester, Gloucester, Peterborough and Westminster while the Augustinians provided Oxford and Bristol. Westminster, which never seems to have acquired a territory of its own, enjoyed only a fleeting period as a cathedral.

70 The parish church at Abbey Dore, Herefordshire, all that remains of the once substantial Cistercian monastery that stood here. The church was restored by the famous local architect John Abel in the seventeenth century

239

Although the events associated with the dissolution, strictly speaking, fall outside the scope of this book, the end of the monasteries in the 1530s perhaps provides a better terminal date to the Middle Ages than the conventional political date of 1485. The dissolution meant the end of monastic communities, a particularly medieval phenomenon, characterised by a combination of piety, learning and economic energy. The dissolution also meant the

71 The abbey church of St Mary, Tewkesbury. At the dissolution of the Benedictine monastery here, the church was bought by the townsfolk and subsequently the great Norman building served as a parish church

72 The gateway at Bromfield in Shropshire is the most substantial surviving portion of a monastic cell of Gloucester Abbey that existed here in the Middle Ages

destruction of some of the finest medieval buildings in Britain, and it saw the break-up of immense estates and the redistribution of land on a scale unknown since the Norman Conquest.

Probably the most noticeable social change associated with the dissolution was the ending of the practice of going on pilgrimages. Most of the famous centres of pilgrimage, such as the shrines of St Thomas at Canterbury or of Our Lady at Walsingham, had been in the custody of the religious orders. In 1538 these shrines were attacked and destroyed on the grounds that the veneration of relics and the making of pilgrimages were undesirable, super-stitious practices, which tended to divert people's atten-tion away from more fruitful good works. The campaign

against relics and pilgrimages ran hand in hand with that against the religious orders. The shrines and the monas-teries fell together. The devotional practices of many English people were, as a consequence, profoundly changed. The suppression of the monasteries thus contrib-uted very significantly to that secularisation of life and society which was to be such an important feature of post Reformation England.

In March 1540 the last remaining abbey at Waltham surrendered. There were no religious houses left anywhere in England and Wales. This was the real end of the High Middle Ages.

73 A fourteenth-century gateway which formed part of Wigmore Abbey in Herefordshire. It was founded in 1179 by Hugh Mortimer for Augustinian Canons of St Victor of Paris who had first settled at Shobdon forty years earlier. The surviving sections of the abbey now form part of a farm complex

Select bibliography

Chapter one The high Middle Ages

Allen Brown, R., Colvin, H.M. and Taylor A. J. (eds), *The History of the Kings' Works,* vols 1 and 2, London, 1963.
Keen, M.H., *England in the Later Middle Ages,* London, 1973.
King, E., *England 1175–1425,* London, 1979.
Lander, J.R., *Conflict and Stability in 15th Century England,* 3rd edn, London, 1977.
Miller, E. and Hatcher, J., *Medieval England: Rural Society and Economic Change 1086–1348,* London, 1978.
Platt, C., *Medieval England,* London, 1978.
Thomson, J.A.F., *The Transformation of Medieval England 1370–1529,* Harlow, 1983.

Chapter two Kings, castles and houses of the great

Allen Brown, R., *English Castles,* London, 1976.
Allen Brown, R., Colvin, H.M. and Taylor, A.J. (eds), *The History of the Kings Works,* vols 1 and 2, London, 1963.
Cantor, L.M. (ed.), *The English Medieval Landscape,* London, 1982.
Renn, D., *Norman Castles in Britain,* London, 1968.
Salzman, L.F., *Buildings in England down to 1540,* Oxford, 1952.

Chapter three Villages in the late Middle Ages

Beresford, M.W., *The Lost Villages of England,* London, 1965.
Beresford M. W. and Hurst, J.G. (eds), *Deserted Medieval Villages,* Guildford and London, 1971.
Beresford, M.W. and St Joseph, J.K., *Medieval England. An Aerial Survey,* 2nd edition, Cambridge, 1979.
Cantor, L. M. (ed.), *The English Medieval Landscape,* London, 1982.
Medieval Archaeology, vols 1–25.
Miller, E. and Hatcher J., *Medieval England: Rural Society and Change 1086–1348,* London, 1978.
Postan, M.M., *The Medieval Economy and Society,* London, 1972.
Roberts, B.K., *Rural Settlements in Britain,* Folkestone, 1977.
Rowley, T., *Villages in the Landscape,* London, 1978.

Rowley T. and Wood, J., *Deserted Villages*, Princes Risborough, 1982.
Sawyer, P.H. (ed.), *Medieval Settlement*, London, 1976.
Swanton, M.J. (ed.), *Studies in Medieval Domestic Architecture*, Leeds, 1975.

Chapter four Medieval agriculture

Ault, W.O., *Open-Field Farming in Medieval England*, London, 1972.
Baker, A.R.H. and Butlin, R.A., *Studies in Field Systems in the British Isles*, Cambridge, 1973.
Cantor, L.M. (ed.), *The English Medieval Landscape*, London, 1982.
Darby, H.C., *The Changing Fenland*, Cambridge, 1983.
Gray, H.L., *English Field Systems*, London, 1915.
Hall, D., *Medieval Fields*, Princes Risborough, 1982.
Postan, M.M., *The Medieval Economy and Society*, London, 1972.
Taylor, C.C., *Fields in the English Landscape*, London, 1974.

Chapter five Woodlands, forests and parks

Beresford, M.W. and St Joseph, J.K., *Medieval England: An Aerial Survey*, 2nd edition, Cambridge, 1979.
Cantor, L. M. (ed.), *The English Medieval Landscape*, London, 1982.
Rackham, O., *Trees and Woodland in the British Landscape*, London, 1976.
Rackham, O., *Ancient Woodland*, London, 1980.
Young, C.R., *The Royal Forests of Medieval England*, Leicester, 1979.

Chapter six Industry, trade and communications

Crossley, D.W. (ed.), *Medieval Industry*, London, 1981.
Darby, H.C. (ed.), *A New Historical Geography of England before 1600*, Cambridge, 1973.
Miller, E. and Hatcher, J., *Medieval England, Rural Society and Economic Change 1086–1348*, London, 1978.
Salzman, L.F., *Building in England down to 1540*, London, 1952.
Salzman, L.F., *English Industries of the Middle Ages*, London, 1973.
Steane, J. M., *The Archaeology of Medieval England and Wales*, Beckenham, 1985.

Select bibliography

Chapter seven Medieval towns

Aston, M. and Bond, J., *Towns in the Landscape,* London, 1976.

Beresford, M.W., *New Towns of the Middle Ages,* London, 1967.

Darby, H.C. (ed.), *A New Historical Geography of England Before 1600,* Cambridge, 1973.

Dyos, H.J. (ed.), *The Study of Urban History,* London, 1968.

Platt, C., *The English Medieval Town,* London, 1976.

Poole, A.L. (ed.), *Medieval England,* Oxford, 1958.

Reynolds, S., *English Medieval Towns,* London, 1976.

West, J., *Town Records,* Chichester, 1983.

Chapter eight The church in the later Middle Ages

Brown, R.A., Colvin, H.M. and Taylor, A.J., *The History of the King's Works,* Vol. 1: *The Middle Ages,* London, 1963.

Butler, L. and Given-Wilson, C., *Deserted Monasteries of Great Britain,* London, 1979.

Deansely, M., *A History of the Medieval Church 590–1500,* London, 1976.

Harvey, J.H., *Cathedrals of England and Wales,* London, 1974.

Morris, R., *Cathedrals and Abbeys of England and Wales,* London, 1979.

Platt, C., *The Parish Churches of Medieval England,* London, 1981.

Index

Index

Index